Occasional Paper 48

Furnaces and Smelting Technology in Antiquity

edited by
P.T. Craddock and M.J. Hughes

Department of Scientific Research 1985

BRITISH MUSEUM OCCASIONAL PAPERS

Publishers: The British Museum
                   Great Russell Street
                   London WC1B 3DG

Production Editor: Josephine Turquet

Distributors: British Museum Press
                   46 Bloomsbury Street
                   London WC1B 3QQ

Front cover: Detail of a smith stoking a furnace from 'Foundry Cup', Staatliche Museum, Berlin,
                F 2294, after A Furtwangler and K. Reichhold, *Greichische Malerei*, III, pl. 135

Occasional Paper No. 48, 1996
Furnaces and Smelting Technology in Antiquity
Edited by P.T. Craddock and M.J. Hughes

First published 1985, reprinted 1992, 1996
© The Trustees of the British Museum 1996

ISBN 0 86159 048 1
ISSN 0142 4815

For a complete catalogue giving information on the full range of available Occasional Papers
please write to:
The Marketing Assistant
British Museum Press
46 Bloomsbury Street
London WC1B 3QQ

Printed and bound in the UK by The Looseleaf Company

CONTENTS

INTRODUCTION

The papers in this volume were read at the Symposium on Early Furnace Technology organised jointly by the British Museum Research Laboratory and the Historical Metallurgy Society and held at the British Museum on 29-30 October 1982.

Research on all aspects of early metallurgy has been gathering momentum during the last decade, and it became clear at the 1979 Archaeometry Conference that there was considerable research interest specifically in extractive metallurgy in early times. The papers from this were published separately in 1980 as *Scientific Studies in Early Mining and Extractive Metallurgy*, (ed. P T Craddock, British Museum Occasional Paper No. 20).

Much work is currently in progress around the world, researching how metal was won from its ores in the past. This requires the coordinated efforts of excavation of the sites of mining and smelting, the scientific study of the stratified remains of ores, slags, refractories and metal, and the experimental reconstruction of the processes based on the researched evidence.

In the short time since the publication of Occasional Paper No. 20 there have been major advances such as the publication of the Bronze Age mining systems at Timna (Conrad & Rothenberg, *Antikes Kupfer in Timna Tal*, 1980); early iron smelting in Europe (*Offa*, 40, 1983); and the study of early slags (Bachmann, *The identification of slags from archaeological sites*, 1982, Institute of Archaeology). Completely new areas of investigation have also appeared recently with topics as diverse as very early copper metallurgy in Africa, south of the Sahara (Echard, *Metallurgies Africaines*, 1983); zinc smelting in India (Craddock *et al.*, Early zinc production in India, *The Mining Magazine*, 1985); and copper mining and smelting in ancient China (*Tonglushan: a pearl amongst ancient mines*, Huangshi Museum).

We look forward to the next five years and beyond.

EXPERIMENTAL SMELTING TECHNIQUES: ACHIEVEMENTS AND FUTURE

R F Tylecote and J F Merkel

Institute of Archaeology, Unversity of London

Abstract

The tendency towards experimental archaeology has put experimental smelting into the limelight. In fact, since the end of the nineteenth century when it was realised that the techniques then being used sometimes had little in common with previous techniques, there has been a tradition in archaeometallurgy of proving your theories by experiment. Cushing's experiments of the 1890s on copper smelting were followed by Gowland's in 1912 and by Coghlan's and others in the 1930s. Since the 1939-45 war much work has been done on the iron bloomery process and latterly the more difficult problem of copper smelting. Side by side with this work has gone the anthropologists' attempt to record and reproduce techniques that were almost extinct in Africa and Asia before the memory of how to do them has died out. This type of work is still continuing as we can see from this volume and is a valuable aid to the work in the laboratory. The experimental work that has been done in northern Europe both in the field and in the laboratory has resulted in a body of people who are skilled in the reproduction of iron smelting processes and it is to be hoped that this tradition will be passed on so that the detailed knowledge of obsolete processes will never in fact disappear. Finally, it should not be forgotten that the simplified techniques of early peoples have an important place in modern teaching institutions. As modern plant, even on a pilot scale, gets more complicated and expensive the small scale processes of antiquity can be pressed into useful service and fully instrumented to teach the principles of modern metallurgical processes.

Keywords: EXPERIMENT, SMELTING, COPPER, IRON, LEAD, TIN, TEACHING, ARCHAEOMETALLURGY, FURNACE, EXPERIMENTAL ARCHAEOLOGY

Definition

The word 'smelting' can be interpreted in several ways. Considering the mass of information now available it is our intention to restrict its meaning more to reduction or oxidation under a controlled environment with a predetermined ore/fuel ratio and airflow, and to omit those reduction experiments in which the reductant is being consumed in the process and not replenished (i.e. crucible smelting) and those where ore is being reduced

4

in a boat in a furnace by a flow of gas of controlled composition.

Experimental smelting and results

(a) Copper

The first experiments on ancient copper smelting may be traced back to 1894 when Cushing (1894) reported on the operation of a primitive furnace based on archaeological evidence from the Salado Valley, Arizona. The furnace remains under investigation were attributed to the Pueblo Indians (possibly AD 1300-1400). The copper ore was first roasted in a separate, open fire. The smelting experiment used a shallow pit or bowl furnace with natural draft; it was started by building a large charcoal fire over the clay-lined pit. The roasted ore was slowly added. The resulting products were copper prills or 'buttons' mixed with slag. The smelted copper was then remelted into ingots for further working.

In 1912 Gowland reported the use of a similar 'hole-in-the-ground' furnace constructed in a laboratory at the Royal School of Mines, London (Gowland 1912, 242) (Fig.1). The purpose of his experiments was to prove that copper ore and tin ore could be smelted together to produce a bronze. Gowland claimed success on every attempt. During an experiment, 7 kg copper ore (30% copper), 4.5 kg tin ore (20% tin) and 3.4 kg limestone were charged with 4.5 kg charcoal. The furnace was blown with a single 2.5 cm diameter tuyere, but the volume of air was not specified. Nothing is said about the air source. After a short period of preheat, the mixed ores and flux were charged in layers with the charcoal. The operation of the furnace was presumably based on Gowland's (1899) observations of copper smelting in Japan and Korea. The quantity or quality of the recovered bronze was not reported. Too few details were published for these experiments to be of much scientific value today.

During 1939 and 1940 Coghlan reported on several experiments using a charcoal fired 'bonfire' or bowl furnace with natural draft. The first experiments demonstrated that an open fire alone was unsuitable for smelting copper. By building a small kiln-like or covered crucible chamber within the charcoal Coghlan (1939, 1939/1940) was then able to produce small beads of copper from crushed malachite. This led him to believe copper smelting may have been first discovered in ceramic kilns. Apparently the optimum products from smelting attempted in a ceramic kiln are only copper prills embedded in slag.

Further experimentation with copper smelting simulations using chalcopyrite was reported by Böhne (1968). The multiple-step process under investigation was based on archaeological evidence from Austria. Work was also conducted on a large scale with a shaft furnace having slag tapping capabilities. The furnace measured about 20 cm in diamter, 1 m high and was built from clay and stones. It operated with one tuyere, an iron pipe 25 mm in diameter placed through the tap hole. An industrial blower with a flow regulator was used to provide the blast. According to Böhne (1968, 50), modern analyses of furnace temperatures, airflow rates, and top gas composition were avoided for authenticity, in order to somehow force intuitive solutions of problems encountered during the smelting experiments. The chalcopyrite ore, from Mitterberg, was first roasted and the sulphur concentration was reduced by roasting from 16.17% to 6.65%. There were many unsuccessful attempts to operate the shaft furnace. The roasted copper ore was mixed with various amounts of limestone and fluorite flux in the empirical approach to slag composition. Charcoal was the fuel. The shaft furnace was used only for the production of matte. No slag was tapped. Even in the furnace, the matte and slag did not separate sufficiently to form distinct layers as expected. The matte/slag mixture needed to be removed from the furnace, crushed and hand-sorted. The matte was again roasted, then reduced in another furnace. This second, bowl, furnace was simply a clay-lined pit or hearth filled with charcoal. It measured 50 cm in diameter and was 20 cm deep. It also used the iron tuyere. The final products of this smelting step were copper prills embedded in slag. The metal prills were about 95 to 96% copper, accompanied with iron as the impurity. Chemical analysis of the slag gave 33.28% silica, 33.38% ferrous oxide, 0.62% copper and a trace of sulphur. It was suggested that ingots could be produced by remelting large quantities of copper prills. Further refining steps would be necessary for the smelted copper, called 'Schwarzkupfer'.

An excellent series of twenty copper smelting experiments, based on archaeological and ethnographic evidence from the Transvaal in Southern Africa, was conducted by Friede and Steel (1975). Three types of furnaces were tested, starting with a tall furnace built of modern firebrick. It measured 18 cm in diameter and about 42 cm in height. The dimensions and operation were based on ethnographic evidence from the Kaonde tribe of Zimbabwe (Chaplin 1961). A single tuyere was positioned through the first course of firebrick, approximately 5 cm above the hearth. Initially an air compressor was used, blowing 60 to 120 litres/min. A pair of bag-bellows, constructed after Zulu examples, were found to deliver only 60 to 90 litres/min worked at maximum speed. The measured airflow was quite less than an estimate based on bag volumes; five litres at 70 double strokes/min equalled 350 litres/min. The low efficiency was attributed to 'poor craftsmanship' and 'inexperienced men working the bellows' (Friede & Steel 1975, 226). The diameter of the tuyere was varied from 2.5 to 4.0 cm internal diameter, but the effects were not reported. To begin a smelting simulation, the hearth was covered with wood ash, sticks and dry leaves. Charcoal, screened to sizes between 10 and 20 mm, was added and the airblast started. A thermocouple placed through the furnace top was used to measure internal temperatures. Malachite ore containing 17.5% copper was layered with charcoal. The Phalaborwa malachite was considered to be self-fluxing. No input weights are given. The blast was increased until the bed reached 800 to 900°C. More charcoal was added. After three hours of firing the blast was increased to raise the bed temperature to about 1000°C. Then the blast was stopped and the furnace allowed to cool. To remove the smelting products the furnace top had to be broken down. 'The conditions of the smelting procedure was varied in a number of experiments, but in each case only a small quantity of reduced copper, in the form of tiny globules and of thin irregular-shaped copper layers coating the surface of the slag, were obtained' (Friede & Steel 1975, 224). The furnace needed to be rebuilt for each experiment.

The copper prills collected from the experiments were remelted in a small crucible furnace. This furnace was a simple design, based on archaeological descriptions by Wagner and Gordon (1929) and ethnographic evidence recorded by Chaplin (1961) and Stayte (1931). A shallow clay-lined pit 20 cm in diameter was built, surrounded with stones. Two tuyeres were used with the compressor or bellows. The crucible was about 8 cm in diameter. It was filled with the smelted copper prills and dry leaves, then covered with a ceramic lid. The crucible was supported by four vertically placed stones and positioned in the charcoal in front of the tuyere. A temperature of 1100 to 1200°C was maintained for about 30 minutes. Many problems were encountered in removing the crucible

from the fire to pour the molten copper into a mould. The product, a cast
bar ingot, was analysed and found to contain 4.4% iron, 0.02% nickel,
0.008% zinc and <10 ppm tin, lead, antimony, bismuth and arsenic; the rest
was copper.

A major difficulty in the experiments may be attributed to the lack
of an iron ore flux as the malachite was not self-fluxing. This error
seems to have originated from the few misleading chemical analyses of
archaeological slag specimens. Most of the 'slag' analyses were actually
slagged furnace lining and slagged tuyeres. This led Friede and Steel
(1975, 223) to consider only calcium, sodium and potassium as possible
flux additions and the importance of the iron flux was not recognized.
The experimental slags were consequently rather viscous.

The excavations of Beno Rothenberg (1962) on the Timna sites in the
years 1960-75 inspired the work started by Boydell (Tylecote & Boydell
1978) and continued by Ghaznavi (Tylecote et al. 1977) and by Merkel (see
below).

Two furnaces have been used; the large one, A (Fig.2), which was
30 cm in diameter and the smaller one, B, which was only 20 cm diameter
(Fig.3). Most of the earlier work was carried out on the smaller furnace
and pure copper oxide, oxide and sulphide ores were smelted with roasting
where required.

Experimentation started with the larger shaft furnace, called type A,
based on archaeological evidence from Timna Site 2 (Tylecote & Boydell
1978). A column of segmental firebricks, measuring 32 cm in diameter and
65 cm high, was built upon a rectangular platform and surrounded with a
sand seal and insulation brick. The furnace was lined with a mixture of
clay, sand and charcoal dust. Seven experiments were conducted with a
single, inclined tuyere. The tuyere was about 25 cm above the furnace
bottom. A mullite tube with a 25 mm diameter served as a tuyere; it did
not protrude into the furnace from the wall. After five experiments the
tuyere diameter was reduced to 19 mm, which improved operation. Airflow
rates were varied between 200 and 370 litres/min.

However,these experiments were not successful and attention was now
concentrated on the operation of a smaller bowl furnace, called Type B
(Tylecote & Boydell 1978). Archaeological evidence from Timna Site 39b
was used to select the furnace dimensions. Smaller firebricks formed the
furnace column, complemented with the same type of sand seal and insulating
bricks. The bowl furnace measured 22 cm in diameter and 30 cm high; it
used a single, inclined tuyere 19 mm in diameter. Usually the tuyere
entered through the furnace wall at a height which was varied between 16 cm
and 18 cm above the bottom. On the second experiment, the tuyere was
placed vertically into the furnace 12 cm above the hearth. A total of
thirteen experiments were completed with this bowl furnace.

The first five experiments used copper oxide or copper metal plus
hematite flux, at various ratios. Airflows from 100 litres/min to 150
litres/min were tested. Preheat times were about 1 hour 30 minutes. Post-
heat charcoal additions after the last ore charge, varied up to 2 hours
30 minutes. A temperature profile was obtained for experiment B3, and the
isotherms showed that the bottom temperatures were too low to melt the
slag. At best the smelting products were copper prills mixed with slag.
Recovery of input copper ranged from 42% to 94.5%.

A second series of experiments with the bowl furnace by Tylecote and Boydell (1978) used crushed (< 4 mm) nodular ore from Timna. The optimum ratio of ore to hematite flux was found to be 1:2. In Experiment B9 no hematite was added so as to demonstrate that the nodular ore was not self-fluxing and the copper could not be separated from the slag. Various ratios of charcoal fuel to mixed ore and flux were tested; empirically the ratio of 1:2 was found superior. A fuel/ore ratio of 1:3 was tried in Experiment B7, but the increase in ore caused the tuyere to block with slag. The subsequent decrease in temperature resulted in poor separation of molten slag and copper.

Plano-convex copper ingots were not produced in any of the experiments. The copper prills contained iron and sulphur as the main impurities. Recovery of arsenic was about 50% of the input values. Trace element analysis was made on the copper prills from Experiments B12 and B13 by Tylecote and Boydell (1978) and Merkel (1977).

Tylecote and Boydell (1978) also reported on eight refining experiments for the impure smelted copper. Iron was the main impurity which needed to be removed. Due to the difference in density and the immiscibility between copper and iron, iron floats to the top in a molten mixture. Under laboratory conditions, the iron metal could be recovered from the top of the copper. Tylecote and Boydell (1978, 45) propose this process may be the source for early finds of iron objects. However, under oxidizing conditions the iron will form ferrous oxide which forms a slag with the charcoal ash and crucible. It was demonstrated that remelting refines the impure copper.

Ghaznavi (1976) completed further experimentation with the bowl furnace. A total of seventeen experiments were undertaken to smelt seven different copper ores and two artificial copper ores. The purpose of these experiments was to study trace element partitioning during copper smelting under simulation conditions.

The first four experiments were conducted using a single inclined tuyere positioned about 11 cm above the bottom. The firebrick furnace measured 23 cm in diameter and was 30 cm high. The airflow was 150 litres/min, which was within a proposed range for bag-bellows. Copper oxide ore from Timna was smelted only in the second and third experiments. Fuel/ore plus flux ratios were tested at 1:1 and 1:2. Only copper prills were produced from the experiments at reported efficiencies of 69% and 80.2%. The experiments with Timna ore were conducted with only one tuyere, not two as stated in Tylecote, *et al.* (1977). The analytical results for the smelted copper from Timna ore by Tylecote and Boydell (1978) and Ghaznavi (1976) are not that different. Thus conclusions based on compositional differences relating to the number of tuyeres require further experimentation.

An additional, second tuyere was placed at the furnace top for twelve subsequent experiments using sulphide ores by Ghaznavi (1976). This change was introduced, according to the author, to increase the burning of carbon monoxide in the exhaust gases.

The benefit of the second tuyere, increasing both airflow and temperatures, was an improved copper and slag liquation. It increased the temperature distribution considerably and allowed the formation of something resembling an ingot rather than isolated prills of copper enveloped in slag. (Tylecote, Ghaznavi & Boydell 1977).

Experiments with the larger shaft furnace were still unsuccessful even after using two tuyeres and a total airflow around 500 litres/min (Tylecote & Boydell 1978). However, results were beginning to improve when this programme was discontinued. A small quantity of molten slag was reported to have leaked through the front wall of the furnace during the last smelting attempt. A suitable tap hole and procedure were still required. It was suggested slag tapping could not be accomplished away from a tuyere. Problems existed with burning rates and heat losses. The furnace bottom was too cold to maintain molten copper and slag. Much more work was required with the shaft furnace. Successful operation demanded solutions very different from copper smelting in a bowl furnace.

In more recent years several other new attempts at ancient copper smelting techniques have been undertaken. A single heating experiment was conducted at Timna using a small shaft furnace and natural draft (Bachmann & Rothenburg 1980). The reconstruction was pear-shaped and built of clay. No ore or flux was charged. The point of the experiment was solely to determine internal furnace temperatures which reached 1260°C.

Based on recent archaeological evidence in China, Hua and Lu (1981) reported on their experiments with copper smelting. A shaft furnace was built of clay and used to reconstruct the process. Few other details are presently available (Fig.4).

(b)   Iron

Perhaps because the bloomery process was still being carried on in the Pyrenees in 1840 (Percy 1864) and in New York State with hot blast in 1889, the early experimenters could hardly claim that the bloomery process was extinct. But by the 1930s metallurgists examining the products of the Roman bloomery process some nineteen hundred years earlier were well aware that they were dealing with something that was not the product of the iron blast furnace and was clearly obsolete.

In order to understand the process producing these materials it was necessary to do simulation experiments. Perhaps the first were carried out by Gilles in Germany, who, being convinced that the earliest furnaces were blown by induced draught, erected a shaft furnace 1.72 m high with a diameter of 0.9 m. There was a single (30 cm diameter) entrance for air at the bottom which could be controlled. These experiments were continued on shaft and hearth furnaces and were reported in 1958 and 1960. Fayalite slags containing iron inclusions were produced. The maximum temperature reached was 1400°C.

The low bloomery hearth was based on that shown by Agricola and blown with a blast of air through a 32 mm diameter tuyere. It was relatively unsuccessful when worked with a mixed charge of charcoal and ore. In fact at this time two groups of workers, Gilles (1958 and 1960) in Germany and Wynne and Tylecote (1958) in Britain, were coming to much the same conclusions that a low shaft furnace had either to be worked on the Catalan hearth principle with ore going in one side and fuel down the other (tuyere) side (Fig.5), or 'manipulated' in such a way as to keep the reduced iron from being reoxidised by the blast from the tuyere.

The only alternative, as Wynne and Tylecote (1958) and Gilles (1958 and 1960) found, was to convert the low hearth into a shaft furnace by putting on top a reservoir for the twin purposes of holding the charge and keeping the heat from being lost by radiation through the top.

During this time Professor M J O'Kelly who had been excavating iron smelting sites in Ireland had been carrying out some smelting experiments which he reported at the Hamburg Conference in 1958. He concluded that the bowl furnace with a depth of 20-50 cm and a diameter of 20 cm at the surface was the commonest type in Britain and Ireland (O'Kelly 1961).

The word 'bowl' used in connection with iron smelting has been generally accepted as applying to a low hearth where the height/width ratio does not exceed ~1.0. But many people have serious doubts about the use of this type of iron smelting furnace in spite of its latter use in the form of the Catalan hearth. This latter furnace was believed to be a developed bowl hearth and, in the form shown by Percy (1864), its height/width ratio exceeds one and it is worked in a special way with the ore going down one side and the charcoal the other.

A recent description of the operation of a bowl furnace in Burundi, East Africa, by J-P Chretien (1982) reminded us of similar descriptions of Scandinavian hearths (Evenstad 1968, Busch 1972). The Burundi type furnace operated for about 2000 years up until the 1930s in the south of the country, to the northeast of Lake Tanganyika. In the 1970s J-P Chretien managed to get together enough people who knew how to work the process.

The rich ore contained 70% ferric oxide and was roasted. The furnace was about 0.5-1.0 m diameter with two opposed tuyeres supplied by double bellows. The two tuyeres were directed downwards towards the bottom where the charcoal was consumed, causing an upward current of carbon monoxide to reduce the ore above. When the reduced ore gets too low and is in danger of oxidation, it is pushed away by a stick to one side and replaced by further supplies of charcoal and ore. Thus it is 'manipulated' and this movement leaves no trace in the archaeological record.

The Scandinavian process reported by Busch (1972) at Nornäs in Sweden seems to adopt much the same principle (Fig.6). The 'bowl' is 50 cm square and 40 cm deep with a single horizontal tuyere; thus it has a height/width ratio ~1.0 and can be said to be a true bowl by our definition although it has a sloping funnel-like top.

As in the furnace described by Evenstad (1968), the charcoal is made in the furnace so that no heat is lost. After filling in this way and adding additional charcoal, the carefully blended ore was charged over the whole surface of the bowl, first at the edges and then in the centre. An air-vent hole was kept open in the middle and charcoal was added as it burnt away near the tuyere. Fuel ash was also added (as flux?).

Then the ore from near the walls was pushed towards the blast while the bowl was topped up with charcoal. At this point slag could be seen to be flowing, presumably away from the tuyere, and the finished bloom was found in the centre of the bowl weighing about 7 kg.

Clearly this is a highly skilled process and manipulation of the contents is the key to success. Evenstad describes a similar process in use in Norway in 1782. The furnace was a truncated cone (Evenstad 1968) about 50 cm diameter at the bottom and 1 m diameter at the top; its height was about 80 cm. Its mean height/width ratio is therefore 1.15 and there is no doubt that it is a true bowl furnace and, although it is circular, has much in common with the furnace at Nornäs. There is a single horizontal tuyere. Just below the tuyere there is a 'plate' of stone. When blowing has started a 'hole' is produced due to charcoal consumption and this is filled with ore and charcoal. Later the 'hole' is filled by pushing material from the sides into the 'hole'. The oxidised ore above the tuyere is removed and placed above the 'hole' where the bloom is forming. All this requires an intimate knowledge of the position and extent of the reducing and oxidising zones of the furnace. Normally, reduction can only take place fifteen charcoal diameters beyond the end of the tuyere. This should be contrasted with a shaft furnace where reduction takes place in the shaft well above the tuyere, and the tuyere level becomes highly oxidising.

The Slav countries have made one of the biggest contributions to iron smelting research. Most of the work has been carried out by Pleiner (1969) in Prague, and Radwan and Bielenin in the Holy Cross Mountains of Poland. In 1964 Pleiner carried out field experiments on the tall narrow shaft furnace - the Scharmbeck type with slag pit. He failed to get this working with induced draught. But the operation of the typically Slav (ninth century) Zelechovice furnace with its inclined tuyere and blind alley was a great success (Fig.7).

Bielenin and Radwan in Poland concentrated on the broader Holy Cross Mountain type of slag-pit furnace. They failed to make the slag go into the pit below the furnace (as indeed did Thomsen (1963) with the Scharmbeck type) but mixed slag and metal were produced in a tuyere zone. Recently, however, it has been shown that by making an inclined hole from the surface into the slag-pit, the air induced is sufficient to cause the residual charcoal in the pit to be burnt, and allow the slag to run into the empty space so produced (Fig.8).

After the slag had run into the pit, the shaft of the furnace was removed and rebuilt over a new hole beside the old. This method of operation left ninety-five enormous 'slag fields' containing over 4053 slag bottoms (Bielenin 1974).

In the 1960s BBC Television encouraged some smelting experiments that were based on the Roman period furnaces at Pickworth in Lincolnshire and Ashwicken in Norfolk. These represented a common type of Roman period shaft furnace about 1.5 m high and 0.30 m internal diameter. After the field experiments recorded in the television programme, the furnace was moved into the laboratory and fully instrumented. The programme resulted in 32 smelts and it was found that with these furnaces very compact and homogeneous all-metal blooms could be made weighing up to 9 kg without the previous mixing of slag and metal. And this was done without any form of 'manipulation', merely by continuous charging of ore and fuel in layers until the metal rose to tuyere level (Fig.8) (Tylecote et al.1971). At the same time many experiments were being made by other groups on similar types of furnace in the United Kingdom (Cleere 1971, Adams 1979). Also a great deal of work has been done in Scandinavia (Thomsen 1963, Hagfeldt 1966), Austria (Straube et al.1965), Hungary (Hackenast et al.1968), and Germany (Ozann 1971), thus producing a great number of people familiar with bloomery technique.

(c)   Lead

Since lead is about the easiest metal to smelt it is surprising, or perhaps understandable, that little work has been done on it. It is possible to produce lead metal from galena (lead sulphide) in a wood-fuelled, brick-built brazier by charging cubes of galena at the top, although the yield is not high (Tylecote 1964).

This is essentially the technique adopted in the 'boles' of the Pennines. The slags were reworked with iron fluxes to extract the remaining 50% lead.

Pleiner (1967) has described reconstruction experiments conducted on lead smelting. Two types of furnaces were used: a bowl furnace and a shaft furnace. The clay-lined bowl or shallow hearth was comparable to that used for copper smelting. The shaft furnace was also built from clay. It measured 70 cm in height and about 35 cm in diameter. One tuyere was connected to a set of goatskin bellows worked by hand. The diameter of the tuyere was 4 cm. The total charge of 8.25 kg mixes of lead ore with iron ore flux was layered with 7 kg charcoal. At the conclusion of the experiment a small quantity of lead was tapped from the surface. When the remaining contents of the furnace were examined, it was found that the slag had solidified round the tuyere zone (Fig.10).

More recently experiments have been carried out by Hetherington (1980). The furnace used was essentially a slightly modified version of the copper furnace Type B (Fig.3).

The ore was a galena concentrate containing 78% lead sulphide, 3% ferric oxide, 2% silica and 2% alumina. Iron ore and sand containing 73-83% ferric oxide was used as a flux.

With an airflow of the order of 150 litres/min there is no difficulty in getting a temperature of 1200°C sufficient to form and run a fayalite slag. However, at such temperatures lead oxide is very volatile (BP = 1490°C), and there is considerable loss as fuming occurs. It became clear that unless one has a 'bag-house' or flue system for collecting dusts, lead smelting must suffer loss either in the slags due to low temperatures and poor fluxing or, under high temperatures and good slagging practice, due to fuming. The two-stage process of low temperature smelting followed by high temperature recovery of lead from slag was probably the best process and was that practised, up to a few years ago, by the ore hearth and blast furnace combination.

As silver has a preference for the metal phase rather than the slag phase, all the silver in the ore is recovered by the first smelt and therefore the silver/lead ratio is higher than in the ore itself. This is an advantage that more than outweighed the loss of the lead in the system. It meant that recovery of lead from the slags was rarely worthwhile until more recent times.

Some work has been done on the cupellation process by R F Tylecote which was reported by McKerrell and Stevenson (1972) (see Table). It was shown that during the cupellation of silver, tin, zinc and copper could be readily removed down to the 0.1% level while lead and bismuth tended to remain at the 0.5-1.0% level.

Since this process is still used today a great deal should be known about it and perhaps this accounts for the lack of attention given to it.

Table: Results of cupellation experiments

Charge (melted)		Product (calculated assuming no losses; %)	
Pb	395 g	Pb	91.88
Ag	25	Ag	5.80
Bi	5	Bi	1.16
Cu	5	Cu	1.16
Total	430 g	Total	402 g

This was cupelled to give:-

21.88 g Ag plus some slag

Analysed composition of the silver bullion:-

Sample	Ag	Cu	Pb	Bi%
1	97.8	0.3	1.0	0.9
2	97.9	0.4	0.9	0.8

(d) Tin

There are so few finds of any type of tin-smelting furnace that it is not surprising that little or no work has been done on this subject. Pure tin-stone can be reduced relatively easily in a crucible, albeit at high temperature and this is the basis of many an assay process for tin ore.

But the remains of early tin smelting furnaces have been reported from South Africa (Friede & Steel 1976). Even here the evidence is meagre and only the foundations of saucer-shaped hearth furnaces were found near Rooiberg. On the basis of these finds and some in Nigeria an experimental furnace was constructed as shown in Fig.11. This consisted of a shaft 60 cm high and 13 cm in diameter, with one tuyere. Ore with a tin content of 6.3% was used which is much below the quality used in Britain in the Medieval and later periods. It was clear that tin oxide was reduced but that the gangue kept the tin particles apart so that no massive amount of tin was found. A better grade of ore (30.88% tin) gave tin prills and larger masses but no plano-convex ingots and it was clear that these could only be made by remelting the prills in a crucible and pouring into a mould. The purity of the tin was in the range 98.8 to 99.15%.

In Britain, however, it was possible to obtain pebbles of pure cassiterite which contains 79% tin, and the problems found in South Africa would not arise. Even so, temperatures as high as 1000°C are needed and care must be taken to see that all the charcoal is burnt away at the end so that it does not keep the tin prills from coalescing.

Conclusions and recommendations

As the preceding shows, a great deal of experimental work has been done on iron and copper and little on the other metals. More people today are familiar with the early and now obsolete techniques of iron-making than they are with copper and there is still room for further work on this metal particularly the sulphide ores.

On iron, recent work by Clough (1985) has shown that the rich sulphide nodules - particularly the limonitized ones - can be smelted so this mineral is now presented as a new source of iron for the south of England. On the whole the problems of iron are well understood. But there is scope for a study of the true bowl furnace and its manipulation.

As far as lead and tin are concerned there is considerable need for more work. No work has been carried out on zinc and antimony.

It is only recently that traces of Roman and Medieval zinc smelting have come to light and investigation and examination of the sites must precede simulation experiments. But it will be of great value to have details of cementation and retorting techniques. One example of the latter is still being used in China and is under investigation by the archaeometallurgy group in Beijing (Tylecote 1983).

How far antimony was recognised as a metal in its own right in classical and medieval times is still in doubt. We know that antimony was being extracted in southwest Scotland in the eighteenth century (Sinclair 1794) and it would be useful to simulate this as it is a simple example of a liquation process.

Precious metals such as gold and platinum are not thought to need much work done on them. Gold is mainly a matter of mineral dressing - a subject that comes into our archaeometallurgical field but which we will not be considering at this conference. Even so we might mention its importance and express the hope that more workers will undertake work on these processes.

Platinum is mainly a South American problem and one of mineral dressing and physical metallurgy rather than smelting. While gold could be melted, platinum could not and could only be consolidated by powder metallurgy or 'brazing' with gold and copper. Considerable work is being done on this subject at the Institute of Archaeology, London by Scott and at the Massachusetts Institute of Technology (Lechtman 1976).

The universities seem the right place for these experiments. They are simple to engineer and fairly cheap to instrument, and teach the principles of extractive metallurgy. They can be integrated as short-term projects into the final year of first degrees or in the more detailed form into post-graduate years. There is only one problem: a good deal of the space once available in universities has been turned over to physical metallurgy and the ventilation and 'dirt' space is no longer available. But such experiments are best carried out in the open in an 'outstation' or field-studies centre and most teaching institutions have such accommodation.

References

Adams, R J 1979. Bloomery experiments. *Wealden Iron*, 15, 11-15

Bachmann, H G & Rothenberg, B 1980. Die Verhüttungsverfahren von Site 30. In *Antikes Kupfer in Timna-Tal*, eds. H G Conrad & B Rothenberg, 215-236. Bochum, Bergbau Museum

Bielenin, K 1974. *The ancient centre of iron metallurgy in the Holy Cross Mountains*. Warsaw, Paustwowe Wydawnictwo Naukowe

Bohne, C 1968. Über die Kupferverhüttung der Bronzezeit. *Archaeologia Austriaca*, 44, 49-60

Busch, J A W 1972. Iron making by the bloomery process at Nornas, Sweden in 1851. *Bull. H.M.G. 1972*, 6 (1), 28-33

Caldwell, J R (ed.) 1967. *Investigations at Tal-I-Iblis*. Illinois State Museum Preliminary Publication, No. 9

Chretien, J-P 1982). La "fonte" du minerais de fer au Burondi etat de la question. Colloque at the College de France, Paris, 11th June 1982

Chaplin, J H 1961. Notes on traditional smelting in Northern Rhodesia. *South African Archaeological Bulletin*, 16 (62), 56

Cleere, H F 1971. Iron smelting experiments in a reconstructed Roman furnace. *Britannia*, 2, 203-217

Clough, R E 1985. This publication, 179-187

Coghlan, H H 1939. Some experiments on the origin of early copper. *Man*, 92, 106-108

Coghlan, H H 1939/1940. Prehistoric copper and some experiments in smelting. *Transactions of the Newcomen Society*, 20, 49-65

Cushing, F H 1894. Primitive copper working: an experimental study. *American Anthropology*, 5, 165-176 (old series)

Evenstad, O 1968. A treatise on iron ore ... and the process of turning it into iron and steel. *Bull. H.M.G. 1968*, 2 (2), 61-65

Friede, H M & Steel, R H 1975. Notes on Iron Age copper-smelting technology in the Transvaal. *Journal of the South African Institute of Mining and Metallurgy*, 76/4, 221-231

Friede, H M & Steel, R M 1976. Tin mining and smelting in the Transvaal during the Iron Age. *Journal of South African Institute of Mining and Metallurgy*, 76, 451-470.

Ghaznavi, H A 1976. 'Trace element partitioning in early copper smelting'. Unpublished M.Sc. thesis, University of Newcastle-upon-Tyne

Gilles, J W 1958. Versuchsschmelze in einem Vorgeschichtlichen Rennofen.
    Stahl und Eisen, **78**, 1690-1695

Gilles, J W 1960. Rennversuch in Gebläseofen und Ausschmieden der Luppen.
    Stahl und Eisen, **80**, 943-948

Gowland, W 1899. The early metallurgy of copper, tin and iron in Europe, as
    illustrated by ancient remains, and the primitive process surviving in
    Japan. *Archaeologia*, **56**, 267-322

Gowland, W 1912. The metals in antiquity. *Journal of the Royal Anthropo-
    logical Institute*, **42**, 235-287

Hackenast, G, Vastagh, G, Zoltay, E & Novaki, G 1968. *History of iron working
    in Hungary in early medieval times*, (in Hungarian). Budapest, Akad, Kiado

Hagfeldt, H 1966. Research on reduction in a forced draught bloomery furnace
    (in Swedish). *Institut fur Järnets Metallurgi*. Stockholm, K.T.H.

Hetherington, R J 1980. Investigation into primitive lead smelting and its
    products. In *Aspects of Early Metallurgy*, ed. W A Oddy, Occasionl Paper
    No. 15. London, British Museum

Hua Jeuming & Benshan, Lu 1981. Restoration of a vertical furnace for
    copper smelting during the Spring-Autumn Age at Tunlushan Relics, (in
    Chinese). *Wen Wu*, 1981, 8, No. 30, 40-45

Lechtman, H 1976. A metallurgical site survey in the Peruvian Andes. *Journal
    of Field Archaeology*, **3**, 1-42

McKerrell, H & Stevenson, R B K 1972. Some analyses of Anglo-Saxon and
    associated oriental silver coinage. In *Methods of chemical and metal-
    lurgical investigation of ancient coinage*, eds. Hall, E T & Metcalf, D M,
    Royal Numismatic Society Special Publications No. 8, 195-210. London

Merkel, J F 1977. 'Neutron activation analysis of copper to examine Timna as
    an ore source during the Chalcolithic and Early Bronze Ages in Israel.'
    Unpublished M.Sc. thesis, University of Minnesota

O'Kelly, M J 1961. The ancient Irish method of smelting iron. *5th
    International Kongress fur Vor- und Fruhgeschichte*. Hamburg, *1958*, 459-
    461. Berlin

Ozann, B 1971. *Rennverfahren und Anfange der Roheisenerzeugung; zur metal-
    lurgy und wissentechnik der alten Eisengewinning*, Vol. 1. Dusseldorf

Percy, J 1864. *Metallurgy; iron and steel*, p. 279. London, Murray

Pleiner, R 1967. Preliminary evaluation of the 1966 metallurgical investi-
    gations in Iran. In *Investigations at Tal-I-Iblis*, ed. J R Caldwell,
    Illinois State Museum Preliminary Publication, No. 9

Pleiner, R 1969. Experimental smelting of steel in Early Medieval furnaces.
    Pamatky Archeologicky, **60**, 458-486

Rothenburg, B 1962. Ancient copper industries in the Western Arabah.
    Palestine Exploration Quarterly, Jan-June, 1-71

Sinclair, Sir John 1794. *The statistical account of Scotland*, Vol. 11, 525-528. Edinburgh

Stayte, H A 1931. *The Bavenda*. London

Straube, H, Tarmann, B & Plockinger, E 1965. Experiments on smelting in Noric-type furnaces. *Karnten Museum Schriften*, **35**

Thomsen, R 1963. Forsog pa rekonstruktion af en fortidig jernudrindingsproces. *Kuml*, 60-74

Tylecote, R F 1964. Roman lead working in Britain. *British Journal for the History of Science*, **2**, 25-43

Tylecote, R F, Austin, J N & Wraith, A E 1971. The mechanism of the bloomery process in shaft furnaces. *Journal of the Iron and Steel Institute*, **209**, 342-363

Tylecote, R F, Ghaznavi, H A & Boydell, P J 1977. Partitioning of trace elements between the ores, fluxes, slags and metal during the smelting of copper. *Journal of Archaeological Science*, **4**, 305-333

Tylecote, R F & Boydell, P J 1978. Experiments on copper smelting based on early furnaces at Timna. In *Archaeo-Metallurgy Monograph* No. 1, ed. B Rothenberg. London

Tylecote, R F 1983. Ancient metallurgy in China. *The Metallurgist and Materials Technologist*, **15** (9), 435-439

Wagner, P A & Gordon, H S 1929. Further notes on ancient bronze smelters in the Waterberg district, Transvaal. *South African Journal of Science* **26**, 563-570

Wynne, E J & Tylecote, R F 1958. An experimental investigation into primitive iron smelting technique. *Journal of the Iron and Steel Institute*, **190**, 339-348

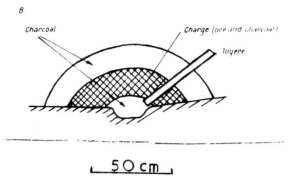

Fig. 1   Furnace used for Gowlands'
direct bronze smelting
experiment (After Gowland
1899)

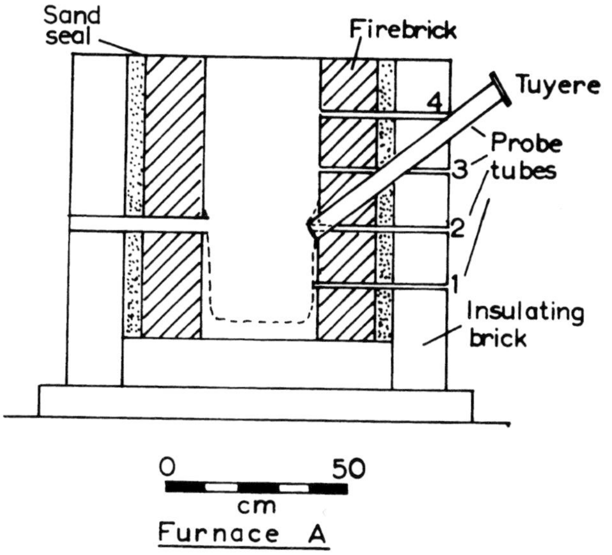

L 50 cm ˥

Fig. 2   Furnace, Type A, used in
Boydell's copper smelting
experiments (After Tylecote
& Boydell 1978)

0   50
cm
Furnace A

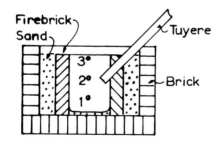

Fig. 3   Furnace, Type B, used in
Boydell's copper smelting
experiments (After Tylecote
& Boydell 1978)

0   50   100
cm

Furnace B

18

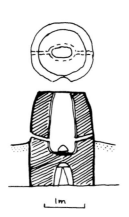

Fig. 4   Reconstruction of Chinese
          furnace based on remains found
          on the fifth century BC site of
          Tonglushan and used for smelting
          experiments (After Hua *et al.*
          1981)

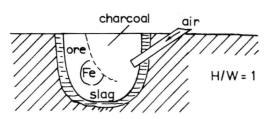

Fig. 5   Iron bloomery furnace based
          on the Catalan principle of
          the divided charge (After
          Wynne & Tylecote 1958)

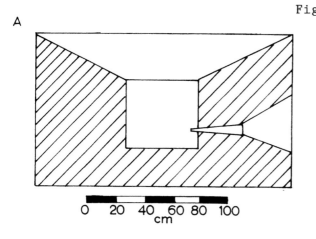

Fig. 6   Scandinavian type of manipu-
          lated bloomery furnace used
          for experiments in the
          nineteenth century AD (After
          Busch 1972)

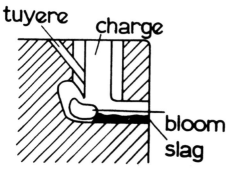

Fig. 7   Section through experimental
          Slav furnace based on the
          eighth-ninth century furnaces
          found at Zelechovice,
          Czechoslovakia (After Pleiner
          1969)

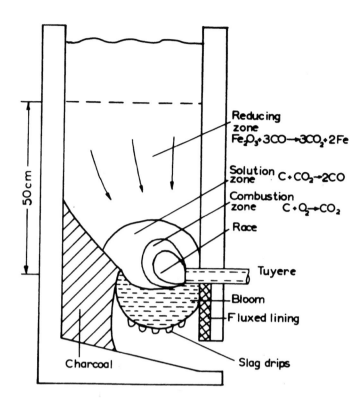

Fig. 8 Details of the working of an experimental shaft bloomery furnace
based on typical Romano-British furnaces (After Tylecote, Austin &
Wraith 1971)

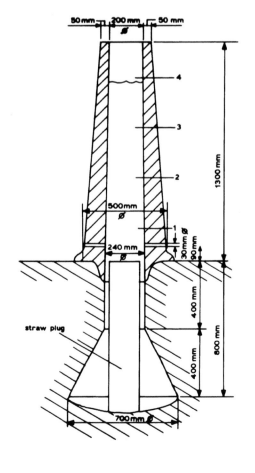

Fig. 9 Details of experimental slag-
pit furnace used by Thomsen and
based on North European types
(After Thomsen 1963)

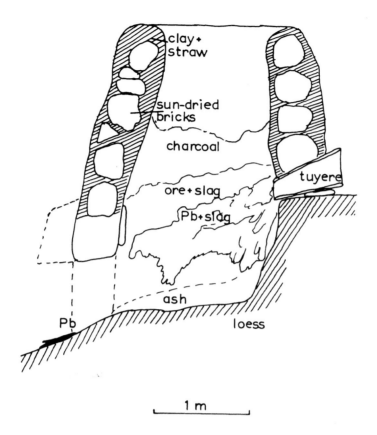

1 m

Fig. 10   Furnace erected in Central Iran for lead smelting experiments (After
Pleiner 1967)

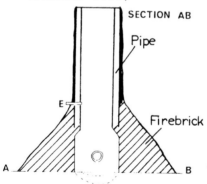

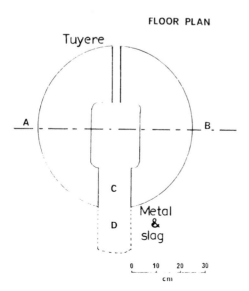

Fig. 11   Furnace used for tin smelting
experiments in South Africa
(After Friede & Steel 1976)

DETERMINATIVE MINERALOGY AND THE ORIGINS OF METALLURGY

J A Charles

Department of Metallurgy and Materials Science,
University of Cambridge, Pembroke Street, Cambridge

Abstract

The important determinative features of the minerals
of lead, copper, arsenic, tin and iron are considered
in relation to the early development of metallurgy,
both in the context of initially accidental alloying
development and then in the purposeful selection of
additions as effects and causes were identified.
Explanations are suggested for the transition from
copper to copper-arsenic alloys and then to bronze.
The production of iron during the Bronze Age and its
eventual dominance will be considered, the latter
particularly as a function of the ability to produce
equivalent properties by carburisation.

Keywords: MINERALS, COPPER, COPPER-ARSENIC, BRONZE,
LEAD, IRON, METALLURGY

Introduction

Firstly, an apology for the broad generalisations and simplifications in what
I am about to say and for presenting what is a very long story, in the sense
of real time, as if it were a smooth and rapid sequential process occurring
uniformly throughout the world unaffected by anthropological considerations.
Nothing could be further from archaeological history. The development of
metal usage and the introduction and use of particular metals and alloys was
very heterogeneous both in location and time. Much depended on the availa-
bility of raw materials and, I believe, on the social structure and the status
of the smith in that social structure. What I believe one can do, however,
is to put together a composite metallurgical picture which assumes the best
possible conditions for innovation and experiment and for the previous traditions to be available, either maintained within one society or diffused from
another society by travel, trade or war with its attendant occupations and
movements.

What I seek to do is to give a sense of the basis for metal discovery
from general archaeological knowledge and how the recognition of minerals and
their connection to smelted products would be established. Putting ourselves
in the position of a late Neolithic man, we have become very 'earth-conscious'.
We are cultivating the soil now, but we are still stone-gatherers always looking
for good stones for tools or for building purposes, or just clearing them away
from our cultivation plots. At such a time coloured minerals are much more
widely abundant on the surface and at outcrops where mineralization exists
than they are today, and such materials attract our attention not only for
their colour but also for their structure and texture. By frequent handling
(as any mineralogy student knows), expected weight in relation to size (i.e.

density) becomes a possible feature for discrimination. Many of the coloured minerals have a veined appearance, some give strikingly facetted surfaces when broken and many are of a very shiny character, reflecting the sun. We collect these, perhaps to use ground up for colouring pictures as a slurry, perhaps for personal adornment (for example, galena could be used as eye-shadow!) or just to keep as attractive possessions in their own right as a matter of aesthetic fancy. We know that many minerals were collected for their own sake in Neolithic times.

There were one or two very strange materials that we would occasionally find. If we lived in certain areas there could be local concentrations of a shiny yellow material, perhaps shining on a stream bed but of very different texture to the rock-like minerals, being ductile such that you could even bend it back and forth if the piece were thin enough; and it only deformed when hammered and did not shatter as all other 'stones' did, being so different in texture and behaviour. We know that such native gold, as we would call it, was collected and used by the late Neolithic people, e.g. at Varna in Bulgaria. Additionally, associated with the strongly coloured copper minerals would be native copper, exhibiting similar properties of ductility: you could bend bits that stuck out of the host rock.

Such native copper, where it was found in large enough pieces, could be worked to a shape directly. It may be that they found that native copper was best freed from associated rock by 'firesetting', a technique already applied for breaking stones. The association of heat with the handling of copper would then be found to ease the hammering process, since the material is softer when hot, and copper which had hardened under the hammer when worked as it cooled, or when cold, could be resoftened by heating again in the fire, the cold-worked copper structure being re-crystallized into new grains, i.e. annealing would have been discovered. Perhaps, even, a copper rod hammered from native copper was found to be a useful tool for manipulating the fire - as a poker - and the softening effect was noted and utilised. Such annealing permitted the working of the native metals to thin sheet or section without cracking.

Once established, the association of minerals and treatment by fire would inevitably lead to the first smelting, i.e. the reduction of compounds to the metal. For example lead would have been collected as the striking and attractive sulphide galena, heavy and easily identified by its facetted, shiny texture. When heated on the top of the fire it would largely convert to lead oxide. Both copper and lead oxides are readily reduced to the metal at temperatures achieved in a fire burning charcoal or dry wood, but it is likely that lead was the first metal to be recovered in this way, since separation of the lead as molten metal from the reduction zone and its collection in the hearth or the separate melting of furnace prill requires only temperatures in excess of 327°C. Copper, on the other hand, could only be agglomerated to a usable form at much higher temperatures in excess of 1083°C, achievable only by a directed draught, whether forced or natural. Eventually, sufficiently hot conditions with draughting were developed to produce melting and, from this, the agglomeration and shaping of copper metal. The distinction has to be made here with gold, which could be agglomerated simply by hammering pieces into close contact, since there are no oxide or other films present which prevent metal bonding. At the beginning of the Chalcolithic, c. 4000 BC, we find cast objects of copper, such as the axes from the Vinca culture in the Balkans. It is difficult to say whether the material melted is native copper or the product of the early smelting of rich copper ores. As already pointed out, the reduction of copper oxide is an easy matter at temperatures in excess of 700°C, above which temperature the CO/CO_2 ratio increases rapidly in equilibrium with carbon, giving efficient gaseous reduction. In pure carbon monoxide supplied from an external source malachite can be reduced to copper at below red heat, since the reaction is no longer dependant on the direct presence of carbon at 700°C plus to produce the carbon monoxide.

How would ancient man have learnt that the highly coloured green and blue minerals were a likely source of copper? In the first place native copper is often associated directly in juxtaposition with oxide minerals, and he may have found that his yield to metal did not suffer, but increased if he did not bother to separate the two before melting for agglomeration. Secondly, he would have noted that heating the coloured minerals alone gave the same strong green flame coloration as produced when he heated metallic copper. Attention would gradually change from the need to find the increasingly rare native copper for melting to the strong heating of strongly coloured 'stones' which gave the green flame. In this respect I do not believe that the discovery of smelting has to be considered as a separate innovative event.

Flame colour has always been used by mineralogists as a simple distinguishing test for the compounds of certain metals, notably copper and lead. Lead minerals give a pale azure-blue flame. Further simple tests relate to the colour and form of encrustations produced by heating and the degree of sublimation of the oxides produced and to the odour produced on heating – the pungent smell of the sulphur dioxide when heating sulphides and the garlic odour produced from arsenic.

It is clear that early smelting was based on the oxidised minerals available at weathered surface outcrops, below the mainly iron oxide surface gossan or iron hat, green malachite ($CuCO_3.Cu(OH)_2$), blue azurite ($2\ CuCO_3$ $(CuOH)_2$) and red cuprite (Cu_2O).

In the Balkans, certainly, we have heard of the first industrial depression at the end of the Chalcolithic period, partly associated with the working out of the oxidised minerals there. But with continued excavation the miners would have eventually encountered the minerals of the secondary enrichment zone, containing the copper-rich sulphide minerals, chalcocite (Cu_2S), covellite (CuS) and the mixed copper/iron sulphides chalcopyrite ($Cu_2S.Fe_2S_3$) and bornite $5\ Cu_2S.Fe_2S_3$, on which the deposit was originally based, together with iron pyrites. These attractive glinting minerals would be tried in the fire, and chalcopyrite and bornite would still have given the strong green flame and all a pungent odour. On roasting they would give a black oxide, just as malachite does, but separation from the iron component requires a somewhat more complex operation, nowadays achieved by the oxidation of a separated molten sulphide or matte, then by some selective reduction at the CO/O_2 ratios employed and the separation of metallic iron from the copper on remelting. It is probably unlikely that the use of the more complex copper-iron sulphide minerals was associated with early copper smelting, although developing later in the full Bronze Age.

The introduction of flux

An important distinction between the mere melting of native copper and the reduction of even hand-picked rich copper ores was the need to separate the mixture of fine copper droplets and high melting point solid oxides – lime, silica, alumina, etc – to give efficient collection either as coarse prill or run-down onto the hearth. It would not necessarily follow that the melting point of the oxide system would need to be lowered to that of copper at 1083°C, but to a temperature achievable in the draughted charcoal furnace, so that a degree of liquid separation could be achieved, the two phases being immiscible. The best flux, easily available, is iron oxide, particularly limonite available from the gossan or iron hat, associated with the copper deposit. The gossan is enriched in iron oxide by the oxidation of the original copper-iron sulphide with the weathering solution of copper salts which drain further down into the deposit. Nonetheless, the gossans still contain evidence of copper association and may have been first included in mixes for smelting for this reason of copper content with eventual recognition that it was an important ingredient for other reasons. This knowledge would then lead to the use of limonite alone by comparison of colour and texture with the bulk of the gossan.

Another possible way in which iron oxide may first have been incorporated when smelting oxidised ores lies in the similarity of cuprite and red iron oxide, haematite, which was used as a flux at Timna. Sometimes cuprite is bright red, as in the crystalline form (isometric-cubes, octahedron, etc, like galena). More often, however, as in the massive lumps associated with native copper, it is a dull red and the similarity to haematite is striking.

The first production of iron

The addition of flux is very important, an addition for an effect rather than for a product. It demonstrates a growing understanding of the behaviour of materials in fire and how their behaviour might be controlled. It also indicates a possible origin for the production of metallic iron even before pyritic ores were employed. In cases where the gangue content of the iron oxide used was low, so that the chemical activity of the iron oxide was not reduced by combination with silica, etc. and if the iron oxide was not very well mixed in with the other components, metallic iron would have occurred as small pieces here and there, not separated to the hearth but held up in the surface cinder. Its characteristics, similarly ductile to copper when forged under the hammer even if a different colour when cold, would have been noted. That such metallic iron can even be produced adventitiously in the smelting of lead is also well established. At this stage it would have been valuable – from early texts more valuable than silver.

Also, under conditions where the activity of iron is high but not leading to some metallic iron formation, some iron reduction into the liquid copper will occur, to be rejected from the copper as it solidifies. Where the originally dispersed smelted copper was remelted in a crucible this iron would separate as a 'rim' of distinct material. It is very likely, therefore, that the earliest iron was obtained by the treatment of ores discovered through association with copper. Certainly the Romans continued to mine iron ore from sites previously excavated for copper and Pliny warns of inferior irons being 'founded upon veins of brass', the main effect of copper impurity in the iron being to introduce hot shortness or cracking under the forging hammer.

With improvement in furnaces, better draughting, bellows, etc, and higher temperatures, more iron would be produced and eventually it could be purposefully made if required, once its association with the brown iron ore was recognised. As Bachmann and Rothenberg have already pointed out in relation to operations at Timna, if it were required to maximise the amount of iron produced in association with copper, the use of manganese oxide instead of iron oxide as a flux would give the desired effect.

The inclusion of haematite instead of cuprite is a sequence by which the connection between iron ore and the white metallic product could be recognised. Yet another possibility is that the collection of iron pyrites of yellow/white metallic lustre would have attracted interest, particularly once the sulphide minerals of copper were being used, giving the same sulphurous smell but an infusible and different-coloured metal in small pieces.

Whatever the explanation, the incidence of occasional iron artifacts (other than meteoric material) in the Bronze Age, from the earliest period, fits with these theories of its adventitious formation during the production of bronze.

The incidence of iron in the cinders of the furnace would increase with improved furnace operation in terms of higher temperature and with maintained CO/CO_2 ratios. It would, in fact, be necessary to maintain a suitably mildly reducing atmosphere in order not to produce too much metallic iron in association with copper. Eventually it would be deduced how to operate the furnace to maximise or minimise the extent of solid-state iron production or simply to use the iron charge to flux silica, etc as free-running fayalite slags at temperatures greater than 1200°C.

Development of copper-arsenic alloys

Copper-arsenic alloys occur as a separate distinct phase of metallurgical development at the end of the Chalcolithic and the beginning of the Bronze Age in many areas, often of considerable duration, before the use of tin to make the copper-tin alloy which is bronze. They then continued in use together with tin-bronze for about 500 years. There are advantages over pure copper in terms of castings where the arsenic acts as a deoxidant, and up to 7% arsenic material can be work-hardened very substantially by cold hammering without cracking to strengths equivalent to tin-bronze. The question that must be asked is how did this material arise? As a mineral arsenic occurs rarely in the form of the native metal and as the sulphides realgar (As_2S_2) and orpiment (As_2S_3), bright orange and yellow in colour, which are associated with volcanic activity. In the copper deposits arsenic is found in each zone, as green arsenates (e.g. olivenite) of similar appearance to malachite in the oxidised zone, and as the sulpharsenides enargite (Cu_3AsS) and tennantite (Cu_3AsS) lower down.

Also in the original deposit would be the ubiquitous arsenopyrite ($FeAsS$). The one feature linking all these arsenic minerals is the garlic odour produced on heating in contact with air, as in the charcoal block test used for determinative mineralogy in the field before modern portable analytical instruments were available. The smell is even detectable when hammering arseno-sulphide ore for breaking.

Presumably the first recognition of the new material came when green stones, of similar but not identical appearance to malachite, initially collected as charge gave better material. The only difference that could be used to be sure of a different charge and thus of a different product would be the smell associated with processing. Other materials giving the same smell, particularly if they gave the same flame colour for copper, would be added to charges. Thus with continued mining the sulpharsenides could have been used. Once the smell was recognized as the important feature, arseno-pyrite could have been employed, mixed in with the copper ores or perhaps used as a separate addition to copper melts since it is found widely and is particularly common in placer deposits with gold.

By this time melting in crucibles as opposed to simple hearth collection was well established and the possibility of re-melting metallic copper with surface additions of concentrated minerals under a charcoal cover becomes a reality, to produce individual alloys under more closely controlled conditions of quantities of addition. It has been shown that tin can be absorbed into copper directly from surface additions of stannite (tin sulphide) as well as from cassiterite under charcoal, and arsenic may have been similarly added from arsenic/sulphide minerals or from a high arsenious oxide product. A possible mechanism for the former can be envisaged as the formation of a surface speiss when the arsenic would diffuse into the copper to balance activity.

Advent of tin-bronze

After the copper-arsenic phase we enter the true Bronze Age. The use of copper-arsenic alloys and the new tin-bronzes goes on hand in hand for a period. The tin-bronzes produced rarely contain significant arsenic and the copper-arsenic alloys are usually free of tin. It seems clear, therefore, that the sort of purposeful alloying that I write of above had become estab-lished, adding selected materials to copper for their effects. In some regions the arsenical phase does not appear to have existed (e.g. Ireland) and the period of alloying commences directly with tin-bronze. How did the effect of tin additions become recognized?

In some sulphidic copper deposits stannite may occur, but it is fairly rare. It usually contains arsenic and where a copper-arsenic tradition was already established could have been selected because of the characteristic odour of the arsenic. It also has the semi-metallic appearance they were used to in the copper sulpharsenides and arsenopyrite, both presumably estab-lished as arsenic sources.

However, as stated, stannite is relatively rare and we are left with the problem of how they made the connection to the only other tin mineral avail-able, cassiterite, available particularly in placer deposits associated with granites and pegmatites at high concentrations.

Cassiterite also occurs in the gossans of some copper deposits. Tin oxide is insoluble and is left behind by the weathering and leaching process often in the wood-tin form. Of a generally brown appearance with no flame colour, it may first have been identified with a magical flux in association with the brown iron oxide. This would initially introduce a low level of tin, but then observation and deduction would lead to the separate component which made all the difference.

Identifying cassiterite is not difficult if you are prepared to handle the material: it is extremely dense and therefore heavy. Together with its inertness, this results in it being concentrated from the breakdown of weathered rock in existing or ancient but now dried stream beds. Once knowing what to look for they would have already known where it was from the earlier mining for gold. Furthermore, in the same placer deposits is arseno-pyrite, already suggested as a possible source of arsenic in the earlier phase.

There remains, of course, the direct approach. Perhaps an ancient smith, already using arsenopyrite collected from a placer deposit or working the gold, just decided to try these very dense brown stones as a surface addition to his crucible surrounded by charcoal just to see what happened - for the smith might be regarded as the earliest scientist experimenting on the basis of that innate curiosity which is part of the human character, particularly developed in skilled craftsmen and the modern-day scientist.

Tin oxide can be reduced relatively easily directly to tin, although with substantial losses to the slag phase unless the furnace is very strongly reducing and the temperature is high, not an easy combination to achieve in a primitive furnace. Some few tin articles have survived from the Bronze Age, but these are not as numerous as one would expect if tin were always added to copper as tin metal in the alloying procedure. Some tin ingots have been found in the Mediterranean, but they are relatively uncommon. There are very few records of any tin metal being found in any Bronze Age founders hoards, although there is always bulk copper and scrap bronze artifacts. Maybe the smaller amount of metallic tin, the vital ingredient, was always kept on his person, as his most valuable possession. But perhaps the archaeologists did not recognize the brown stones that might have been near the hoard - the cassiterite - for the smith could perfectly well have added the tin this way, crushing it and putting it into the copper surface under charcoal. Reduction is, in fact, more easily achieved in the presence of copper, since the copper in dissolving the tin away from the reaction (decreasing its chemical activity) increases the thermodynamic driving force for the reduction reaction and it is achieved at lower temperature.

Eclipse of copper-arsenic alloys

Eventually, after about 700 years at most, copper arsenic alloys were no longer employed, and tin-bronze alone was made. Why? Technical reasons may be advanced. Once the arsenates were exhausted in deposits the addition of arsenic from such materials as enargite, tennantite and arsenopyrite would involve substantial losses of arsenic in the roasting stage of heating, and the volatility of arsenious oxide would make control of arsenic content difficult. Once the arsenates were no longer available and once the lead to tin-bronze had become established, perhaps the somewhat better properties of the tin-bronze and certainly its consistency from measured additions of cassiterite would have eventually won the day.

Personally I believe that it was almost an evolutionary change, based not only on the increasing difficulty of finding arsenical minerals and inconsistent results, but also on that very garlic odour used to determine the mineralogy. Of the Greek gods in the Homeric record only Hephaestus the the smith was imperfect: he suffered with a limp, and was a bit of a joke, presumably the mark of smiths generally - and terminal neuritis is a sympton of arsenic poisoning.

Eventually, the smiths concentrating on tin-bronze would be clearly seen to be in better health and live to greater ages than those making the terrible smell! Eventually understanding would work itself into the smiths' code, just as we now recognize the dangers of working with carcinogenic materials. In later history alchemists in particular were fascinated by arsenic in potions and clearly a tradition of its strange effects on human beings had been handed on.

The change from bronze to iron

We have established that small quantities of iron were produced in the Bronze Age and that, eventually, selective smelting for iron blooms would have been possible with high enough temperatures, as in the primitive African iron furnaces of today. Levels of metallurgical skill had been achieved in the Bronze Age which make these present Iron Age smiths, who in some instances have no social status in their tribes, look positively neolithic. For example, the Minoans invented 'Sheffield Plate', diffusion bonding silver to copper at each end of the rivets holding the handle to the tang of a dagger. The Mycenaeans bonded both silver and gold to bronze as inlay on the famous shaft grave daggers, presumably also by diffusion bonding. The addition of lead to bronze for the marked effect it has on castability was identified as a metallurgical technique of particular value in the production of thin walled castings.

Such people and their successors were able to assess material and its potential. They had status in their social life and patronage to produce superior products, both for war and for the aesthetic sense in forms of decoration and design. They would have recognised the need for change as cassiterite from easy placer deposits effectively disappeared with the need for journeyings further and further afield. In producing iron in more complex furnace structures at higher temperatures and with changes in manipulative techniques giving more carburisation external to the blast zone, superior material would be produced which began to have strength properties at least as good as bronze, for iron containing carbon can be progressively cold-worked and annealed to the same hardness as bronze for a sword. Separate carburisation using a charcoal hearth after initial forging of the bloom could also have emerged as part of a hot forging process for blades. Eventually, impatient to cool down such carburised hot metal, dowsing into cold water from bright red heat gave the smith a remarkable material, extremely hard and brittle, particularly at the thin cutting edge which could be progressively softened and toughened by reheating, and the true 'steel' age was born, probably in Egypt, around 900 BC.

Reference

Bachmann, H G & Rothenberg, B 1980. Die Verhüttungsverfahren von Site 30. In *Antikes Kupfer im Timna-Tal in der Arabah (Israel)*, eds. H G Conrad & B Rothenberg, 215-236. Bochum: Der Anschnitt, Beiheft 1

METHODS OF ORE ROASTING AND THE FURNACES USED

J R Marechal (translated by P T Craddock)

Le Miramar, 4 Avenue Foch, F-14390 Cabourg, France

Abstract

This paper deals with the process and structural remains of ore roasting as applied to both non-ferrous and ferrous ores in Europe, particularly France, over the past two thousand years. Most ores require a preliminary roast in air prior to smelting to break down compounds such as sulphides and carbonates, to evaporate moisture, or just to prepare them for smelting. The process and its furnaces have so far received scant attention by those studying ancient metallurgy and the archaeology of metal smelting sites.

Keywords: ROASTING, FURNACE, FRANCE, KILN, ORE, IRON, COPPER, SILVER, LEAD, SILVER-LEAD, SMELTING, SPEISS, MATTE

Introduction

The first operation that ores used to undergo was usually heating to a temperature below that necessary to melt the metal or the gangue. We will call this process by the more specialised name *roasting*, during which a chemical change takes place. This will be either an oxidisation (of sulphides - a *sulphatising roast* or *dead roasting* depending on the degree of oxidisation), a chlorination (when sodium chloride is added as in the case of argentiferous ores), or a calcination (when there is only decomposition as in the cases of carbonates, sulphates, arsenates etc). These changes can take the form:

1 Agglomeration or sintering as in the treatment of some galenas

2 Volatilisation as in the case of sulphides, arsenides and antimonides

3 Concentration by partial oxidisation of the iron and the formation of mattes and speiss.

Copper

Before sulphate roasting, suitable ores could be easily processed when they
contained bituminous materials. There are many examples such as those found
in the district of Mansfeld-Eisleben-Hellstedt, situated at the southern
edge of the Harz in central Germany, or the cupiferous marls of Hesse and
Waldeck which contain fossil plant material (wood, jet, grass, nutshells
with imprints of plants and even insects) and are rich in copper (8-20%
and averaging 13%) and which also contain silver (up to 1 kg te^{-1}).
There are also the cupiferous 'Mergelschiefer' ores of the northern foot-
hills of the Riesengebirge (Lower Silesia) which are already degraded by
the atmosphere and roast very easily producing copper granules (globulisa-
tion) which the miners call 'Graupen' (grain) because of the similarity to
grains of wheat. This class of ores was sometimes decomposed in the atmosphere and could be concentrated by washing. According to the old writer
F L Cancrinus (1767), who described the deposits of Hesse and Waldeck,
there was at Goddelsheim and at Niederense green or brownish 'Graupen' of
couvellite (Cu_2S) capable of producing 25 tonnes of copper per year lying
just beneath the turf.

Roasting in heaps first drove off the moisture and broke down the
carbonates and sulphides, completing the breakdown already started by exposure to air. The combustibles naturally present in the ore burned easily
and reduced the residual oxides and sulphides, forming globules of metal
which grew in varying degrees according to the duration of the roasting.
One must not forget that the sulphur in the sulphides is also combustible
and that if they are placed in heaps surrounded by refractory stones one
has only to start the combustion and the reaction proceeds until almost all
the sulphur is removed. Up to 600°C the reaction is:

$$Cu_2S + 2O_2 \quad ---> \quad 2CuO + SO_2$$

and at 800°-850°C:

$$2Cu_2S + 2CuO \quad ---> \quad 4Cu + SO_2$$

The copper oxides are then reduced in the appropriate furnace. If the ore
contains too much pyrites it is obviously necessary to concentrate the
copper and iron sulphides (matte) after the partial oxidisation of the iron.
Some of this iron is removed in the slag. If there is arsenic or antimony
in the ore one sometimes obtains a lighter matte than the sulphidic matte,
known generally as speiss (containing high melting point iron arsenides and
antimonides). The operation is repeated several times in the roasting
furnaces, the mattes becoming increasingly richer, to obtain more than 20%
of copper. In practice more than eight and sometimes up to fifteen or six-
teen separate roasting operations have been known to take place (Liege 1778).

Lead and Silver

With lead ores roasting in air gives a mixture of oxides and sulphates
with a varying residue of sulphides, depending on the temperature. When
the temperature is quite low (500-600°C) then the product has more sulphide
than oxide, but accordingly if the temperature is raised (800°-900°C), then
the formation of the oxide predominates. To moderate the heat, faggots of
wood, peat or dry wood were added. First there is the formation of a
yellowish crust which covers the mass of the ore which must be stirred and
mixed with the untouched galena, producing new sulphates and oxides which
react with the galena to give the oxy-sulphide. This is known as the

'Schlicks', which is ready to be reduced by carbon. If there is silica in the gangue, or if it has been deliberately added, lead silicates are formed which can be reduced by limestone:

$$Pb\ SiO_3\ +\ CaO\ \longrightarrow\ \ Ca\ SiO_3\ +\ PbO$$

$$2PbO\ +\ C\ \longrightarrow\ \ 2Pb\ +\ CO_2$$

If the gangue contains barytes (barium sulphate) as well as silica (which is the case in certain regions such as in Ceilhe, department-Herault, see Fig. 1), barium oxide is formed which facilitates the desulphuring of the galena. It is thus a useful substance in the treatment of lead sulphate, acting as a very necessary flux which will improve the fluidity of the shaft furnace slags, especially if mixed with fluorspar (CaF_2).

If one adds iron ore in the form of an oxide or limonite to the lead ore, they form a matte consisting of the sulphides of lead, copper (if present in the ore), and iron, together with a slag principally of iron silicate. In order for the air to be able to circulate through the contents of the furnace, one must adjust the openings in the bottom of the furnace interior, such as is shown in representations of several furnaces depicted on the lead plaques found at Lascours (Ceilhe, Herault). More than a score of these circular cast lead seals were found in 1936 by Dr J Brunel, and depict ore-roasting furnaces and other apparatus.

As most of the lead veins lying to the west of the upper Orb have barytic gangues, the origin of this metalliferous district is to be explained not only by the galena, but also by the stibnite (Sb_2S_3), grey copper, mispickel and bournonite ($CuPbSbS_2$). As well as lead, antimony (especially from silver) was extracted.

The massif is formed of Hercynian microgranites (Mont Faulat) giving rhyolithic veins towards the edges. Towards the north the 'Grand Mourgis' of basalt with veins of argentiferous galena and stibnite was considered by the German geologist Trautmann as the 'Harz' of the South of France.

The local archaeologist Robert Gourdiolle considered that mining and metallurgy started in the area towards the end of the second century BC, or the beginning of the first century BC, which does not mean that earlier prospectors did not collect the native silver found in the upper veins of the lead-antimony deposits. A sacred place was established during the first century BC on the site of an ancient roasting area at Lascours (Mange-Homme, see Fig. 1). The roasted products were washed in the River Rabasse and sent as concentrates to the smelter, the site of which has not yet been found. The processing, traces of which have been found, took place at an early stage in the process, which was temporarily abandoned and then restored at the beginning of the first century AD. The site of Mange-Homme has a slag heap in which 'ingots' of waste metal, plates, and slags have been found, which M Boyer of the Societe de la Vieille Montagne, Viviez, has analysed (Table 1). These samples could be identified as matte (sample 1) or speiss, where the sulphur had been eliminated by roasting, leaving arsenic and antimony in the product (samples 2, 3 or 4). Nickel, which is resistant to oxidisation, was possibly concentrated in these speiss after roasting. Analyses of the three speiss samples from Mange-Homme (2, 3 and 4 in Table 1) can be compared with those given by Witter from Guschau (Kr Sorau) produced by treating fahlerz, and those given by Werner (1976) in Table 2.

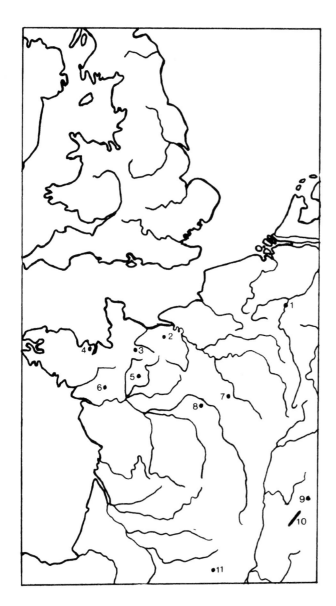

1 Lustin, province de Namur (Belgium).

2 Mesnil – Germain, dép. Calvados.

3 La Coulonche, dép. Orne.

4 Alet, près de Saint – Malo, dép. Ille – et – Villaine.

5 Lavardin au nord – ouest du Mans, dép. Sarthe.

6 La Meilleray, dép. Loire – Atlantique.

7 Fontaine, près de Toucy, dép. Yonne.

8 Châtillon – sur – Loire, dép. Loiret.

9 Peisey – Nancroix (formerly Pesey) & the
   mine of Macot or Plagne, dép. Savoie.

10 Chalanches,
   Allemont
   La Gardette   dép. Isère
   Le Pontet
   Le Grand Clot

11 Upper Valley of the Orb, dép. Hérault :–
   Lascours (Mange – Homme)
   Mont Faulat
   La Rabasse

Figure

It can be seen by comparing Tables 1 and 2 that the speiss from Mange-Homme has more nickel, arsenic and antimony, coming from the local ore bodies, than the fahlerz, which gave the speiss from Guschau, rather than the German speiss dating from the first part of the twentieth century AD, as a by-product of lead smelting given by Werner. However, the Mange-Homme speiss contains some lead (8-12%) coming from the galena and bournonite which both occur in the region.

When one comes to the so-called slags they must be considered rather as roasting residues of which a single analysis from Mange-Homme is compared with those found on the island of Helgoland (Table 3). The low copper content of the Helgoland samples is consistent with them being from lightly fritted gangue.

What did they do with these apparently useless speiss? They could only have mixed them with molten copper to make the complex alloys so common in central Europe and in the South of France. Did the Romans know how to treat them to eliminate the volatile elements by remelting in the furnaces for handling other more easily reduced copper ores?

Table 1

	1 ropelike waste %	2 granular waste %	3 Thick Plate %	4 Conical waste %
Cu	40.00	30.00	50.00	64.00
S	20.00	1.50	1.40	0.22
As	0.12	20.00	11.60	19.40
Sb	0.20	20.00 by difference	15.00 by difference	1.98
Ni	0.20	20.50	10.00	14.00
Pb	32.50	8.00	12.00	1.98 by difference
Density	6.20	7.00	8.20	-

Table 2

	'SPEISS' from Guschau (Witter)		'SPEISS' from Germany (Werner 1976)		
	No 6 %	No 7 %	Oker-Hutte %	Lautenthal %	Mean %
Cu	33.17	44.54	51.73	33.50	35-40
S	4.38	2.23	-	-	-
As	16.76	16.94	2.75	8.20	5-10
Sb	13.09	12.97	3.34	17.00	4- 8
Fe	5.72	0.55	1.60	7.20	3-15
Ni	19.10	15.92	0.30	1.20	5-12
Pb	0.07	0.83	35.20	28.50	10-35
Ag	0.428	0.579	-	-	-

Table 3

	Mange-Homme (analysed for Vieille-Montagne) %	Helgoland (analysed by Marechal) %	
SiO_2	29.40	42.60	43.57
Al_2O_3	12.40	13.66	14.66
FeO	7.04	2.40	3.22
CaO	3.78	10.25	8.56
MgO	0.41	1.59	1.11
Pb	48.00	-	-
Cu	0.35	0.75	7.20
Ag	0.10	0	trace
As	2.00	0	0
Sb	1.20	-	-
Ni	0.15	0	trace
S	-	0	0

Traces can remain, as in the case of the copper from Lauthental known under the title of 'Mica du Cuivre', a double copper nickel antimonate partially oxidised by the reprocessing of copper containing rather too much antimony, which is very difficult to break down, and which makes the metal very brittle when present in quantities over 1.5%. It is proposed here to call this metal 'hampite' in memory of the German metallurigst W Hampe (1841-1899) who was the first to study it scientifically around 1870 and who gave it the chemical formula $6Cu_2O.8NiO.2Sb_2O_3$.

Another example of a special treatment of mixed copper/lead/silver ores was that carried out at the site of Alet (Sant-Malo department Ille et Villaine, Fig. 1) where slightly concave ingots of waste 10-15 cm in diameter, consisting of lead oxides completely converted to the carbonate and of copper oxide and carbonate, were found. These were produced by an oxidising roast and were probably destined for cupellation on account of their silver content which could reach 5%. It was not possible to reconstruct the shape of the furnaces because of the fragmentation of the burnt clay debris found with these 'cakes', but it was possible to date them by the associated coins and ceramics. It was before the disappearance of the gallic sintering process found at Alet, around 20-15 BC. This metallurgical roasting was thus carried out by the local tribe called the Curiosolites before the arrival of the Romans and the Romanisation of the region (Marechal 1978).

J E Dayton (1981) has attempted to reconstruct the shape of a furnace for treating silver ores found in the metals district of Schneeberg in the Saxon Erzgebirge. This region is very rich in silver, thus containing nickel, cobalt and bismuth, which makes it very characteristic and almost unique in the ancient world. But as the ores contained volatiles which had to be removed, such as sulphur, arsenic and antimony, a preliminary roasting had to be carried out before utilising the furnaces described by Dayton. He claims that the slag was the source of the much prized blue cobalt glass and that the calcareous speiss was the celebrated 'Kyanos', described by Homer! Bismuth is a good indication of the source of silver, especially when accompanied by cobalt as in the region of Schneeberg. The silver from this area contained traces of tin, bismuth, and cobalt as found in the silver coins struck in Bohemia and, more astonishingly still, traces of copper, cobalt, nickel, and bismuth are found in silver objects from Greek tombs and from the Hyksos period in Egypt.

The presence of stannite, which is a mixed ore of copper, tin and iron, in the western part of the Erzgebirge could have produced a natural bronze after roasting and reduction. This, according to Dayton, would be an interesting clue indicating a local invention of bronze metallurgy, thus supporting the hypothesis of the famous German metallurgist W Witter, which was previously so much ridiculed. He clamined that the paragenesis of the ores in mining districts in the Harz, Erzgebirge and in Thuringia was too characteristic for one to doubt a local origin for the torcs and axes of the earliest Bronze Age. (It should be noted that the properties of complex copper minerals arising from successive roastings, have still not been adequately studied in spite of the researches of S L Archbutt and W E Prytherch (1937) and other English experts at the British Non-Ferrous Metals Research Association.)

Now let us return to silver and the work of John C Allan (1968) on the recovery of that metal by roasting the jarositic earths of Rio Tinto. Jarosite is a basic hydrated sulphate of iron and potassium which is able to undergo substitution by variable amounts of other metals such as lead or silver as in plumbo-jarosite and argento-jarosite. Allan gives chemical analyses of these ores showing a silver content of 166-3110 g te^{-1} as well as a little gold (2-40 g te^{-1}). He cites the example of deposits at Matagente in Peru where the pockets of jarosites low in iron and high in friable silica made it easy for the Indians to extract silver by using a globulising roast before smelting. The description of this process from South America has made it possible to identify the analagous primitive round furnaces found at Rio Tinto dating from 800-600 BC also consisting of clay-lined hollows in the ground.

Advancing technology permitted an increase in the temperature, improving the fusion of the silica and iron oxide but in turn leading to the formation of slag, which led to the development of shaft furnaces similar to those used later by the Romans, about 2 m tall and 75-100 cm in diameter. One imagines that it was above all the silver extracted from this mine which made the fabulous wealth of the kingdom of Tartessos so famous. Rio Tinto also supplied between 60,000-70,000 tonnes of copper to the Romans (Allan 1968). Another classic example, but clearly more recent, are the argentiferous ochres of Chalanches (department Isere, Fig.1) arising from the alteration of a very complex network of ore-bearing veins, situated 2000 m upon the southern slopes of the Grande Lance d'Allemont above the tree line. This deposit, in France in the *serie satinee* of the Alps, is composed of gneiss, micaschist, and amphiobolite with enhanced nickel and cobalt originating from a profound metamorphsim of Hercynian type at the time of the alpine orogeny. As well as the silver this deposit contains more than 60 other different minerals which makes it a paradise for the geologist (Clavel 1964). It resembles neither the formations of Sainte-Marie-aux-Mines in the Vosges nor those found in Saxony. The silver was discovered by chance in 1767 by a shepherdess, Marie Payen, who collected a lump which was recognised to be of silver and was soon sought by the amateur prospectors. But it was a metallurgist from Saxony, Johann-Gottfrief Schreiber, who discovered the complex network of the ore fields. The complexity of the argentiferous earths caused by alteration underlined the inadequacy of the first furnaces used for their treatment. He substituted small shaft furnaces, which immediately allowed an economy of 30% in fuel, then Scottish type furnaces, and finally reverbatory furnaces which did away with all the intermediary roasting stages and allowed further reduction in fuel consumption and an increase in silver recovery. The remains of this process have been found at the most ancient sites of metallurgy.

But this region of the Oisans had other riches, notably about ten kilometres to the south of the Chalanches deposit, where Schreiber extracted gold from a placer deposit. This was then the only gold mine, apart from the gold-bearing sands usually worked at this period. Then there are the deposits at Pontet, near to the Gardette, and finally those of the Grand Clot, the mine of Pesey (really Peisey-Nancroix) 1300 m high in the Tartentaise mining district (see Figure), known in antiquity for 'Sallustius Copper' (Pliny) of the Ceutron district, although copper was exhausted in Pliny's time. But the area was rich in argentiferous lead which the Romans also worked.

More recently the workings prospered between 1745 and 1791, and produced in total 14,670 tonnes of lead and 36,670 kg of silver. The mine, called Macot, in a valley running parallel to that of Pesey but higher, at 2,000 metres, was rediscovered by a local child, Francois Pelissier, and Schreiber worked it under the name of La Plagne Mine. Galena in a gangue of quartz and barytes was washed downstream from the mine. The ore also contained a significant percentage of cerusite (lead carbonate) which helped the roasting and reaction process become standard practice. The metallurgical processes were carried on in an old saltworks bought by Schreiber at Conflans, at the confluence of the Isere and the Arly rivers. He applied his experience acquired at Pesey, notably the installation of a Scottish type furnace and a cupellation furnace.

Iron ores

Turning to iron ores, they are roasted when they come from vein deposits, and could contain sulphur, or they may be carbonates (siderites) or again they may be dense magnetites which are difficult to process. The breakdown of the anhydrous carbonate is an exothermic reaction when there is an excess of air:

$$4FeCO_3 + O_2 \dashrightarrow 2Fe_2O_3 + 4CO_2 + 30 \text{ calories}$$

The reaction evolves 65 calories per kilo of carbonate or 134 calories per kilo of iron. This corresponds almost exactly to the quantity of heat needed to raise a kilogram of iron carbonate to a temperature of 400°C which is the dissociation temperature of the carbonate. Theoretically with pure iron carbonate, once the furnace is heated and the first load of ore is raised to the dissociation temperature by burning a little wood or charcoal, the reaction should continue indefinitely without appreciable combustion of fuel. But in practice it is not so, as some calories are necessary to heat the ore and the gangue, to drive off moisture from the ore, and to compensate for heat losses by radiation, conduction, and by convection with the fume.

It can be said that with ore which is not too friable and with shaft furnaces of height and capacity to suit the size of the ore fragments and to avoid crushing, the average consumption of charcoal need not exceed 10 kg te^{-1} of roasted carbonate, and say 7.5 kg te^{-1} of crude ore. It is the same for the roasting of magnetite ores, which could theoretically proceed without appreciable expenditure of heat as the oxidisation reaction is exothermic:

$$4Fe_3O_4 + O_2 \longrightarrow 6Fe_2O_3 + 94 \text{ calories}$$

This reaction evolves 101 calories kg^{-1} of magnetite and 140 calories kg^{-1} of iron (Angles d'Auriac 1930). For the same reasons as in the case of carbonates, it is necessary in practice to supply heat. This is all the more important when one wants to achieve a complete removal of the sulphide for which a higher temperature is required and which is often the principal objective in roasting magnetite anyway as it is often mixed with pyrites.

The original process of roasting in heaps or stalls was applied to all spherosiderities (Black-bands), which provided their own fuel, on account of the simplicity of the process and the trifling cost of installation. The heaps are in the form of a truncated pyramid with a rectangular base, whose height must not exceed 2.5 m to facilitate the circulation of gases through the mass. The breadth depends above all on the size of the ore fragments and their resistance to the movement of the gases; it is usually 4-18 m depending on the ore. The length is only limited by the tonnage of ore to be roasted and, naturally, by the available space; it can reach 60 m. The length of the process varies between 15 days and several months. Roasting in stalls or in compartments depends on the cost of installation. The first furnaces used were discontinuous in operation: they were emptied after each roasting, whereas with continuous furnaces the roasted ore was removed from the bottom in such a way as to help the gradual descent of material charged at the mouth. The simplest furnaces of Siegerland and those of Erzberg in Styria and of Carinthia have been described elsewhere as well as those of Dannemora in Sweden where the air entry is controlled by holes in the plates of the openings for removing the roasted ore. The large cylindrical furnaces of Sommorostro, Italy, 10 m in height and 4 m in diameter at the base, are somewhat reminiscent of those shown on some of the plaques found at Lascours (see p.31).

It is appropriate here to correct an error which has appeared in several publications on the early iron industry and which concerns the discovery in 1870 of the remains of large furnaces in a brick earth quarry at Lustin, 10 km to the south of Namur in Belgium. The furnaces were found at a depth of 70 cm beneath the foot of an outcrop of calcereous tuffa (Rochers de Frenes) and were apparently 4.3 m by 3.3 m in diameter. The two hollows were found about 10 m apart. They were erroneously described by Berchem (1872) as low bowl furnace. In fact the diameter of the broad, low bowl furnaces never attains these exceptional dimensions. One can only interpret them as furnaces for the roasting of ores mined nearby. This could include the ores found either in the Civetien or in the Famennien, or again in the substitution pockets along the length of the contact between the limestone and the schistes forming a string of deposits at varying depth, now empty (Delmer 1913). Since at depth these ores usually change to iron carbonate with a varying degree of pyrites, it was necessary to roast them to help their reduction in cylindrical furnaces, of a diameter clearly less than those of Lustin! Nevertheless, elsewhere iron ore roasting furnaces are beginning to be recognised and described as such. Thus the Polish expert A Pawlowski (1979) has recently recognised a dozen furnaces of this type associated with a Roman-period site at Dobrzen Maly (Community of Dobrzen Wielki, province of Opole, Poland). Two heaps of roasted ore accompanied the furnaces as well as five reduction furnaces and twenty hearths. Similarly Leube (1980) has described four roasting furnaces of the third to fifth centuries AD at Waltensdorf (Kr Königs WusterHausen, Germany) where there were 51 areas paved with stone showing traces of heating, and a few fragments of charcoal. An excursion of the Erzberg Symposium held at Vordrenberg in Upper Styria (Erz, Holzkohle, Schlacke und das Frühe Eisen, 12-15 October 1981) enabled us to see the eighteenth and nineteenth century roasting installations not far from the thirteenth century ironworks.

Another example, of nineteenth century date, lies near to the farm of Ronceray, to the west of the commune of the Coulonche (department Orne, France). This furnace probably roasted iron carbonate ores from the area of the Ferté-Macé and of the Ferrière-aux-Etangs not far distant. Blocks of armorican sandstone were found weighing between 2 and 10 kg. Some of them have one face greenish and vitrified, together forming the bottom of an inverted cone one metre in depth, mixed with burnt clay strongly coloured red. This is all in the mound, 10 m in diameter at the base and 6 m in height, covered by coppice which extends for about a hectare. A raised road about 5-6 m wide runs east-west through this coppice, which used to lead to iron carbonate workings at the Ferriere-aux-Etangs on one side and the Ferté-Macé on the other. The wood probably came from the forests near to Dampierre, Messei and Andaines.

Two fragments of the sandstone, one of which had a vitrified face, have been analysed (Table 4). One can see from these figures that the vitrification of the surface of some of the sandstone blocks is a result of the action of the alkaline ashes on the silica of the blocks with the formation of potassium silicate in the main, which proves that wood was the fuel used with the aim of heating at relatively low temperatures compared to those at which slag is formed.

Petrological study of the sandstone has shown the structure to be that of a type of local armorican sandstone of Silurian age. This quarzitic sandstone resists heat well, it does not usually split in the fire, and is well-suited to the construction of roasting furnaces. Some of the blocks show areas somewhat reddened beneath the vitrification layer resulting from the action of heat on the small quantities of iron occurring naturally in this sandstone. The reddened clay shows a variety of characteristic tints which show that it was heated to differing temperatures. The ceramist Salvetat has established a table of temperature-related tints from orange-yellow (850°C) to purple-red (1000°C), as given in the following sequence: orange-yellow, flesh-coloured, carmine, lacquer-red, red-brown, and purple-red. These terms although old-fashioned may be used to estimate the temperature to which the furnace clay was exposed.

We see from these considerations that the scientific study of roasting processes in former times would deserve to be completed by careful scientific examination of the remains found on metal working sites when excavated further.

Table 4

	Unmodified sandstone %	Vitrified surface %
loss of ignition	1	0
SiO_2	93.60	83.50
Al_2O_3	3.45	2.98
Fe_2O_3	1.10	0.95
CaO	0.40	0.30
MgO	0.45	0.28
K_2O	-	9.6
Na_2O	-	1.9
P_2O_3	-	0.40

Discussion

We will finish with a discussion of certain furnaces of which traces have been recovered, even complete examples, but which unhappily were often destroyed by the workers at the time of their accidental discovery owing to the fragility of their burnt clay walls.

In about 1860 a group of approximately ten furnaces was discovered in the slag heaps at Lavardin, about a dozen kilometres northwest of Mans (department of the Santhe). The furnaces were of unusual dimension and unlike the smelting furnaces in the same region. The ore used was called Roussard locally (Marquis n. d.) and definitely must have been roasted in these furnaces before being reduced not far from the old chapel of Saint-Nicolas (Jeanne Chapin, personal communication). Their form is similar to the furnaces discovered in 1907 and described by the mining engineer L Davy de Chateaubriant (1913), and to that of Blars uncovered in 1912 by the Marquis de Tryon-Montalembert on the lands of the commune of Fontaines near to Toucy (department Yonne). The interior diameter of 1.85 m greatly exceeded that of the smelting furnaces usually employed in the Gallo-Roman period (Tryon-Montalembert 1955).

A bank of four pear-shaped furnaces of the same dimensions was uncovered in the hamlet of Puits-d'Havenas in the commune of Chatillon-sur-Loire (department Loiret) under one of the five slag heaps covering about a square kilometre, and described by L Dumuys (1898).

To conclude, G Vallois (1884) called attention to furnaces of badly burnt clay mixed with sand and easily crushed by pressure. This fragility is again well-attested by F de Mely (1906) for a furnace at Mesnil-Germain (department Calvados). Tryon-Montalembert (1955) expresses doubts on the purpose of this type of badly burnt furnace, easily crushed between the

40

fingers, but he does not suppose that their function was to give the ore a brief preliminary roast in order to concentrate it.

Acknowledgement

We thank Brenda Craddock for preparing the Figure for this paper.

References

Allan, J C 1968. The accumulation of ancient slag in the southwest of the Iberian peninsula. *Bulletin of the Historical Metallurgy group*, 2 (1), 47-50

Angles d'Auriac, P 1930. *Lecons de siderurgie* esp. chapter III, 128-142. Paris, J Estour Gounod

Archbutt, S L & Prytherch, W E 1937. *Effects on impurities in copper* esp. chapter III. London, British Non Ferrous Metals Research Association

Berchem, A 1872. Histoire du fer dans le Pays de Namur Le bas-foyers de Lustin. *Comptes-rendus du Congres international d'Anthropologie et d'Archaeologie prehistoriques*, 6th session. Brussels

Cancrinus, F L 1767. *Beschreiturg der vorzuglichsten Bergwerke in Hessen, in dem Woldekkischen, an dem Haarz*. Frankfurt

Chermette, A 1981. *L'or et L'argenc?* Presses Universtaires de Grenoble

Chevalier de, W 1778. *Encyclopedie pratique du chevalier*, II, p 269. Liege

Clavel, 1964. *Thesis of the Geology Laboratory of the faculty of science of Grenoble* volume 40

Davy, L 1913. Etude des scories de forges ansiennes. *Bulletin de la Société de l'industries Minerale*, April, 448-449, fig. 5

Dayton, J E 1981. Geological evidence for the discovery of cobalt blue glass in Mycenaean times as a by-product of silver smelting in the Schneeberg area of the Bohemian Erzgebirge. Revue D'archeometrie, Supplement *Actes du XX Symposium internationales d'Archeometrie III*, 57-61. Paris

Delmer, A 1912. La question du mineral de fer en Belgique. *Annales des Mines* 17, 853-940

Delmer, A 1913. La question du mineral de fer en Belgique. *Annales des Mines*, 18, 325-448

Dumuys, L 1898. *Proces-verbaux des seances du Congres archeologique de France*, p 117. Bourges

Gourdiole, R 1977. Exploitations metallurgiques antiques dans la houte vollee de l'Orb. In *Federation historique du Languedoc mediterraneen et du Roussillon*, 69-87. Mont Pellier

Leube, A 1980. Germaische Rostofen zur Eisengewinnung aus Waltersdorf Kr Konigs Wusterhausen. *Zeitschrift fur Archeologie*, 14, 217-224

Marechal, J R 1970. Debut et evolution de la metallurgie du cuiure et ses alliages en Europe. *Janus*, **57**, 16-18

Marechal, J R 1978. Note sur un produit metallurgique plombo-cuprifère découverte à Alet. In *Dossiers du centre régional archéologique d'Alet*, 7, 25-30

Marquis, and The Abbe, Manuscript study on Lavardin

Mely, F de 1906. *Bulletin de la Societe de Antiquaires*, p 139

Pawlowski, A 1979. *Sprawozdania Archeogilzne*, **31**, 193-204

Tyron-Montalembert, R de 1955. La sideriergie en Gaule. *Techniques et Civilisation*, **24**, 191-196

Vallois, G 1884. Le fer dans l'Antiquité. *Mémoires de la Sociéte de Antiquaries du Centre*, **XI**, 103

Werner, O 1976. Westafrekanische Manillas aus Deutschen Metallhutten. *Erzemetall*, **29**, 448-455

Witter, W. *Die Ausbeutung der mitteldeutschen Erzslager statten in der fruhen Metallzeit* Mannus 60 Leipzig 12-13 & 137 analyses 6 and 7

ILLUSTRATIONS OF METALWORKING FURNACES ON GREEK VASES

W A Oddy[1] and Judith Swaddling[2]

1   British Museum, Conservation Division, London
2   British Museum, Department of Greek and Roman
     Antiquities, London

Abstract

Shaft furnaces, which may reasonably be associated
with metalworking operations, are depicted on seven
known Greek vases, and may be inferred from existing sherds on three others. These scenes have
been used as illustrations on numerous occasions
by historians of technology, but often with
different interpretations as to what is actually
depicted. The purpose of this paper is to illustrate the furnaces and associated activities and
to point out what can actually be seen. The two
main conclusions are first that where metalworking
activities are in progress the operations are all
concerned with the manufacture of metal objects
and not with the smelting of ore, and second that
where finished objects can be associated with the
scenes, the objects are always things which were
made of bronze and not iron.

Keywords: FURNACE, METALWORKING, BRONZE, GREEK,
             VASE, PAINTING

Introduction

Knowledge of metalworking techniques in Iron Age Greece is available from
four sources. First there are the excavated remains of metalworkers' furnaces
and forges (e.g. Schwandner 1983, 57ff; Mattusch 1977 A & B; Miller 1977, 17ff;
Heilmeyer 1981 and 1969; Schmidt 1972, 178-81; Mallwitz and Schiering 1964,
42ff; Hampe and Jantzen 1937, 29ff) and surviving examples of tools (e.g. Kent
Hill 1949, xxii). Second there is the scientific study, including analysis
and metallographic study of metal artefacts, (e.g. Craddock 1975 and 1977).
Third there are references to some of the processes in the contemporary
literature, which are all too often tantalisingly vague or obscure (e.g.
Mattusch 1975, Gray 1954) and finally there are scenes of metalworking processes painted on vases (Schwandner 1983, Zimmer 1982, Ziomecki 1975, Mattusch
1980, Kluge and Lehmann-Hartleben 1927, 11-13; Blumner 1887, 363-7). It is
the last of these, the vase-paintings and their use and abuse as evidence,
which is the subject of this paper.

The painted scenes showing furnaces on Greek vases have been used as
evidence by numerous historians of technology, but in many cases different
interpretations have been put on the same scene, and questions as fundamental
as whether it is the working of bronze or iron that is depicted have not been
argued.

Altogether, seven vases have been traced on which a complete shaft furnace is depicted, and in addition there are three fragments on which the
adjacent presence of shaft furnaces has been inferred.

The vases

Pride of place must be given to the so-called Foundry Cup in the Staatliche
Museen, Berlin (F2294, about 490-480 BC), which shows a number of metalworking
techniques including a scene of a smith poking a long rod into the base of a
furnace (Mattusch 1980, 435-6, 442, fig. 2; Burford 1972, pl. 39, 40; Beazley
1971, 370 and 1963: 400; Thompson 1964, 323-8; Cloché 1931, pl. 24; Kluge and
Lehmann-Hartleben 1927, 10-13, 152, 169) (Fig. 1).

Perhaps next in order of importance is a column-krater in the museum at
Caltanisetta, Sicily (20371, about 470-460 BC), which shows a smith hammering
in front of a furnace (Beazley 1971, 354; Gempeler 1969, 16-21, pls. 13, 1
and 14, 3-4) (Fig. 2).

Then follows an *oinochoe* in the British Museum (GR 1846.6-29.45, about
500-475 BC), which shows a smith holding a lump of hot metal either on a low
anvil or in the mouth of a furnace (Mattusch 1980, 435; Boardman 1974, 150,
fig. 285; Orlandos 1966, 110, fig. 72; Forbes 1968, 79 fig. 15; Beazley 1956,
426, 670; Cloché 1931 , 233; Kluge and Lehmann-Hartleben 1927, 11 fig. 46;
Walters 1893, B 507; Blumner 1887, 364, abb. 51) (Fig. 3).

Four other vases depict shaft furnaces with which no metallurgical
activity is directly related. A *chous* in the Agora Museum, Athens (P15210,
about 420-400 BC), has two rather grotesque figures standing in front of a
furnace (Van Hoorn 1951, 90) (Fig. 4) and a cup in the Ashmolean Museum,
Oxford (518, about 480-470 BC), depicts a seated youth working on a helmet
with a furnace in the background (Beazley 1963, 336, 1646) (Fig. 5).

A vase that is now lost apparently depicted male and female figures
standing by a furnace, but as this is known only from an old drawing, the
extent of any restoration is unknown. The vase may have been a *lekythos*
(Kluge and Lehmann-Hartleben 1927, 11, fig. 4c; Christie 1825, 64-7) (Fig. 6).

Finally as far as the complete scenes are concerned, there is an interesting *hydria* in the Antikensammlung, Munich (1717, about 520-500 BC), which
shows a potter's workshop in which there is a shaft furnace with burnt-out
fuel piled up in front of its mouth (Beazley 1971, 161, Beazley 1956, 362,36)
(Fig. 7). This type of furnace was not suitable for firing ceramics, though
it can also be inferred on a fragment of a vase in the Acropolis Museum,
Athens (166, about 510-500 BC), which shows a potter's wheel. However the man
sitting beside the furnace is almost certainly a smith with a bellows-operator
in the background (Beazley 1963, 92, 64; Beazley 1944, pl. 1, 3; Burford 1972,
fig. IV) (Fig. 8).

The ninth scene is on another fragment in the Acropolis Museum (607 S,
about 570-560 BC), showing a helmeted Hephaistos with a small portion of what
has been interpreted as the top of a furnace behind him (Moore 1979, 88, ill.
1, pl. 12. 6; Beazley 1971, 44, 21; Beazley 1956, 107, 1) (Fig. 9).

Lastly, a fragment in the Ashmolean Museum, Oxford (1966: 469, about
490-480 BC), shows two workers beside what is presumably the rim of the mouth
of a furnace, but there are no metallurgical tools present (Beazley 1967,
189 pl. XX) (Fig. 10). One worker is probably poking the long rod that he
holds into the fire while the other man leans well back, perhaps to avoid the

heat of the hearth. He appears to be operating two pairs of bellows made of hide with two long pointed nozzles (cf. Gempeler 1969, 17). On the frieze of the Siphnian Treasury at Delphi Hephaistos also appears with two pairs of bellows (De la Coste-Messelière 1943, pl. 80).

The furnace and its associated vessel depicted on a lekythos in Providence, Rhode Island, (Bleecker Luce 1933, Zimmer 1983, 69) will not be considered here as the furnace is of a different type with tall tapering chimney, while the cauldron is placed on a low platform and does not appear to have a lid of any kind.

Discussion of the scenes

This then is the evidence, but what does it tell us? Two of these paintings seem to impart no information about the use of the furnace. The small jug in Athens (Fig. 4) depicts a furnace which appears to be open at the bottom, although an object on the ground between the two figures may represent the door. The significance of this scene is uncertain, but the smaller figure may be offering a sacrificial basket to the larger figure, or it may merely represent a servant offering food to a smith. It has also been suggested that the figures are actors in costume (Van Hoorn 1951, 90).

The second painting from which nothing metallurgical can be inferred, not even the type of metal that was heated in the furnace, is the lost vase, once belonging to Mr James Edwards (Fig. 6), which appears to have been destroyed in an accident (Christie 1825, 67). The explanation of the metal-working scene on it will thus no doubt remain obscure, for all surviving illustrations seem to be based on one drawing, and it is not clear whether the dotted line which divides the picture indicated a break, or a division between the original and the restored parts of the vase. If the latter is the case, then either the upper or the lower zone may be a draughtsman's reconstruction. Identification of the characters is also uncertain: the figure second from the left who is holding a pair of tongs may be Athena in her capacity as patron goddess of crafts. Alternatively it has been suggested that she may be the nymph Aitna, assisting either Hephaistos or the Cyclops Briareos in his workshop on Mount Etna (Pauly-Wissowa 1933, s.v. Aitna; Blümner 1887, 365). The furnace is interesting. It has the appearance of being but-tressed with clay or hewn out of rock, a characteristic which either the ancient or the modern artist may have thought appropriate for a foundry set in the mountainside, but which was often the case with shaft furnaces, for numerous excavated examples have been found built into a bank or a hillside. The hearth itself is enclosed by a short tunnel, rather like the stoke-hole of a potter's kiln, and it has been suggested (Kluge and Lehmann-Hartleben 1927, 11) that the tunnel might enclose the channel that conveyed the metal down into the mould.

On five of the vases the furnaces may possibly be associated with the craft of the armourer, although in two of them, the fragments in the Acropolis Museum (Figs. 8 and 9), the presence of a furnace is implied rather than depicted.

On the fragmentary cup in the Acropolis Museum (Fig. 8), made about 510-500 BC, a potter's wheel is present with a vase on it apparently being painted, while a smith with a hammer sits beside a furnace; a man plies the bellows from behind, while tongs and two more hammers hang in the background. Another fragment from the same vase shows the lower part of a group of a horse and three men, two of whom appear to be working on the horse, which is almost certainly a statue (Beazley 1944, 10) (Fig. 8). (Compare the well known *oinochoe* in Berlin, F 2415, Beazley 1963, 776, 1 Mattusch 1980, 438, pl. 55, 3.) The seated figure of Athena beside the smith may also be a statue, although the goddess herself occasionally appears in pottery- and metalworking-scenes in her capacity as patron-goddess of crafts. As a warrior-goddess it was quite normal for her to be depicted with a helmet, though here the helmet could be interpreted as a representative product of the workshop.

The undoubted presence of pottery-making in the same workshop seems strange, but links up with the scene in Munich of a potter's workshop with a shaft furnace at one end (Fig. 7). It is certainly not a potter's kiln, which would be low and dome-shaped (Noble 1966, 72, figs. 231-8; Cook 1960; Eisman 1978, 397). No metal products are evident, but below the scene is a parade of hoplites, the plumes of whose helmets impinge on the representation of the potting activities.

It may be that some workshops produced both pottery and metalwork. Alternatively, such scenes may be intended to represent craftsmen's quarters in general, or particularly the Agora in Athens, the industrial area where many crafts were carried on side by side. Such telescoping of location is a frequent convention in Greek art. Hephaistos, who appears in several of the scenes, is commonly known as the smith-god, but he was also the patron god of craftsmen in general. He is shown alongside a potter working at a wheel on a wall-painting in Naples (Brommer 1978, 74, 173, 236, pl. 39).

The interior medallion of the Foundry Cup shows a scene from mythology with the nymph Thetis, who has come to collect the arms and armour made for her son Achilles by Hephaistos (Mattusch 1980, pl. 54. 1). It must be admitted, however, that medallion scenes cannot always be associated with scenes on the exterior of cups, which is where the shaft furnace is depicted on this vase (Fig. 1).

The third vase that possibly associates a shaft-furnace with the armourer's craft is the other Acropolis fragment, which depicts the battle between gods and giants. A recent reconstruction sees the object by the elbow of Hephaistos as the top of a shaft-furnace (Fig. 9) (Moore 1979, ill. 1). Hephaistos, who made armour for the gods, is himself in full armour; he often used his furnace as an instrument of war for heating up lumps of metal to throw at the enemy, and this would support the argument for the presence of a furnace in this scene (cf. the frieze of the Siphnian treasury at Delphi; De la Coste-Messelière 1943, pl. 80).

The fourth of these vases is the drinking-cup in Oxford, which actually shows an armourer with an anvil at his feet putting the finishing touches to a helmet (Fig. 5). Part of this scene is restored, including the face, arms and torso of the figure and lower part of the furnace.

To summarise so far, all that has been inferred from the furnace scenes on the vases is a link with the manufacture of statues and armour. Surviving examples indicate that in the mid-first millennium BC armour and helmets were most often made of bronze and what little analytical data is available shows that this usually contained 7-12% of tin (Craddock 1977).

The so-called 'Foundry Cup' in Berlin gets its name from the various bronze-working activities which are depicted on it. The scenes on the exterior appear to be taken from everyday life: on one side apprentices are scraping off the fire-coat from a statue of a warrior; on the other side a statue of an athlete is being assembled while nearby are two men working a furnace (Fig. 1). One man thrusts a long hooked poker into the fire: it has been suggested that he is manipulating the door of the furnace and is

about to release the molten metal (Thompson 1964, 324), but there is no repre-
sation of such a door and if casting is in progress then the metal must
already be pouring out and the men merely adjusting the charge to increase
the flow of metal. Behind the furnace is a man operating the bellows, and
modern experiments with shaft furnaces have shown that a continuous draught
is essential to maintain a high temperature for either the smelting of ore,
or for melting bronze in a crucible inside the furnace.

The plaques and masks hanging beside the furnace on the Berlin cup are
probably *apotropaia*, offerings to propitiate the *daimones* who watched over
bronze-castings. Various tools hang in the background and also two feet,
which could be clay or plaster matrices, or waxes waiting to be cast, or the
finished bronze articles ready for attachment to another statue. Here the
evidence points exclusively to the working of bronze, and analyses of statues
of approximately this date have shown that the usual composition was copper/
tin containing 8-11% of tin and up to 1% of lead (Craddock 1977).

Finally, two other complete vases depict the forging of hot metal, but
in neither case is an end product shown, and so it is impossible to say
whether bronze or iron is intended.

On the British Museum jug a workman squats on a stool by the furnace,
shielding his face from the heat (Fig. 3). Kluge and Lehmann-Hartleben
(1927, 12) believed that the vase-painter had here chosen to represent the
crucial moment in casting, when the metal was released from the furnace to
run down a channel into the mould, which was embedded in a pit. The seated
man, they thought, had just removed the stopper, which he holds with a pair of
tongs; he considered the object on the ground to be the removable door of the
hearth. However, in view of the fact that the standing figure holds a hammer,
smithing is a more likely subject and the seated figure should be seen as
holding the metal in the furnace to get it sufficiently hot to work. In
this operation he appears to rest his tongs on the low anvil, a very
necessary aid when supporting a lump of heavy metal for any length of
time.

The inscriptions on the vase are mainly nonsensical but beside the seated
man is written "Is Mys a fine man? Yes". It is not always clear whether such
inscriptions refer to the figure by which they appear, or to some contemporary
of the vase-painter. However, in the later fifth century BC there was a
metalworker named Mys who carried out the designs of the artist Euenor, most
notably the figures on the shield of the statue of Athena Parthenos by Pheidias
(Pausanias, *Description of Greece* I 28, 2; Lippold 1933, 1186). As certain
names tended to run in craftsmen's families, the Mys on this vase was perhaps
an ancestor of the one mentioned by Pausanias (cf. Webster 1972, 67; Mys also
occurs as a vase-painter's signature: Beazley 1963, 663-4).

The krater in Caltanisetta shows the forge of Hephaistos (Fig. 2). Like
the figure on the British Museum vase, the god sits holding a lump of metal
on the anvil before the furnace, which is here seen in profile; he is about
to strike the metal with the hammer in his right hand. Assisting him are two
satyrs, one with an axe and the other with a pair of bellows made from an
animal skin. The satyr depicted on the furnace is probably another apotropaic
device. Unfortunately, the scene on the reverse of the krater gives us no
clue as to what is being made, but the furnace is interesting in having an
asymmetric top, rather like that on the Munich vase.

The tops of the shaft-furnaces themselves are the last but not the least
piece of evidence for what the scenes depict. The six complete vases illustrate a large globular vessel sitting on the furnace and what may well be

examples of two such vessels have been found in the excavations at Samos and Olympia.

The vessel from Samos was discovered in a foundry context in the sanctuary of Hera (Schmidt 1972, 77). It is 41 cm high and 70 cm wide and its suggested date is the late sixth century BC. The bottom was covered with a thick layer of soot and had been patched twice, indicating that the cauldron had been used repeatedly for long periods over considerable heat.

The Olympia vessel was found beneath the so-called workshop of Pheidias where, it is believed, the cult statue of Zeus was made for his temple nearby. On the basis of its proximity to the furnace Mallwitz and Schiering (1964, 43-5) and Kunze (1959, 280) associated the cauldron with the casting process, but thought that it was probably used to hold water for cooling castings. It is larger than the Samos vessel, 70 cm high and about 105 cm wide, while the mouth has a diameter of 63 cm, all of which dimensions apparently agree well with those of the cauldrons represented in the furnace scenes on the vases. The vessel was placed at the bottom of a pit next to the furnace between 460 and 440 BC (Heilmeyer 1982) and was therefore buried before construction of the cult statue took place in the late 430s and early 420s. However its proximity to the furnace and the parallel of the Samos vessel in a foundry context may well indicate that it was used during metalworking of an earlier date.

One might adduce as supporting evidence the graffito plaque from Pheidias' Workshop, a corner of which may show the lid of a vessel sitting on top of a furnace with two workmen and a herm of Dionysos beside it (cf. reconstruction drawing, Mallwitz and Schiering 1964, Abb. 68). Unfortunately, however, not enough of the graffito survives to be sure about the restoration.

Numerous explanations have been offered in the past for the vases depicted on top of the furnaces, for example:

1. That they are actually part of the furnace, being a sort of damper to control the flow of air (Beck 1884, 463).

2. That they are crucibles for preheating the lead and tin before they were alloyed with the copper inside the furnace proper (Kluge & Lehmann-Hartleben 1927, 13; Hampe & Jantzen 1936-7, 35).

3. That they are crucibles for melting bronze or for making steel (Mattusch 1980, 442; Livadefs 1956, 64-5; Pleiner 1969, fig. 8; Orlandos 1966, 110).

4. That they serve as stoppers of apertures for stoking the fire and cleaning out the furnace (Schwandner 1983, 70; Orlandos 1966, 110).

The first explanation can be discounted because the vessels are obviously not an intergral part of the furnace, and they cannot be crucibles because the furnace could not work at full blast with a large curcible blocking the top; even if a sufficiently high temperature to melt bronze could be achieved at the top of the furnace, which is very unlikely, such a large vessel full of molten metal would need a crane or other lifting device to handle it. As for Schwandner's suggestion, there is no reason why a straightforward lid or damper should not have been used for closing the aperture.

It is more than likely that the vessels depicted on top of the furnaces held some sort of liquid, and possibilities include a pickling solution for removing oxide, or oil for tempering wrought iron. However, all these large globular vessels have a strange but identical lid, and it will be argued elsewhere (Swaddling and Oddy, in preparation) that these vessels are double-boilers (or water-baths) for melting the wax used in making patterns for cire-perdue casting. This is clearly a necessary part of the production of statuary. Indeed, an *oinochoe* in Berlin shows Athena modelling a horse (Beazley 1963, 776, 1; Mattusch 1980, 438 pl. 55, 3; Burford 1972, pl. 38), which can only be in clay or wax. Its scale suggest that it is a wax model for casting, as representations of horses on this scale seem rarely to have been made in terracotta outside Etruria.

But what of the armour-making operations, as armour and helmets are generally thought to be wrought rather than cast? In this context, it is relevant to note the existence of limestone moulds (Schroder 1920) presumably for making wax models of helmets from which metal versions could be cast. The moulds are from Egypt and although the helmets cannot easily be paralleled they appear Greek in type, perhaps dating to about the fourth century BC (cf. those depicted on Praenestine cistae, e.g. British Museum GR 1859.8-16.1, Walters 1899, no. 638). Might not, therefore, the armourer on the drinking cup in Oxford be working on a wax model, rather than a metal helmet? In this case the wax may have been heated in an inner vessel in the cauldron on the furnace behind him.

Conclusion

Shaft-furnace scenes on vases seem to depict only processes associated with the casting of bronze or the forging of bronze or other metals. In reality furnaces were also used for smelting, but the vase-paintings cannot be interpreted as representations of this aspect of metalworking.

Acknowledgements

The authors wish to thank Mr Brian F Cook and Professor P E Corbett for reading the text and making helpful comments. Dr Mary B Moore and Dr Michael Vickers kindly drew our attention to the Acropolis fragment (607s) and the Ashmolean fragment (1966:469). We are grateful to Sue Bird of the Department Greek and Roman Antiquities for the drawings of Figs. 2, 3, 4, 5, 7, 8 and 9.

References

Beazley, J D 1927. *Corpus Vasorum Antiquorum*, Great Britain Fasc. 3, Oxford Ashmolean Museum Fasc. 1

Beazley, J D 1944. *Potter and painter in ancient Athens*, reprinted from the *Proceedings of the British Academy*. London

Beazley, J D 1956. *Attic black-figure vase-painters*. Oxford, Clarendon Press

Beazley, J D 1963. *Attic red-figure vase-painters*. Oxford, Clarendon Press

Beazley, J D 1967. *Select exhibition of Sir John and Lady Beazley's Gifts to the Ashmolean Museum, 1912-1966*. Oxford, Clarendon Press

Beazley, J D 1971. *Paralipomena, additions to Attic black-figure vase-painters and to Attic red-figure vase-painters*. Oxford, Clarendon Press

Beck, L 1884. *Die Geschichte des Eisens in technischer und kulturgeschichtlicher Beziehung I*

50

Bleecker Luce, S 1933. *Corpus Vasorum Antiquorum*, Providence Fasc. 1

Blumner, H 1887. *Technologie und Terminologie der Gewerbe und Künst bei Grichen und Römern* IV. Leipzig, Teubner

Boardman, J 1974. *Athenian black-figure vases*. London, Thames and Hudson

Brommer, F 1978. *Hephaistos, der Schmiedegott in antiken Kunst*. Mainz, Von Zabern

Burford, A 1972. *Craftsmen in Greek and Roman society*. London, Thames and Hudson

Christie, J 1825. *Disquisitions on the painted Greek vases*. London, Longmans

Cloche, P 1931. *Les Classes, les Métiers, le Trafic*. Paris, Les Belles Lettres

Cook, R M 1960. The double stoking tunnel of Greek kilns. *Annual of the British School at Athens*, **56**, 64-7

Craddock, P T 1975. 'The composition of copper alloys used in the classical world'. Ph.D. thesis for Institute of Archaeology, London University

Craddock, P T 1977. The composition of the copper alloys used by the Greek, Etruscan and Roman civilizations-2: the Archaic, Classical and Hellenistic Greeks. *Journal of Archaeological Science*, **4**, 103-123

Daremberg, C & Saglio, E 1876. *Dictionnaire des Antiquites Grécques et Romaines*. Paris, Hachette

De la Caste-Messelière, P 1943. *Delphes*. Paris, Editions du Chêne

Eisman, M M 1978. Robinson's Kiln Skyphos. *American Journal of Archaeology*, **82**, 394-399

Forbes, R J 1966. *Studies in ancient technology* VI. Leiden

Gempeler, R D 1969. Die Schmiede des Hephäst - eine Satyr-spieleszene des Harrow-Malers. *Antike Kunst*, **12**, 16-21

Gray, D H F 1954. Metalworking in Homer. *Journal of Hellenic Studies*, **74**, 1-15

Hampe, R & Jantzen, W 1936-7. *Bericht uber die Ausgrabungen in Olympia*. Berlin, Walter de Gruyter

Heilmeyer, W-D 1969. Giesserbetriebe in Olympia. *Jahrbuch des Deutsches Archaeologisches Instituts*, **84**, 1-28

Heilmeyer, W-D 1981. Antike Werkstattfunde in Greichenland. *Archaölogischer Anzeiger*, 440-453

Heilmeyer, W-D 1982. (Information provided by Prof. Heilmeyer at the symposium for which these papers were presented.)

Kent Hill, D 1949. *Catalogue of classical bronze sculpture in the Walters Art Gallery*. Baltimore, Trustees of the Walters Art Gallery

Kluge K & Lehmann-Hartleben, K 1927. *Die Antiken Grossbronzen*. Berlin & Leipzig

Kunze, E 1959. *Neue deutsche Ausgrabungen in Mittelmeergebeit und im vordern Orient*. Berlin, Deutsches Archaeologisches Institut

Lippold, G 1933. Mys. 6. *Paulys Real-Encyclopadie der Classischen Alterthumswissenschaft*. Herausgegeben von G Wissowa. Stuttgart, Metzersche Verlagsbuchandlung

Livadefs, C J 1956. The structural iron of the Parthenon. *Journal of the Iron and Steel Institute*, **182**, 49-66

Mallwitz, A & Schiering, W 1964. Die Werkstatt des Pheidias in Olympia. *Olympische Forschungen* V. Berlin, Walter de Gruyter

Mattusch, C C 1975. Pollux on bronze-casting. *Greek, Roman and Byzantine Studies*, **16**

Mattusch, C C 1977 A. Bronze and ironworking in the area of the Athenian Agora. *Hesperia*, **46**, 340-379

Mattusch, C C 1977 B. Corinthian metalworking: the Forum area. *Hesperia*, **46**, 380-389

Mattusch, C C 1980. The Berlin Foundry Cup: The casting of Greek bronze statuary in the early fifth century BC. *American Journal of archaeology*, **84**, 435-444

Miller, S G 1977. Excavations at Nemea. *Hesperia*, **46**, 19-20

Moore, M B 1979. Lydos and the Gigantomachy. *American Journal of Archaeology*, **83**, 79-99

Noble, J V 1966. *The Techniques of painted Attic pottery*. New York, Faber and Faber

Orlandos, A K 1966. *Lex Materiaux de Construction*, Suppl. 16. Ecole Francaise d'Athenes

Pauly-Wissowa 1893. *Paulys Real-Encyclopadie der Classischen Alterthumswissenschaft*. Herausgegeben von G Wissowa

Pleiner, R 1969. *Iron working in ancient Greece*. Prague, National Technical Museum

Schmidt, G 1972. Heraion von Samos: Eine Brychon-Weihung und ihre Fundlage. *Mitteilungen des Deutsches Archaeologisches Institut, Athenische Abteilungen*, **87**

Schroder, B 1920. Aegyptische Helm-Modellen. *Archaologischer Anzeiger*, **35**, 3-14

Schwandner, E L, Zimmer, G & Zwicker, U Zum 1983. Problem der Ofen Griechischer Bronzegiesser. *Archäologischer Anzeiger*, 57-70. In this article, which appeared shortly after the colloquium at which this paper was presented, the authors arrived at the conclusions that the furnaces on the vases can be associated with forge-work only.

52

Swaddling and Oddy (in preparation)

Thompson, H A 1964. *Essays in memory of Karl Lehmann*. Marsyas, Supplement I, New York University

Van Hoorn, G 1951. *Choes and Anthesteria*. Leiden, E J Brill

Walters, H B 1893. *Catalogue of the vases in the British Museum*. London, Trustees of the British Museum

Walters, H B 1899. *Catalogue of the bronzes in the British Museum, Greek, Roman and Etruscan*. London, Trustees of the British Museum

Webster, T B L 1972. *Potter and patron in classical Athens*. London, Methuen

Ziomecki, J 1975. Les representations d'artisans sur les vases attiques. *Bibliotheca Antiqua*, 13. Warsaw, Academie Polonaise des Sciences, Institut d'Histoire de la Culture Materielle

Zimmer, G 1982. Antike Werkstattbilder. *Bilderhefte der Staatlichen Museen Preussischer Kulturbesitz Berlin*, **42**

Fig. 1 'Foundry Cup', Staatliche Mussen, Berlin F 2294, after A Furtwangler
& K Reichhold, *Greichische Malerei* III pl. 135

Fig. 2 Column-krater, Museo Caltanisetta, Sicily, inv. no. 20371

54

Fig. 3 Oinochoe, British Museum, reg. no. 1846.6-29.45

Fig. 4 Chous, Agora Museum, Athens, inv. no. P15210. Drawing after a photograph kindly provided by the American School of Classical Studies in
Athens

Fig. 5 Kylix, Ashmolean Museum, Oxford, inv. no. 518

Fig. 6 Vase now lost, once in the collection of James Edwards. After
J Christie *Disquisitions on the painted Greek vases* pl. IX

Fig. 7 Hydria, Antikensammlung Munich, inv. no. 1717

Fig. 8 Fragment of a vase, Acropolis Museum, inv. no. 166

Fig. 9 Fragment of a vase, Acropolis Museum, inv. no. 607S

Fig. 10 Fragment of a vase, Ashmolean Museum, Oxford, inv. no. 1966:469.
        After J D Beasley *Select exhibition of Sir John and Lady Beasley's
        Gifts to the Ashmolean Museum, 1912-1966*, no. 189, pl. 20

ANCIENT INDIAN COPPER SMELTING FURNACES

K T M Hegde[1] and J E Ericson[2]

1   M S University of Baroda, Baroda - 390 002, India.
2   University of California, Irvine, California - 92717, USA.

Abstract

Scores of Copper-Bronze Age sites, two of them located
within the Aravalli Hill copper ore belt, have been excavated in India. But none of them has revealed stratified
evidence of structures that could be identified as copper
smelting furnaces. Nevertheless, there is evidence
to believe that copper was smelted from the Aravalli
Hill copper ore deposits during the Chalcolithic
period. For example, one of the Aravalli Hill sites,
Ahar, has yielded, together with copper tools, chunks
of semifused glasslike material which we have identified as copper smelting slag. A trace element impurity pattern comparative study on excavated artifact
samples with the Aravalli Hill copper ore deposit
samples has also suggested the possibility of linking the artifacts with the Aravalli Hill copper ore
deposits. In order to gain a greater degree of cer-
tainty for this observation a lead isotope assay of
ore and artifact samples is now in progress. To
increase our understanding of ancient Indian copper
ore mining and smelting methods, therefore, we carried out a survey of six ancient copper ore mining
and smelting sites in the Aravalli Hills. In this
survey we have found interesting evidence enabling
us to reconstruct the early methods of locating
copper ore-bearing hills, methods of gouging superficial gossan cap and ore dressing near the mouths of
mines. We have also found ore-crushing pits near
the foot of ore-bearing ridges where roasted ore was
crushed into fine powder; gravity separation devices
where powdered ore particles were concentrated, and
extensive slag heaps associated with broken pieces
of tuyere and the remains of small, crucible-shaped
furnaces.

Keywords: MINING, SMELTING, COPPER, INDIA,
            CHALCOLITHIC, METALLURGY, GEOLOGY,
            FURNACE

Introduction

Numerous Chalcolithic sites, many of them dated by radiocarbon to the third
and second millennium BC (Sankalia 1974) have been excavated in the northwestern part of India during the last thirty years. All these sites have
yielded a variety of copper and bronze objects, some of them in good numbers.

60

But none of the sites has yielded stratified remains of structures that could
be identified as copper smelting furnaces. There is, however, evidence to
support the belief that copper was smelted in northwestern India during the
Chalcolithic period and it appears that copper and bronze objects were probably indigenously made. For example Ahar, one of the early metal-using sites
located near Udaipur, within the copper ore belt in the Aravalli Hills in
Rajasthan (Fig. 1), has yielded in levels dated between 1800 and 1600 BC
(Sankalia *et al.* 1969) a number of copper axes, chisels, rods and other
heavily corroded copper objects of indeterminate use, together with heaps of
chunks of semifused glasslike material. The excavators of the site had sent
us the copper tools and samples of the glasslike material for examination.
Analysis of the glasslike material revealed a high percentage of silica, iron
oxide and 0.67 to 0.91% of copper oxide (Hegde 1969). We have been able to
identify the glasslike material as copper smelting slag. Ahar therefore could
be said to be a copper smelting centre of the Chalcolithic period.

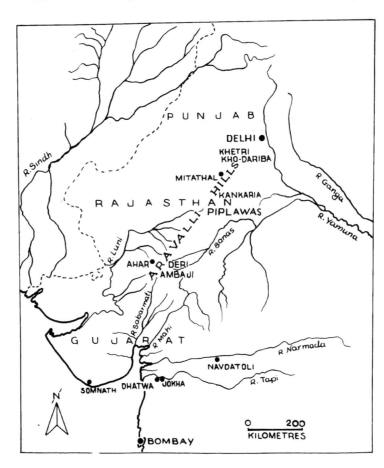

Fig. 1 Map showing the position of Chalcolithic sites and copper ore mining
and smelting sites mentioned in the text

Identification of Ahar slag shows that it is likely that the Indian
Chalcolithic metal objects were indigenously made. In order to gain a degree
of assurance for this hypothesis it was necessary to link the metal objects
with the Indian copper ore deposits through a comparative study of the trace
element impurity patterns and lead isotope ratios in the ore and artifacts.

Within the area inhabited by the Chalcolithic communities in northwestern
India, extensive copper ore deposits in the form of chalcopyrite, malachite
and azurite are found in discontinuous belts in the Aravalli Hills. At a
number of places these deposits are marked by shallow gouged pits as well as
deeper shafts and extensive slag heaps, representing marks of ancient mining
and smelting activity. A spectrometric study of copper ore samples obtained

from these ancient mining pits and metal samples cut from representative artifacts selected from widely distributed sites located at Mitathal, Ahar, Somnath, Navdatoli, Jokha and Dhatwa (Fig. 1) showed an agreement of over 92% in impurity patterns and, more important, artifacts did not show any elements that were not present in the ore samples (Hegde 1965). In collaboration with the Muroran Institute of Technology in Japan, we have obtained the lead isotope assay of copper ore samples collected from eight old mining and smelting sites in the Aravalli Hills (Table). As lead in ore deposits has a set of characteristic ratios among its isotopes, it is possible to determine the source of ancient copper and bronze objects which contain about one percent or more of lead, with a degree of fineness.

LEAD ISOTOPE RATIOS OF COPPER AND LEAD ORE DEPOSITS IN THE ARAVALLI HILLS

SITE	NATURE OF THE SAMPLE	Pb 206/Pb 204	Pb 207/Pb 204	Pb 208/Pb 204	Pb 207/Pb 206	Pb 208/Pb 206
AMBAJI	CHALCOPYRITE WITH PbS & ZnS	17·315 ± 0·016	15·649 ± 0·010	37·387 ± 0·016	0·90405 ± 0·00046	2·1596 ± 0·0015
ZAWAR	GALINA	16·583 ± 0·005	15·698 ± 0·007	36·535 ± 0·046	0·94671 ± 0·00019	2·2031 ± 0·0020
RAJPUR DARIBA	GALINA	16·061 ± 0·014	15·477 ± 0·040	35·815 ± 0·089	0·96543 ± 0·0020	2·2345 ± 0·0021
PIPLAWAS	CHALCOPYRITE WITH PbS	15·685 ± 0·042	15·444 ± 0·0049	35·218 ± 0·025	098446 ± 0·00004	2·2451 ± 0·0008
KANKARIA	CHALCOPYRITE WITH PbS	16·122 ± 0·008	15·524 ± 0·007	35·925 ± 0·057	0·96301 ± 000040	2·2284 ± 0·0032
KHO-DARIBA (DARIBA NALA)	CHALCOPYRITE WITH PbS.	33·39 ± 0·12	17·04 ± 0·08	61·44 ± 0·26	0·5167 ± 0·0002	1·844 ± 0·001
KHETRI (GHATIWALI)	CHALCOPYRITE WITH PbS	45·91 ± 0·10	18·24 ± 0·05	50·09 ± 0·18	0·3976 ± 0·001	1·091 ± 0·002

The suggestion that the copper ore belts in the Aravalli Hills possibly supplied copper to the Indian Chalcolithic communities settled over an extensive area was encouraging. We considered that an investigation of six selected mining and smelting sites in the Aravalli Hills might reveal details of the ancient mining and smelting techniques. Since none of the excavated sites revealed any evidence of the early smelting furnaces, we thought that we might find evidence of their structures at the ancient smelting sites.

Copper mines

The Aravalli Hills (Fig. 1) form one of the most dominant as well as picturesque geomorphic features in northwestern India. They extend over a thousand kilometres from Gujarat in the southwest to Delhi and beyond in the northeast. These hills include steep, discontinuous ridges that were formed by repeated folding and faulting of the Archaen ultrabasic rocks. These deformations resulted from pre-Cambrian plate tectonics of the proto-Indian subcontinent. Geologists have given a detailed account of the mechanism of plate subduction that gave rise to metallogenesis through hydrothermal deposition along the shear zones. They have located seven shear zones in the hills (Sychanthavong and Desai 1977). All the shear zones are rich in base metal ore deposits. The northeastern zones are rich in copper and contain negligible lead and zinc, which together constitute less than 0.004%, while the central and southwestern zones are rich in lead and zinc but rather poor in copper, containing only 0.5 to 2.5% of copper. But all the seven shear zones show evidence of their exploitation for extraction of copper in the past.

We selected six copper ore mining and smelting sites distributed within the Aravalli Hills shear zones for investigation. They are: Khetri and Kho Dariba in the northeastern part of the copper ore belt, Kankaria and Piplawas in the central part, and Deri and Ambaji in the southwestern part. We studied the site at Ambaji in detail (Fig. 1).

Analysis of copper and bronze objects of the Chalcolithic period excavated from sites in northwestern India, has shown about one or more than one percent of lead in their composition (Hegde 1965). Their metal, therefore, was not obtained from the copper ore belt in the northeastern part of the Aravalli Hills. It would be interesting to know if the metal was obtained from the copper ore in the central or southwestern part of the hills, for the host rocks surrounding the base metal minerals in these parts are soft. In the central part the host rocks are soft graphitic schists. In the southwestern part they are not too hard tremolite-chlorite schists. In the northeastern part copper ore minerals occur in very hard quartzites. The lead isotope assay on the archaeologically dated artifact samples may indicate the stages through which the ancient Indian copper ore miners improved their skills to move from the soft host rock mines, where the percentage of copper was poor, to rich copper ore deposits embedded within hard quartzites. We will soon be obtaining the lead isotope ratios for representative Chalcolithic period artifact samples.

At the central and southwestern zones of the copper ore belt in the Aravalli Hills we found much evidence of superficial gouging of the oxide-rich gossan cap. A large majority of these pits measure seven to eight metres in diameter and three to four metres in depth. There is evidence of fire-treating of the host rocks on the mine walls to widen the rock joins and thus facilitate extraction of copper ore bearing minerals.

According to Bateman (1950) the weathered upper part of a metal ore has two characteristic zones. The primary metal sulphide ore veins are converted by the action of oxygen and water into metal oxides, carbonates and sulphate. These are concentrated immediately below the ground water level and also at the top gossan zone. We therefore wanted to find out if the early miners exploited only the shallow, three-to-four-metre deep, poorly represented gossan cap, or whether they also penetrated deeper to exploit the richer redeposited minerals and also the primary chalcopyrite lenses below the weathered zones.

At all the six sites we visited we also noticed mine shafts that were very deep. All these deep mines opened into galleries and narrow tunnels following the natural configuration of ore veins at different levels. These galleries were provided with ventilation holes at regular intervals.

We consider the superficial shallow gouging pits as the earliest attempt at mining copper ore in the Aravalli Hills. Deep shafts complete with galleries, stopes, adits and ventilators may perhaps represent later mining acitvity.

There is, however, evidence to believe that at least some of the deep mines were worked during the Chalcolithic period. Timber supports recovered from a gallery at a depth of 120 metres at Rajpura-Dariba mines in Udaipur District were dated by radiocarbon to 3120 $\mp$ 160 years before the present (Hindustan Zinc Ltd 1980). That is the last quarter of the second millennium BC when the Chalcolithic communities were still active in many parts of northwestern India.

In the field we also wanted to look for any telltale evidence that would enable us to understand how the ancient miners prospected in the Aravalli Hills to locate copper ore deposits. These hills are extensive; only a few ridges among them contain copper ore. The hills are sharply dissected, steep, craggy and thorny. They do not form an easy terrain to explore. We tried to find out from the botanists in the Department of Botany at the M S University of Baroda if there was any identifiable floral clue to the copper rich ridges. They were not able to point out any such clue. However, we noticed that the ridges enclosing the shear zones were marked by an abundance of quartz veins. When we climbed up on those ridges we noticed a heavy scatter of chunks of quartz on those hill slopes. When we climbed further up, we encountered an abundance of chunks of green malachite-stained rocks. There were also pieces of blue azurite-stained rocks. It appears therefore that the presence of chunks of quartz, green malachite- and blue azurite-stained rocks, specially found in the beds of hill streams near the foot of the ridges, formed the clue for the identification of the copper ore-bearing hills.

Concentration of copper ore

We found the evidence for the first step towards ore concentration near the mine mouths. Near all the mine mouths we found large heaps of road metal size waste debris and road metal size chunks of malachite-bearing rocks. These selected ore-bearing rock pieces were roasted, crushed, concentrated and smelted. We have not found any evidence for reconstructing the method of ore roasting. But the small size of furnace that was used for smelting and the high yield of metal that was extracted in it, suggest that the ore was roasted and the smelting technology was efficient. Such an efficiency would not have been possible if the ore was not well roasted to convert all copper minerals in the ore into copper oxide and render the ore pieces porous and fragile and hence easy for crushing. We have found many groups of ore-crushing pits near the foot of the hills. Larger pits among them measure 60 cm in diameter and 70 cm in depth. Smaller ones measure 30 cm in diameter and 40 cm in depth.

The finely crushed ore was concentrated by gravity separation at the smelting sites which were invariably located near the banks of hill streams. Plate 1 illustrates one of the many such ore separation devices found by us. It is a smooth, gently inclined rock surface, neatly marked with rows of round shallow pits, 3 to 4 cm in diameter and 3 to 4 cm in depth. The finely crushed ore was allowed to slowly flow down the inclined plane and thus, by repeating this process, much of the gangue was effectively separated from the ore.

Smelting furnace

At the smelting sites were found large slag heaps spread out in terraces, littered with broken remains of furnaces (Plate 2) and broken tuyere. On some of the slag pieces was found the clear cylindrical flow structure, suggesting that the furnace used for smelting the metal had provision for tapping slag. Among the slag pieces we also found large, circular, 18 to 20 cm diameter chunks which the present day local farmers have used for building hedge walls around their fields and homes near the smelting sites.

Using the evidence of broken parts of furnace, tuyere, tapped and massive chunks of slag, shape, size and weight of the extracted copper ingots recovered at Chalcolithic sites, we have made an attempt to reconstruct the ancient Indian copper smelting furnace and its technology.

Furnace remains show that they were all broken at the bottom. It appears that there was no provision to tap the extracted molten metal out of the furnace. The ingot was left in the furnace and allowed to cool. Then the bottom part of the furnace was broken to take out the ingot. The furnace therefore was used for a single smelting operation.

An examination of the unbroken upper part of the furnaces shows the following interesting features: the furnaces were all of the same size, small, simple and inexpensive. They were made of coarse, not much elutriated, locally available, stream bank clay. All the broken parts show near uniformity in their curvature and thickness. They show finger impressions on their inner side only, indicating that they were made on moulds by spreading a 2 cm thick layer of clay. These curved pieces also show intact rim portion and lateral edges, thereby further indicating that the ancient furnace was a composite structure, made up of three separate curved parts, each part representing one third of a conical structure. One of the three segments of the furnace had a tuyere luted to it when it was leather hard. The angle of luting was approximately 30°. On another segment a hole was made at a height of 5 to 6 cm above the bottom, for tapping slag. Production of furnaces in three separate segments and assembling them together appear to have facilitated their manufacture in large numbers at less expense (Fig. 2).

The interior of the tuyere pipes shows bamboo bark impression indicating that they were made by rolling a layer of 1 cm thick clay over 15 cm long, 3 cm diameter bamboo pieces. It is not without interest here to note that this was also the method that was used for making tuyeres for iron smelting furnaces until about 50 years ago in our country. Verrier Elwin (1942) who studied the Agaria, an iron working community in central India, in the 1930s, has given a picture of an Agaria woman making tuyere pipes using bamboo pieces.

The furnace was assembled by putting the three curved parts together, one of them containing the luted tuyere, another with the slag tapping hole and a plain third one.

We did not find the bottom part of the furnace. We have reconstructed it using the size and shape of the copper ingots recovered in the excavations of Chalcolithic sites at Lothal, Harappa and Mohenjodaro. At all these sites the ingots were shaped like buns. Since the flat portion of the bun is uneven and irregular and the curved portion is regular, we have inferred that the curved portion represents the curved bottom of the smelting furnace.

No report of metallographic study of these buns has so far been published. We do not know if they are porous, or contain cuprous oxide and slag inclusions. The Lothal bun is 10 cm in diameter, 4 cm in height and weighs 1438 g (Rao 1973). We have used the curvature of the bun and its diameter to reconstruct the bottom part of the furnace.

The assembled furnace therefore was small, barely 35 cm in height, 18 cm in diameter at the rim, 14 cm in diameter at a mid-level and 10 cm in diameter near the base (Fig. 3). If we assume the mid-level diameter as the average diameter of the furnace, its capacity, $\pi r^2 h$, is 5390 cc. This small capacity of the furnace and the relatively high yield of the metal as represented by the weight of the copper ingot buns, enable us to infer that the ancient smelting process was rather efficient. To attain that efficiency adequate roasting of the ore to convert all copper minerals into copper oxide was necessary. Only copper oxide contains over 80% of copper. It is also the easiest mineral for reduction into metal. It therefore appears that the hand-picked, road metal size chunks of copper

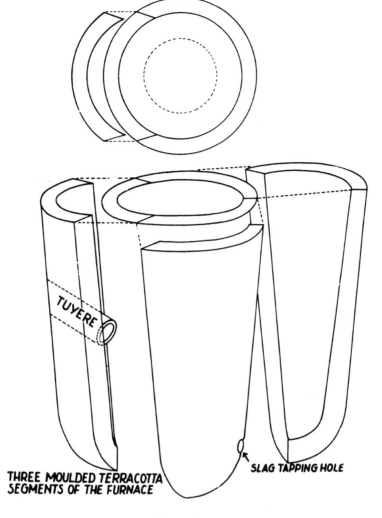

TUYERE

THREE MOULDED TERRACOTTA
SEGMENTS OF THE FURNACE

SLAG TAPPING HOLE

Fig. 2

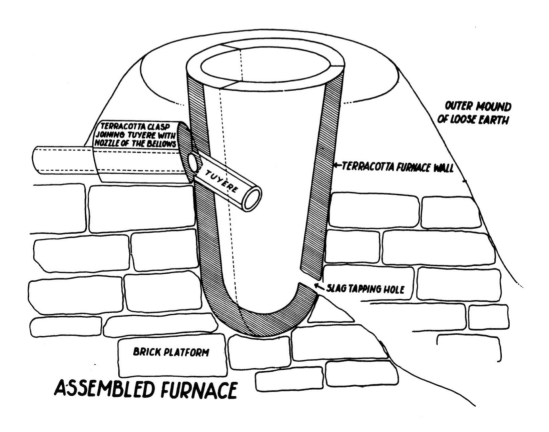

OUTER MOUND
OF LOOSE EARTH

TERRACOTTA CLASP
JOINING TUYERE WITH
NOZZLE OF THE BELLOWS

TERRACOTTA FURNACE WALL

TUYERE

SLAG TAPPING HOLE

BRICK PLATFORM

ASSEMBLED FURNACE

Fig. 3

ore were well roasted to convert all copper minerals into copper oxide.
The roasted ore was finely crushed. It was then well concentrated under
gravity separation. For preparing the smelting charge it was mixed with
crushed quartz, about equal weight of the ore and crushed charcoal, and
about twice the weight of the ore. Quartz was used to flux the ore and more
important, to sequester iron in the molten slag. Good quality quartz was
locally available in abundance. We have noted above that the Aravalli Hills
are rich in quartz veins and the hill slopes are littered with chunks of
quartz. We have also noted large quantities of these chunks at the smelting
sites.

The evidence of tuyere luted to the furnace wall suggests that the
smelting process in the furnace was carried out with the help of the forced
draught. But it is not easy to force a draught into a furnace when it is
filled with a mixture of finely powdered smelting charge. This prompted
us to re-examine the interior of the broken furnace remains more closely
to find out if there was any telltale evidence to indicate how the furnace
was charged. This examination revealed spherical, fist-size lumps sticking on to the interior of the furnace walls (Plate 3). Samples cut from
these lumps under the microscope showed vesicular structure, crushed particles of quartz and slag. These lumps therefore appear to be the remains
of smelted charge. Their fist-size and small, spherical shape indicate
that the crushed ore, flux and fuel mixture was charged into the furnace
in the form of small, handmade, fistfulls of spherical lumps. From the
capacity of the furnace, it appears that about 40 lumps, each weighing
about 100 g, could have been charged into it at the first instance. Above
the lumps excess fuel was continuously added to maintain the domination of
reducing atmosphere through an excess production of carbon monoxide over
carbon dioxide. This reducing atmosphere would ensure the reduction of
copper oxide. As the first charge was smelted more lumps and fuel were
added until an optimum was reached.

The main component of the slag is fayalite; it melts at 1170°C. The
cylindrical flow structure of the tapped slag suggests that the charge
was smelted in the furnace at a temperature much above 1170°C. As copper
melts at 1083°C the extracted liquid metal collects at the bottom of the
furnace, because of its high specific gravity of 8.89, below the molten
slag whose specific gravity is four. Towards the close of operation slag
was tapped by opening a way out for it through the slag tapping hole and the
loose earth surrounding the furnace. It appears that the slag tapping
segment of the furnace was arranged towards the edge of the terrace so as to
let the slag drain out easily. When much of the slag flowed out in this
way the slag in the upper part of the furnace, along with the still burning
fuel, piled up over it and collapsed into the furnace forming the massive
circular chunks of slag which the present day local farmers have used to
build hedge walls. When the furnace was cooled, the copper ingot was
taken out by breaking its bottom.

Conclusion

From the foregoing discussion it appears that the ancient Indian copper
smelting furnace was a small, crucible-shaped, clay-walled, slag-tapping
furnace worked on forced draught blown into it from bellows. It was a
composite structure made of three moulded segments. Evidence found at the
smelting sites shows that it was set up on a brick platform and was surrounded with bricks and earth to keep the three segments of the furnace tightly
in position (Fig. 3) and also to conserve the heat within the furnace. At

these sites we have also found terracotta clasps that joined the tuyere and the nozzle of the bellows (Plate 4). This simple furnace appears to have been continuously used in India over the millennia without any innovation.

References

Bateman, A M 1961. *Economic mineral deposits*, 245-288. Bombay, Asia Publishing House

Elwin, V 1942. *The Agaria*, 86, pl. xxiv. Oxford, O.U.P.

Hegde, K T M 1965. 'Chalcolithic period copper metallurgy in India'. Unpublished Ph.D. thesis, M.S. University of Baroda, Baroda

Hegde, K T M 1969. Technical studies in copper artifacts from Ahar. In *Excavations at Ahar*, H D Sankalia, *et al*. 225-29, pls. xxvi-xxviii. Deccan College, Pune

Hindustan Zinc Limited 1980. Pamphlet on Rajpura Dariba Mines

Rao, S R 1973. *Lothal and the Indus Civilization*, 80-85, pl XVIIIA. Bombay, Asia Publishing House

Sankalia, H D, Deo, S B & Ansari, Z D 1969. *Excavations at Ahar*, 8-12, 99 Deccan College, Pune

Sankalia, H D 1974. *Prehistory and proto-history of India and Pakistan*, 309-470. Deccan College Pune

Sychanthavong, S P & Desai, S D 1977. Proto-plate tectonics controlling the Precambrian deformations and metallogenetic epochs of northwestern peninsular India. *Minerals Science Engineering*, **9** (4), 218-236

Plate 1 Gravity separation device for concentrating copper ore at copper smelting sites in the Aravalli Hills

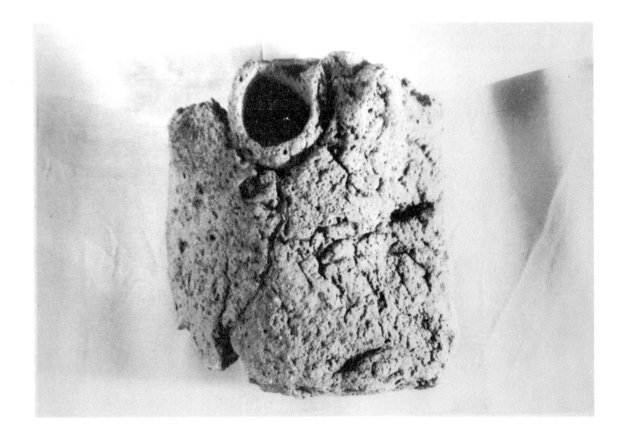

Plate 2 Fragment of a copper smelting furnace with tuyere

Plate 3   Interior of a furnace fragment, arrows showing the position of two
spent smelting charge lumps sticking on to the furnace wall

Plate 4   Terracotta clasp for joining tuyere with nozzle of bellows

METAL WORKING IN THE AGADEZ REGION (NIGER): AN ETHNO-ARCHAEOLOGICAL APPROACH

Suzanne Bernus[1] and Nicole Echard[2]

1 Centre National de la Recherche Scientifique, 27 quai
   de la Tournelle 75005 Paris
2 Centre National de la Recherche Scientifique, 2 rue
   du Loing 75014 Paris

Abstract

This paper presents some of the results of studies
undertaken since 1977 as part of a regional survey.
Archaeological, ethnological and ethno-archaeolo-
gical methods have been used together for the comparative study of ancient and recent metallurgies.
Copper was worked froma round 1000 BC up to the
fifteenth century AD. During the early period
furnaces were used. In the Middle Ages crucibles
were used in Azelik. In contrast to copper there
have been no radical changes in iron work
procedures. Since the fourteenth century the
furnaces have assumed a form comparable to what
could be seen twenty years ago in southern
regions of Niger.

Keywords: COPPER, IRON, MELTING, SMELTING, FURNACES,
             CRUCIBLES, TECHNICAL SYSTEM, HISTORY OF
             TECHNIQUES, AFRICA, NIGER, NATIVE COPPER,
             METALLURGY, EXPERIMENTAL ARCHAEOLOGY,
             ETHNOLOGY, ETHNO-ARCHAEOLOGY

Introduction

In the north-central region of the Republic of Niger, on the southern border
of the Sahara, plains of clay soils surround the volcanic massif of the Air
(Fig.). In the area around the town of Agadez, a French multi-disciplinary
team including geographers, anthropologists and archaeologists, has undertaken a regional survey. Some members of the team have been working in
this region for more than ten years. This paper presents the point of
view of the anthropologists.

This systematic research was facilitated by the interest which the
government of Niger took in planning the industrial and economic development
of the region consequent to the discovery of uranium.

In the present period the climate is of the sahelian type (short rainy
season from July to September, very long dry season of nine months) and
permits no other style of life than pastoral nomadism, which is practised
in the region by Tuareg and Fulani. There are no cultivated fields and
permanent settlements are limited to three, which are of an urban type:

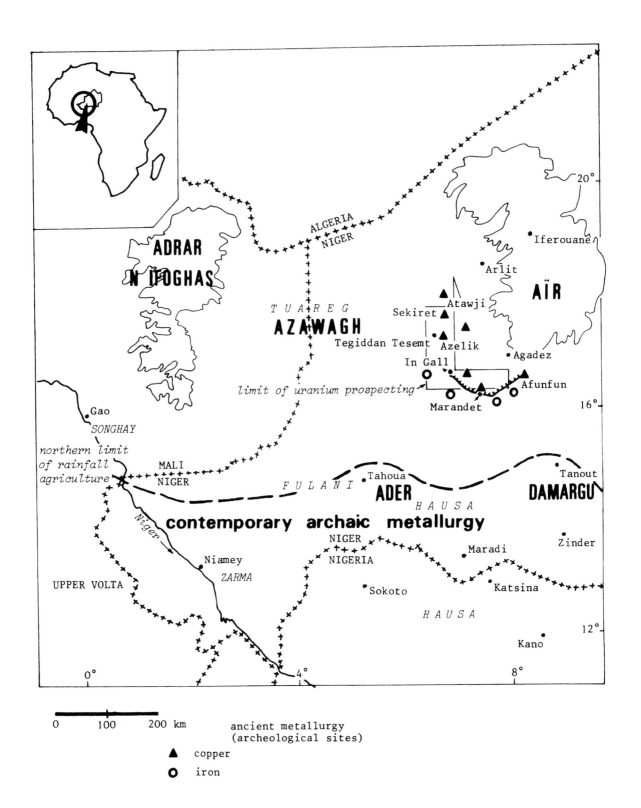

ADRAR
N'IFOGHAS

T U A R E G
AZAWAGH

AÏR

ALGERIA
NIGER   20°

• Iferouane

• Arlit

▲
Atawji ▲
Sekiret ▲
▲ ▲
Tegiddan Tesemt   Azelik
In Gall   • Agadez
limit of uranium prospecting   ○   ▲ ▲   ▲
○   Afunfun
○ ○   16°
Marandet

• Gao
SONGHAY

*northern limit
of rainfall
agriculture*   MALI
NIGER   *F U L A N I*   • Tahoua
ADER   *H A U S A*   **DAMARGU**   • Tanout

contemporary archaic metallurgy

Niger   NIGER
NIGERIA   • Maradi   • Zinder

• Niamey
UPPER VOLTA   *ZARMA*
• Sokoto   • Katsina

H A U S A
12°
• Kano

0°   4°   8°

─────────────
0   100   200 km

ancient metallurgy
(archeological sites)

▲ copper

○ iron

Figure

Agadez, the historical and political centre; In Gall, an important market and palm grove; and Tegiddan Tesemt where salt mines are worked. The people living in these three places differ from the nomadic herders; linguistic analysis and oral traditions suggest they are residual groups belonging to a prior stock.

In a course of the regional archaeological survey undertaken, however, very numerous traces of earlier permanent habitation have been discovered: concentrated settlements, necropolises, human and animal cemeteries, suggesting a higher population density than that observed in the present.

A rigorous survey of the ground surface has revealed:

-    copper artifacts in certain sites;

-    deposits of copper ores (chrysocolla, malachite, and dolomite containing inclusions of native copper);

-    accumulations of slags accompanying remnants of burned clay structures.

A series of carbon-14 dates extending from the beginning of the second millennium BC to the contemporary period led to the formulation of this hypothesis: despite changing climatic conditions, the permanence of human occupation in this area is associated with the exploitation of mineral resources (copper, iron, salt and uranium).

The general problem to be resolved is the place of metal exploitation in this regional continuity. This paper will present the way in which the treatment of the metals was studied (generally speaking: extraction, reduction, shaping etc), the results obtained and the questions which these results raise.

Methods

Archaeological and ethnological methods have been used together. With regard to archaeology, systematic surface surveying and as complete an inventory as possible have been deliberately favoured over the classical focus on the excavation of particular sites. In fact, the study of prior habitation and human activity in the distant past cannot be limited to the comparison of artifacts collected at random in chance discoveries. The distribution of remains within a region, on one site or among a group of sites, is not random. The cartography of this distribution provides important indications concerning the extension of a particular human group, the nature of its activities, the limits of its territory etc. The means utilized have been (1) aerial photographic coverage and satellite imagery, (2) geological studies, (3) the heterogeneous data collected by geographers and anthropologists in collaboration with the current inhabitants of the area, and (4) the cartography of the data and the formulation of research hypotheses on the basis of preliminary mapping of the distribution of various items (copper, burials, furnaces etc). This knowledge of the regional space allowed us to formulate a provisional classification of the vestiges of occupation and activities.

We also need to define the contribution of ethnology to such an investigation in order to formulate the questions in the perspective of a 'history of techniques', as it has been established in France through the work of B Gilles, for example. This approach also defines in advance and in part the methods we intend to use, such as:

1. The observation of the contemporary practice of metallurgy: how are the nomadic and sedentary workplaces for the treatment of metals constituted, and how do they function technically and socially?

2. The collection and study of oral traditions currently held by the different populations in the area: is there a technical memory associated with the current treatment of metals? Does one find mytho-historical schemes which provide information as to origins?

3. The extension of the same observation and collection to neighbouring populations considering that the region is inserted in a larger whole. Thus far samples have been taken among populations established in three districts in the sedentary zone to the south: the Damargu, the Kurfey and the Ader. The comparison with metallurgical traditions in the Ader seems especially promising, since contemporary populations in the region claim descent from groups who emigrated from the region of Agadez around the tenth century AD.

The investigation has benefited from the cooperation between the two disciplines in two specific ways: first, the knowledge held by current populations concerning the past has led to numerous discoveries. For example, the nomads are very well-informed concerning the location of places covered with ceramic sherds. They refer to them as 'villages of the People from Before', and it is on or near these places that they attempt to dig wells.

Secondly, this interdisciplinary cooperation has allowed us to formulate a project in experimental archaeology which has drawn on the contributions of ethnology and archaeology, namely a reconstruction of the manufacture of copper as one can suppose it to have been done in the medieval period at Azelik (Pls. 1 and 2). In this project the classical methods of archaeology contributed a knowledge of the materials used in the past: debris of treatment, ore, crucibles etc. The methods of ethnology suggested the specific form taken by the reconstruction, in that it was carried out by a local smith, who used his own charcoal together with his usual crucibles and tools.

The lessons drawn from this experiment benefit the ethnologist as well as the archaeologist. The dialogue with and the participation of the current holders of technical knowledge singularly enlarges the field of hypotheses to be tested by anthropologists as well as archaeologists. The work which we will present here results from the application of these methods of investigaiton. It constitutes a part of the general study of the zone.

Copper

Azelik is probably the site of Takedda, a town described and visited in the Middle Ages by the Arab traveller Ibn Batuta. It was established by our previous research that the site had been an important centre for the treatment of copper. The presence of residues of ore and finished or semi-finished artifacts (ingots, filaments, plates) on the site of settlement led us to extend the survey to discover the copper-bearing deposits and the sites of treatment.

Plate 1   Copper melting (in Gall, 1982).   The Tuareg smith is pouring
          melted copper in the ingot mould (reconstruction).

     To the southeast of the site of settlement, the attentive examination of
a zone covered with grey-blue slags yielded remains of round structures of
burned clay which were identified as the bases of furnaces. Extending the
survey still further, very numerous locations bearing such remains of round
form were discovered, sometimes accompanied or replaced by more complex
structures of elongated form, whose use is not clearly established. The
correlation between these structures of burned clay and the working of copper
(presence of residues, drops of melted metal, ingots and finished artifacts)
appears well-established throughout the first millennium BC for a series of
sites: Afunfun, Tuluk, Azelik, Sekiret, Atawji (Grébénart 1983). The upper
parts of the furnaces are destroyed down to ground level.

     The diameter varies from 50 cm to one metre, the depth of the depression
rarely surpassing 35 cm and is of cylindrical or truncated conical form.
Several fragments of tuyeres have been found nearby.

     A few older dates have been obtained from charcoal collected in the
complex structures which are found sometimes in proximity to these furnaces
and sometimes in isolation. However, the mode of functioning of these
structures has not yet been firmly established, nor have incontestable
slags been found in their immediate proximity. Without more ample informa-

76

Plate 2   Iron smelting in Ader (Hausaland 1967): pouring charcoal into the
          fire

tion these structures cannot be considered as indices of an older period of copper production ('Copper I', according to Grébénart) employing a different technology.

The later traces of copper working are much more recent and show a clear difference in the technical procedure used. Marandet and Azelik, the largest copper-working sites from the medieval period, have yielded no trace of furnaces. However, the working of copper is clearly and certainly attested there, both by the presence of ore residues (an estimated fifteen tonnes on the surface of the site of Azelik) and by the presence of work-places (45,000 crucibles at Marandet).

The technique used at Azelike was reconstructed with the help of Tuareg smiths. Copper-bearing calcite was crushed to extract the nodules of native copper. These nodules were melted in a small clay crucible, to which charcoal powder was added (Pl. 1). The melted copper was cast into small ingots, which were subsequently worked by hammering.

Thus one can summarize the preliminary conclusions concerning the production of copper:

1. The results of the analyses conducted on the ashes and slags by Professor Tylecote as well as by J R Bourhis of the Laboratory of Rennes demonstrate that in all cases native copper was being melted. A single procedure was used, although with variations (furnaces during early period, crucibles during medieval period).

2. One can draw from this some suggestions regarding the populations concerned. Copper was manufactured during the early period outside the places of settlement and doubtless this implies specialized artisans working in cooperation. During the medieval period the work was conducted in the settlements in individual fashion, and a finer range of techniques was used. These were applied, for example, to the manufacture of jewellery, padlocks, knife and sword handles and other small decorative pieces.

3. The production of copper is discontinuous historically and ends definitively toward the end of the fourteenth century. Various hypotheses have been advanced to account for this discontinuity: exhaustion of copper-bearing deposits, climatic change, migrations of populations modifying the balance of the political economy in the region.

Iron

The production of iron is attested to beginning around 500 BC and appears to have occured in two periods. In the earlier period cylindrical furnaces of clay 80-100 cm in diameter resting on the ground are sometimes found near settlements. They are not the same as those used for the melting of copper, although their destruction is also required to recover the metal. The question of the relation between the Neolithic men, the producers of copper, and the iron-makers has not received a satisfactory answer thus far (Grébénart 1983).

The second period of iron manufacture begins 500-600 years after the end of the first. The earliest date from this second period is 490 AD. The furnaces used during this period appear first as clay chimneys in the form of conical or cylindrical trunks partially buried in the ground, as for the melting of copper. Then the technique seems to have evolved pro-

gressively until it presents, in the fourteenth century, the same characteristics observed contemporarily in the sedentary regions to the south
(Ader, Kurfey, Damargu). The main characteristics are:

    1.   a cavity created in the ground; the ground itself is then used
as part of the furnace;

    2.   tuyeres placed around the edge of the cavity;

    3.   a chimney of clay resting on the tuyeres.

It does not appear that any auxiliary blowing system was used, in contrast
to the apparatus used in melting copper.

    Comparison of the sum of observations for the two periods indicates:

    1.   the area of geographical extension was not the same: the
second period of iron-working was in a more southerly zone;

    2.   the furnaces were modified during the second period (beginning
in about the fourteenth century) by the introduction of a chimney. This
eliminated the need to destroy the furnace to recover the bloom: it
sufficed to remove the chimney;

    3.   the smelting areas of the second period are never associated
with a settlement.

Thus the main characteristics of the furnaces of the second period are a
detachable chimney and the distance of the operation from the settlements.
This implies work in cooperation and a corresponding social organization
of work.

    We should note concerning this final proposition that other furnaces
have been observed during the second period which require neither cooperation nor any particular organization of work. Among other interpretations,
these furnaces might correspond to the need to produce a small quantity of
metal under urgent circumstances.

    Thus copper production and iron production contrast in a number of
ways. Three major areas of contrast are summarized in the following
table (p. 79).

Conclusion and questions

At this point in the development of our research other questions still remain
concerning the production of the metals and their role in the technical and
economic systems in which they appear.

    Concerning copper, let us raise two principal questions:

    1.   To what factors should one attribute the technical descontinuity
observed (the passage from melting in furnaces to melting in crucibles)?
Might these factors relate to the change in ore utilized, to data of a micro-
geographical order, or might they be associated with a change in population?

    2.   To what factors should one relate the total disappearance of copper
production at Azelik and in its region toward the beginning of the fifteenth

	COPPER	IRON
Technology: structure and functioning of the apparatus	furnace destroyed after melting auxiliary blowing system	furnace re-utilized (in part) after smelting no auxiliary blowing system
Social Organization of Work	First period: cooperation (?) outside the settlement (furnaces) * * * Second period: individual work inside the settlement (crucibles)	near the settlement cooperation outside the settlement
Chronology	discontinuity: -850 BC to 90 BC -"medieval" (disappearance since around fifteenth century in Azelik)	continuity 500 AD to the present

century? Were the copper-bearing deposits exhausted as the current state of the strata may eventually indicate? Or were the imperatives of production transformed instead - demanding higher yields, for example?

Other hypotheses are possible, among them the replacement of copper by another metal, in this case iron, which would have been both suited to the uses to which copper had previously been put and sufficient to satisfy regional demands. This hypothesis would explain the cessation of copper production in furnaces and would assume a differential utilization of the two metals beginning in the medieval period, iron for weapons and tools, copper for decorative work and jewellery-making. Thus far the manufacture of bronze is not attested in the region, although a few objects of this material have been discovered.

The problems posed by iron metallurgy are of an entirely different order; (we will not consider here the questions raised by the first period of iron manufacture, which would have lasted for some 400 years). The smelting of iron ore from the fourth century AD to the contemporary period presents such a remarkable continuity that one can speak of 'technical blockage'. The problems of 'technical blockage' - or more precisely of the couple innovation-blockage - have been raised principally by ethnology. The archaeologists probably have elements to contribute to this debate.

To consider these diverse facts concerning the metals also presupposes their placement in the perspective of given technical systems. What light can these investigations shed on the transition from the end of the last Stone Age (Neolithic) to the beginning of the Age of Metals? Are the vestiges of ancient metallurgy associated with particular geographical regions? What relations existed between metallurgical practice and other technological practices? Various working hypotheses remain to be explored, which demand the cooperation of several disciplines.

Bibliography

Bernus, S & Gouletquer, P L 1976. Du cuivre au sel, recherches ethno-archéologiques sur la région d'Azelik (campagnes 1973-1975). *Journal des Africanistes* **46**, 1-2, 7-68

Bernus, S 1983. Découvertes, hypothèses, reconstitution et preuves: le cuivre médiéval d'Azelik-Takedda. In *Métallurgies africaines. Nouvelles contributions*, 153-172. Paris, Mémoires de la Société des Africanistes

Bucaille, R 1975. Takadda, pays du cuivre. *Bulletin de l'Institut Fondamental d'Afrique Noire*, **37** B, 4, 719-778

Echard, N 1983. Scories et symboles. Remarques sur la métallurgie hausa du fer au Niger. In *Métallurgies africaines. Nouvelles contributions*, 209-224. Paris, Mémoires de la Société des Africanistes

Grébénart, D 1983. Les métallurgies du cuivre et du fer autour d'Agadez (Niger). Vues générales. *Métallurgies africaines. Nouvelles contributions*, 109-126. Paris, Mémoires de la Société des Africanistes

R C P 322 1983. *Programme archéologique d'urgence (région d'In Gall, Niger) Rapport final.* To appear in *Etudes Nigeriennes*, **47, 48, 49**

Poncet, Y 1983. Minerais et exploitations métallurgiques: une réflexion géographique. In *Métallurgies africaines. Nouvelles contributions*, 199-208. Paris, Mémoires de la Société des Africanistes

Tylecote, R F 1982. Early copper slags and copper-base metal from the Agadez region of Niger. *Journal of Historical Metallurgy Society*, **16** (2), 58-64

COPPER SOURCES AND COPPER METALLURGY IN THE AEGEAN BRONZE AGE

N H Gale[1], A Papastamataki[2], Z A Stos-Gale[1] and
K Leonis[2]

1   Department of Geology, University of Oxford, Parks
    Road, Oxford
2   Institute of Geology and Mineral Exploration,
    70 Messoghion Street, Athens

Abstract

Copper ore sources have been investigated on the
Cycladic islands of Seriphos and Kythnos; two
ancient copper slag heaps on Seriphos (Avyssalos
and Kefala) and one on Kythnos have been surveyed.
Each of these slag heaps is located high above sea
level in a situation exposed to the north winds.
In each case pieces of oxidised copper ore can be
found scattered amongst the slag together with
abundant clay fragments of furnaces, but no intact
furnace remains have certainly been located so far.
The Avyssalos slag heap is on a scale comparable
with those on Cyprus and probably does not relate
to the Bronze Age. Indeed the antiquity of copper
metallurgy on neither of these islands has yet been
determined, but there are indications (granite crushing hammers, large copper prills, pottery, obsidian
artefacts) that the Kythnos slag heap may date to
the Bronze Age. Bulk chemical and lead isotope
analyses have been made of the slags, together with
some microprobe analyses of the abundant copper
prills which they contain. Petrographic examination
shows that dominant phases of the slags are fayalite
and iron oxide, consistent with their classification
into Bachmann's System 2. Determination of empirical
free running temperatures of the Kythnos slags show
that liquidus temperatures predicted by the SiO_2-FeO-
CaO ternary diagram are very much too high. Predictions made by the proper AN-FeO-SiO_2 diagram are much
better, but may still be one or two hundreds of
degrees too high. Microprobe analyses of the copper
prills show nickel contents up to 1% and arsenic
contents up to 4.5% resulting accidentally from the
smelting of oxidised copper ores with no deliberate
addition of arsenic. Lead isotope analyses suggest,
but do not yet prove, that some Early Cycladic bronzes
from Amorgos may be made of copper from Kythnos.

Keywords: COPPER, SLAG, PRILLS, ANALYSIS, PHASE
             DIAGRAMS, LIQUIDUS TEMPERATURES, ARSENICAL
             COPPER, OXIDISED ORES, AEGEAN BRONZE AGE,
             GREECE, SMELTING, FURNACE, CYCLADIC

Introduction

This paper presents some of the first results of a cooperative research programme between the Institute of Geology and Mineral Exploration, Athens, and the Department of Geology, University of Oxford. The objectives of the research are the search for metal sources and the study of ancient mining and metallurgy in the Aegean Bronze Age.

Lead isotope studies have already shown that the two major sources of lead and silver for the Early Cycladic culture were Siphnos and the Laurion in Attica, with a swing almost wholly to the Laurion by Late Bronze Age times in Thera (Gale & Stos-Gale 1981). A comprehensive study of Early to Late Bronze Age artefacts from Ayia Irini, Kea, shows that sources dominantly in Siphnos and Laurion were used in the Early Bronze Age, swinging almost wholly to the Laurion in Late Bronze Age, and a very similar picture holds for the Minoan culture (Stos-Gale & Gale 1982b). On mainland Greece the source of silver and lead in the Late Bronze Age was almost exclusively the Laurion for those sites so far investigated (Stos-Gale & Gale 1982a). One exception is that in the Shaft Graves of Circle A at Mycenae silver was obtained both from the Laurion and from another source. This work demonstrated also the existence of a trade route in lead and silver linking Crete via the Cyclades to Attica in Middle Minoan to Late Minoan times.

Since, in addition to lead-silver ores, oxidised copper ores also occur in the Laurion (Gale & Stos-Gale 1982) and since the smelting procedures and temperatures needed to extract metal from impure ore are very similar for copper and lead, it seemed not improbable that the proof of Bronze Age lead-silver production there might imply also copper production in the Laurion at these times. That is now proved by the demonstration that many Minoan bronzes from Middle Minoan 111 to Late Minoan 111 times are made of copper from the Laurion and that the same is true of some Early Cycladic bronzes from Amorgos, Naxos and Syros and for the few Mycenaean bronzes so far analysed (Gale & Stos-Gale 1982, 1985). The work which proved the Bronze Age exploitation of Laurion copper showed also that at least five other non-Cypriot copper sources were used by either the Minoans or the Cycladic people. Since more than seventy copper ore sources are known in Greece, Crete and the Cyclades (see the Metallogenetic Map of Greece, IGME, 1965 and the accompanying handbook) and many Greek copper slag heaps are known (Papastamataki 1975), it is necessary to establish whether any of these local sources were exploited in the Bronze Age. The ancient metals trade route between Crete and the mainland via the Cyclades suggests that copper sources in the Cyclades might be especially important; in this paper we concentrate particularly on copper sources in Seriphos and Kythnos.

Copper sources in the Cyclades

Copper ores are known on Andros, Syros, Paros, Kythnos and Seriphos and copper slag is known on each of these islands except Syros (Davies 1935). In July 1982 a joint IGME/Oxford team made a preliminary investigation of ores and slags on Kythnos and Seriphos.

Seriphos

There is evidence that mining was carried on at least as early as the fourth century BC in Seriphos, and Galanos (1962) gives an account of the history of mining on Seriphos which shows that there was intense activity in the Venetian period and in the nineteenth century AD. This modern mining was chiefly for iron, but licenses to extract copper, zinc, manganese and argentiferous lead were issued at various times between 1869 and 1886. It is clear that pyritiferous copper ores were exploited at Kalavatsena in the southwest (Fig. 1), that argentiferous lead ores were exploited at Moutsoula in the north, and that there was extensive exploitation of iron ores in the southwest in a region stretching from Koutala to Avyssalos; much of the iron ore was shipped to Newcastle for smelting. The silver-lead ore at Moutsoula was certainly exploited anciently for silver (Gale & Stos-Gale 1981).

The antiquity of copper exploitation on Seriphos is not yet known. We found oxidised copper ores (chrysocolla) on top of the headland between the bays of Mega Livadi and Koundouro and sulphidic copper ores (iron pyrite plus chalcopyrite, together with some secondary oxidised ores) at Kalavatsena where there was much modern exploitation of copper ore. The iron ores in the southwest generally bear small localised amounts of copper. Davies (1935) mentions malachite at Koundouro and at Aspropyrghos; he mentions also copper slag heaps at the top of the hill at Koundouro which we could not find; perhaps he is in fact speaking of the slag heap at Avyssalos which lies about one km north of Koundouro Bay. Fiedler (1841) mentions copper ores in the iron ores at Koutala, but does not mention the slag heap on Seriphos.

In fact an enormous copper slag heap of at least 100,000 tonnes lies on the hill slopes above and to the South of Avyssalos Bay; it lies in a high position open to the winds but well away from the sea or other water supplies (Plate 1). The heap is full of broken slabs of tap slag and of broken fragments of clay furnace walls or lining. In places the slag heap is three to four metres thick (Plate 2). Throughout the slag heap rare pieces of oxidised copper ore were found. The antiquity of the copper smelting is not yet known, but the scale of the operation at Avyssalos is comparable with that recorded by the Cypriot copper slag heaps (whose age also remains poorly established, but is probably Geometric to Roman).

A smaller (perhaps 3000 tonnes) copper slag heap exists on Seriphos at Kefala (Fig. 1); this seems not to have been reported before. The slag heap is on the north facing slope of Cape Kefala, facing Piperi and Kythnos, about 100 metres above the sea and fully exposed to the winds (Plate 3). This heap is extensive but not above about 50 cm thick anywhere; there is much broken clay lining mixed with the slag. Much of the heap consists of large broken slabs of tap slag but there are abundant regions where the slag is broken into centimetre-sized fragments, perhaps to extract copper prills (Plate 4).

Table 1 gives representative chemical analyses of slags from Avyssalos and Kefala, showing that the copper content ranges from about 1 to 19%. The sulphur content is low, consistent with the smelting of oxidised copper ores. The chlorine content of the slags from Kefala no doubt records weathering due to exposure to salt-laden spray carried by winds up to the slag heap during the winter months. The specific gravity of the slags from Kefala and Avyssalos ranges from 3.25 to 3.90.

Table 1 Copper slag heaps in Seriphos: Avyssalas and Kefala

SLAG NO:	AVY 1	AVY 2	AVY 3	AVY 4	AVY 5	AVY 6	AVY 7	AVY 8	KEF 1	KEF 2	KEF 3	KEF 4
FeO	32.19	40.91	32.81	40.30	41.76	56.2	37.18	50.0	37.03	55.31	31.29	44.3
MnO	0.66	0.23	0.22	0.31	0.25	1.84	0.23	0.47	0.31	0.24	0.20	0.28
MgO	6.22	5.14	5.79	5.09	5.64	2.07	5.15	2.4	4.13	1.95	2.85	4.6
Al_2O_3	5.95	1.59	1.67	2.27	3.65	4.63	1.74	2.3	1.93	5.84	2.91	4.5
SiO_2	37.41	39.89	42.83	41.22	37.0	29.0	45.0	36.5	42.89	28.85	35.31	38.0
CaO	7.79	8.35	4.78	6.85	7.56	2.52	8.00	8.8	3.99	2.28	3.23	9.8
BaO	-	-	-	-	-	-	-	-	-	-	-	-
K_2O	0.66	0.30	0.21	0.34	0.55	0.50	0.30	-	0.32	0.70	0.29	-
Na_2O	0.49	0.26	0.13	0.29	0.40	0.30	0.36	-	0.21	0.71	0.15	-
TiO_2	0.16	0.06	0.06	0.08	0.10	0.07	0.08	-	0.07	0.25	0.15	-
P_2O_5	0.15	0.09	0.05	0.13	-	-	-	-	0.16	0.17	0.12	-
CuO	6.97	1.36	9.81	1.81	1.64	1.56	0.57	0.63	6.31	1.01	18.77	0.35
PbO	0.05	0.25	0.05	0.04	0.05	0.08	0.06	0.10	0.02	0.01	0.19	0.06
ZnO	0.05	0.06	0.00	0.07	0.72	0.82	0.70	0.17	0.15	0.06	0.01	0.04
As_2O_3	0.00	0.00	0.32	0.00	0.15	0.0	0.0	0.0	0.00	0.00	0.56	0.00
Sb_2O_5	0.12	0.13	0.03	0.09	-	-	-	-	0.11	0.10	0.09	-
S	0.15	0.17	0.13	0.08	0.34	0.15	0.16	0.40	0.17	0.60	0.26	0.47
Cl	0.18	0.04	0.18	0.02	-	-	-	-	0.57	0.14	2.62	-
Ni	-	-	-	-	0.04	0.05	0.04	0.04	-	-	-	0.05
Co	-	-	-	-	0.04	0.06	0.03	0.04	-	-	-	0.03
Au (ppm)	-	-	-	-	0	0	0	0	-	-	-	0
Ag (ppm)	-	-	-	-	2.5	3.0	1.0	0	-	-	-	0

-- not determined   AVY: Avyssalos;   KEF: Kefala

Kythnos

Iron ore occurs in the marbles on Kythnos principally in the northwest of the island and in the Ayios Ioannis, Zogaki and Milyes regions (Fig.2), but also in the Kanalia region and in the extreme south of the island. It was exploited in the nineteenth and early twentieth centuries AD and also by the Italians in 1940/41; the Italian exploitation has destroyed much of the remains of ancient mining.

Fiedler (1841) observed that malachite occurs in the iron ore in the Ayios Ioannis region and that ancient mines exist in iron ore at a place which he called Lefties; this seems most probably to be Zogaki, which is near Lefkes Bay. Fiedler (1841) knew also of the large slag heap exposed to the north winds on the cliff side to the north of Ayios Ioannis, and that no mineralisation occurs actually at this place. Davies (1935) knew of three ancient mining regions on Kythnos, at Zogaki, Kanalia and Milyes, but he does not seem to have suspected that the ancient mining was for copper contained in the iron ore. Honea (1975) briefly mentions the copper ore on Kythnos and a copper slag heap; he ascribes this slag heap to the Bronze Age.

On our visit to Kythnos we went to the Milyes and Zogaki mining regions and also to the copper slag heap. At Milyes and Psathi we saw many vertical shafts through the marble and several entrances to the mines underground; all are now blocked, but we collected ore, which was predominantly iron ore with a little copper. Davies (1935) describes the mines at Milyes as the most perfect specimen of an ancient mine which he had seen, but the evidence of Roman Imperial coins found in them suggests that they may have no relevance to the Bronze Age. At Zogaki the ancient mines are badly destroyed by the Italian exploitation in 1940/41 AD, but there are still remnants of the ancient galleries (Plate 5) seen by Davies and Fiedler; these ancient galleries tunnel through the iron ore as though iron was not the ore primarily sought, and the iron ore does contain copper. There are scattered pieces of slag on the Zogaki peninsula.

The Kythnos copper slag heap is about 150 metres above sea level at the cliff top about two km to the north of Cape Ioannis; part of it covers the steep plunge of the cliff down to the sea (Plate 6); the rest forms a medium-to-thin scatter on top of the cliff and also forms a scatter in a saucer-shaped valley inland from the cliff. Much of the slag is copper stained and it is mixed with abundant fragments of clay furnace lining, many undecorated brownware pottery sherds which Honea believes to date to the Bronze Age, many pieces of oxidised copper ore (malachite in iron ore) and many fragments of quartz (quartz veins are abundant in the nearby schist outcrops and would have been ideal as a source of flux). The slag has a specific gravity of between 3.0 and 3.7. It occurs in the heaps both as broken slabs of tap slag and as large regions of small fragments crushed to liberate prills of copper. The slag was crushed with spherical hammers (Plate 7) of imported granite.

Copper prills of centimetre size were found also, and obsidian blades suggestive of, but not proving, Bronze Age exploitation here. The largest intact piece of furnace lining reconstructs to a diameter of about 50 cm, perhaps indicative of the typical furnace dimensions (Plate 8). Perhaps indeed these clay fragments which average three cm in thickness are not furnace lining, but rather pieces of the walls of small shaft furnaces similar to those reported by Bernus in Echard (1983) still in use in the Niger today. Possibly the reason we do not find more substantial furnace remains in Seriphos, Kythnos and Siphnos is that the furnaces were deliberately destroyed in a ritual such as that recorded by Bernus in Echard (1983) in the Niger, where the clay shaft furnaces were ritually destroyed and deliberately reduced to small fragments after the smelt was completed.

Typical slag from the Kythnos heap still contains copper prills of one to several millimetres in diameter, confirming an overall impression that we are dealing with a fairly primitive smelting process here. Bulk analyses of slags from Kythnos, given in Table 2, show that copper fluctuates between 0.5 and 12% averaging 3.7%; lime is rather high at a mean of 8%, fluctuating up to 17%; it is at too high a level to have come from the charcoal, but may well not have been added as a flux. Instead it may have come from the ore, which occurs in marble and commonly contains siderite. Lead, zinc and arsenic are substantial, averaging 0.8, 1.1 and 0.3% respectively.

Sulphur is low at an average of 0.2%, consistent with the oxidised copper ores found on the slag heap. Electron microprobe studies of a polished section of Kythnos slag No 1 (Plate 9) show however that the copper prills are often surrounded by copper sulphide; the point is reinforced by the mixture of copper metal and sulphide in Kythnos slag No 3 (Plate 10). These slags have bulk analyses of 0.36% and 0.08% sulphur respectively. It would seem dangerous to use such microscopic evidence either in slags or in copper artefacts to propose that sulphide ores were smelted; they certainly were not in the present instance. The small sulphur content of the oxidised copper ores (about 0.2% for the Kythnian ores) shows a tendency to be taken up by the copper, for which it has a high affinity; that is all that is shown by these polished sections.

Phase diagram analyses

In order to extract further information from the bulk chemical analyses of the Kythnian slags and to classify them for comparison with copper slags from other ancient smelting sites, one may attempt to represent them in one of the five ternary systems discussed by Bachmann (1980).

One of the most useful parameters that one might obtain from such a phase diagram approach is the liquidus temperature as an estimate of the minimum furnace temperature used in the production of a suite of ancient smelting slags. This was attempted by Conophagos (1980) for the lead-silver slags of the Laurion using the simplest SiO_2-FeO-CaO phase diagram; this diagram can in fact not be a very good representation for these alumina rich slags. Conophagos deduced a furnace temperature for the Laurion slags of the order of 1300°-1400°C, but this seems rather too high a temperature to have been obtained in the large Classical shaft furnaces whose remains can still be inspected at Panormos and Megala Pefka in the Laurion. In fact our unpublished melting point determinations for Laurion lead-silver slags show them to melt at very much lower temperatures.

Milton *et al.* (1976) also attempted to classify a copper slag from Timna using the SiO_2-FeO-CaO phase diagram. They deduced a liquidus temperature of *c.* 1380°C and reinforced the estimate by appealing to the high iron content of a copper prill in the slag which, in the Fe-Cu binary phase diagram, predicts a melting point of *c.* 1380°-1400°C. However the Fe-Cu binary phase diagram probably does not describe well the phase relations in impure copper produced within molten slag, and the copper prill in question also contained lead, nickel, cobalt and zinc in amounts which may well

Table 2   Copper slag heap on Kythnos

SLAG NO:	1	2	3	4	5	6	7	8	9	10	11	12	13	14	15	16	17	18
FeO	39.95	27,95	23.26	32.88	32.32	31.01	41.04	32.70	22.20	13.15	8.90	25.84	24.90	31.89	28.24	56.0	44.00	30.60
MnO	0.40	0.36	0.38	1.00	0.42	0.35	0.44	0.42	0.26	0.17	0.30	0.33	0.63	0.50	0.36	0.23	0.27	0.20
MgO	3.26	1.16	1.06	0.84	2.11	3.25	2.99	2.57	1.20	0.60	3.21	1.77	2.35	1.33	1.00	0.50	0.83	0.40
Al_2O_3	4.42	3.91	6.92	1.98	6.99	3.11	4.78	6.72	6.05	2.54	14.17	9.24	6.71	3.60	6.15	5.53	4.54	9.92
SiO_2	32.63	43.19	50.43	38.48	44.16	40.52	32.98	43.93	42.85	74.97	64.36	44.99	39.45	41.39	44.20	29.70	34.40	43.40
CaO	5.27	16.74	7.90	8.98	8.46	8.73	7.04	8.73	8.63	2.28	2.25	6.64	11.91	8.75	12.60	3.50	6.30	7.00
BaO	-	-	-	-	-	-	-	-	-	-	-	-	-	-	-	-	-	-
K_2O	0.75	0.79	1.32	0.56	1.08	0.51	0.73	1.02	1.01	0.43	2.56	1.53	1.07	0.65	1.09	0.86	0.76	1.49
Na_2O	0.49	0.02	0.62	0.32	0.75	0.56	0.50	0.57	0.35	0.24	0.81	1.11	0.48	0.35	0.48	0.36	0.40	0.98
TiO_2	0.12	0.34	0.30	0.09	0.27	0.11	0.17	0.27	0.25	0.09	0.76	0.48	0.34	0.22	0.33	0.51	0.33	0.70
P_2O_5	0.38	0.16	0.10	0.07	0.10	0.17	0.18	0.16	0.13	0.10	0.08	0.23	0.17	0.08	-	-	-	-
CuO	7.43	1.49	4.73	11.22	0.62	0.56	1.58	0.75	12.07	2.86	0.45	4.23	8.78	0.48	1.38	1.25	3.25	3.29
PbO	2.81	1.17	0.08	0.69	0.15	0.08	4.87	0.11	0.15	0.92	0.16	0.24	0.44	0.27	0.14	0.26	2.06	0.28
ZnO	0.01	1.41	0.15	0.26	0.39	0.28	0.07	0.40	0.17	0.25	0.10	0.26	0.26	8.06	1.46	0.17	0.10	0.22
As_2O_3	0.66	0.03	0.60	0.83	0.60	0.55	0.64	0.12	0.45	0.04	0.00	0.36	0.07	0.02	0.0	0.0	0.0	trace
Sb_2O_5	0.18	0.18	0.23	0.12	0.17	0.12	0.20	0.18	0.19	0.08	0.30	0.20	0.15	0.15	-	-	-	-
S	0.36	0.04	0.08	0.16	0.06	0.46	0.06	0.11	0.86	0.02	0.02	0.19	0.08	0.80	0.28	0.37	0.35	0.39
Cl	n.d.	0.05	n.d.	-	-	n.d.	-	0.07	1.17	0.08	0.06	0.47	1.02	0.07	-	-	-	-
Ni	-	-	-	n.d.	n.d.	n.d.	n.d.	n.d.	n.d.	n.d.	n.d.	n.d.	n.d.	n.d.	0.03	0.05	0.04	0.08
Co	-	-	-	n.d.	n.d.	n.d.	n.d.	n.d.	n.d.	n.d.	n.d.	n.d.	n.d.	n.d.	0.03	0.03	0.03	0.06
Ag (ppm)	-	-	-	n.d.	n.d.	n.d.	n.d.	n.d.	n.d.	n.d.	n.d.	n.d.	n.d.	n.d.	3.0	3.1	1.6	4.2
Au (ppm)	-	-	-	n.d.	n.d.	n.d.	n.d.	n.d.	n.d.	n.d.	n.d.	n.d.	n.d.	n.d.	0.0	0.0	0.0	0.0
BASN	1.283	0.964	0.573	1.010	0.849	1.131	1.454	0.879	0.662	0.196	0.238	0.669	0.893	0.901	0.838	1.590	1.232	0.726
VISC	1.353	0.998	0.602	1.102	0.883	1.201	1.397	0.908	0.688	0.218	0.230	0.686	0.896	0.966	0.869	1.744	1.350	0.763
SYSTEM	2	2	2	2	2	2	2	2	2	2	-	2	2	2	2	2	2	2

BASN = basicity number, VISC = viscosity number, SYSTEM = ternary system, all as defined by Bachmann (1980).

affect the melting point. At all events the estimated liquidus temperature
of *c.* 1400°C seems high when compared with the experimental melting points
determined experimentally for similar Timna slags by Bachmann and Rothenberg (1980), which are mostly in the range 1120°-1140°C, with only two as
high as 1200°C.

These two examples lead one to ask whether the use of the very simple
SiO_2-FeO-CaO phase diagram to represent ancient slags may be rather misleading. The more sophisticated approach of Bachmann (1980) should be a
considerable improvement, but of course any ternary diagram is something
of an approximation to a complex slag. We therefore determined directly
the free running temperatures of our analysed Kythnos slags for comparison
with the liquidus temperatures predicted by these phase diagrams.

In the simple SiO_2-FeO-CaO phase diagram (Fig 2) the Kythnos slags
plot chiefly in the Tridymite-Cristobalite region, with 65% of the predicted liquidus temperatures over 1400°C.

However, according to the Bachmann classification all these slags fall
into System 2, fayalite type tap slags, properly treated by the Anorthite-
FeO-SiO_2 diagram (thin sections indicate that a major phase is indeed
fayalite). In this diagram (Fig. 3) the Kythnos slags fall chiefly in the
anorthite-fayalite region, with very much lower predicted liquidus temperatures of less than 1100°C to about 1220°. These temperatures seem much
more reasonable for primitive furnaces but, since they are strikingly
different from those predicted by the simple SiO_2-FeO-CaO diagram, direct
determination of the free running temperatures of the Kythnos slags seemed
necessary to determine whether either phase diagram gives approximately
correct predictions.

Experimental determination of slag-free running temperatures

Free running temperatures were determined on 0.2 g aliquots of powdered slag
using a miniature graphite tube furnace; the furnace temperature was measured with an infrared pyrometer calibrated against the melting points of
silver (961.9°C), gold (1064.4°C), copper (1083°C) and nickel (1453°C).
The tube furnace used was a standard Perkin Elmer atomic absorption spectrometry graphite furnace with digitally programmable heating current and
heating times. Slag samples were placed in molybdenum boats within the
furnace and heated to preset maximum temperatures in an argon atmosphere.
The heating cycle consisted of ten seconds preheat at 200°C to expel
volatiles followed by 90 seconds at the full current necessary to achieve
a preset maximum temperature; this temperature was achieved after about 60
seconds. The cooling water to the furnace current leads ensured rapid
quenching to room temperature within fifteeen seconds at the end of the
heating cycle. This rapid heating and quenching cycle in an argon atmosphere prevents further chemical reactions in the slag melt, and no attack
of the molybdenum boats has been observed for any slags yet studied.

A given slag sample was heated to maximum temperatures successively
increasing from 950°C in 15° steps; after each heating cycle the boat was
withdrawn to examine the slag sample. A typical sequence of changes in the
slag powder samples would be: light sintering; strong sintering and con-
traction into a sintered block; slumped semi-glossy glass block; finally
either a glossy glass spheroid or glass covering the bottom of the boat.
Either of these final stages was taken to imply that at the corresponding
temperature the slag had been a free running liquid. A very few highly

siliceous slags, such as Kythnos No 10, did not become free running even at a temperature of 1400°C.

All of the analysed Kythnos slags were free running at temperatures below 1150° except for No 10 and No 11. Slag No 11 (free running at 1250°C) is highly silica- and alumina-rich and probably represents slagged furnace lining; slag No 10 (still viscous at 1450°C) is very silica-rich and iron-poor, highly atypical of the Kythnos slags and was probably never fully molten in the furnace.

Fig. 4 gives a comparison of liquidus temperatures predicted from the phase diagrams with the empirically determined free-running temperatures. Predicted liquidus temperatures might, if anything, be expected to be lower than empirical free-running temperatures. Fig. 4 shows that the reverse is true. The simplest SiO_2-FeO-CaO diagram clearly predicts liquidus temperatures which are much too high, often by many hundreds of degrees.

The Anorthite-FeO-SiO_2 diagram is clearly very much better, but still often predicts temperatures which are one or two hundred degrees too high. It seems that at present the best way to find the slag free-running temperature, and thus an estimate of furnace slag bath temperature, is to measure it directly.

For the Kythnos slags the free-running temperatures lie roughly between 1050°C and 1150°C, which is similar to the slags from Timna discussed by Bachmann and Rothenberg (1980). It seems unnecessary to postulate furnace temperatues at Kythnos above 1200°C to 1250°C; in this respect one would have been led very much astray by using predictions from the SiO_2-FeO-CaO diagram.

Analyses of copper prills

Some preliminary electron microprobe analyses have been made of copper prills within the slags from Kythnos; a few analyses of different prills within two slags are given in Table 3. They show the usual content of iron for primitively smelted copper (Craddock 1980) and a rather variable lead content. The antimony content is at a level much the same as in the bulk slag, whilst the sulphur content is low.

The most interesting results are those for nickel and arsenic. Branigan (1968) singled out a class of Minoan bronze artefacts for their high nickel content (about 1-2%) and suggested that this implied use of Cretan copper sources, believing nickel not to be present in copper ores accessible to other east Mediterranean or Aegean cultures. Though nickel is less likely to be associated with copper than with iron (present either in the copper ore or introduced as a flux), the high nickel content of copper prills in Kythnos slag 3 give evidence of at least one non-Cretan Aegean source of copper containing high nickel.

The copper prills in slag No 3 also contain 3.9-4.5% of arsenic. The slags from the Kythnos slag heap are quite unequivocally copper smelting slags. The analyses of the copper prills in slag No 3 therefore clearly show that copper smelted directly from its ores can contain accidentally up to at least 4.5% of arsenic (and at least 1% of nickel). There is no question here of deliberate addition of arsenic in any form; indeed Table 4 shows that arsenic occurs at levels of up to 2% in the copper-iron ores found at Milyes, Zogaki and in the slag-heap itself. More analyses are

Table 3 Microprobe analysis of copper prills in Kythnos slags

Prill No:	1A	1B	1C	3A	3B	3C
FeO	0.64	0.47	0.55	2.65	1.88	1.51
MnO	0.01	0.07	0.01	0.02	0.00	0.01
Al_2O_3	0.82	1.41	1.40	0.29	0.33	0.29
Cu	96.26	97.37	95.25	92.42	92.44	92.11
Pb	1.08	0.14	0.04	0.01	0.01	0.01
As	0.11	0.17	0.17	3.88	4.28	4.50
Sb	0.28	0.19	0.17	0.19	0.27	0.59
Ni	0.02	0.03	0.03	1.06	0.98	1.08
S	0.10	0.06	0.01	0.01	0.01	0.01

needed, but it seems quite likely that arsenical copper-alloys found as artefacts in Aegean Bronze Age cultures were often the accidental result of smelting, though their properties no doubt resulted in their being selected as an especially good sort of copper for casting and cold working to produce a tougher metal. It is interesting to note that Branigan (1968) comments specifically that the Minoan objects containing 1-2% of nickel contain higher than usual amounts of arsenic, in the range 1.5-4.1% arsenic, although there is no correlation between nickel and arsenic in the copper of the Early Cycladic artefacts forming the Kythnos hoard (Craddock 1976).

Lead isotope analyses

Finally, Fig. 5 shows that lead isotope analyses of slags from the Kythnos copper slag heap define in general a rather tight linear array which accommodates also the isotopic analyses of ores from Zogaki, but not those from Milyes. However two Kythnos slags lie away from this line (numbers 1 and 6), unless the Kythnos slags really occupy the whole of this region in the lead isotope diagram. If this is so, then the four Early Cycladic bronzes from Amorgos also shown on Fig. 5 could then have their copper source ascribed to Kythnos. At present we believe that it is premature to make this claim.

Conclusions

Field and laboratory studies have established that oxidised copper ores exist on Kythnos island and that both oxidised and sulphide copper ores occur on Seriphos island in the Cyclades. Two ancient slag heaps on Seriphos (Avyssalos and Kefala) and one on Kythnos have been surveyed; in each case fragments of ore found in the slag heaps prove that oxidised copper ores were smelted. Each of these slag heaps is situated high above sea level and well away from the nearest copper ore source; their location

Table 4 Copper ores from Kythnos

Ore No:	MIL 1	MIL 2	ZOG 1	ZOG 2	ZOG 3	KYTO 1	KYTO 2	KYTO 3
FeO	26.00	32.50	33.89	1.20	13.8	7.67	13.45	13.90
Fe_3O_4	63.50	57.10	-	7.60	61.8	23.10	27.70	38.65
MnO	0.52	0.82	2.98	60.28	3.43	0.47	0.12	1.52
Al_2O_3	0.25	0.53	1.69	0.93	1.18	4.48	6.71	0.70
SiO_2	1.47	2.65	6.37	2.63	10.86	39.82	41.63	7.82
CaO	0.43	0.47	21.82	2.20	5.18	17.00	2.42	33.51
MgO	0.07	0.09	0.39	0.42	0.54	1.01	0.96	0.51
TiO_2	0.02	0.02	0.02	0.08	0.03	0.20	0.31	0.02
P_2O_5	0.03	0.03	0.08	0.05	0.03	0.20	0.10	0.07
CuO	3.68	2.83	0.54	1.48	0.57	0.31	4.44	0.56
PbO	1.10	0.52	0.45	0.40	0.24	0.64	0.05	0.41
ZnO	0.09	0.24	0.12	0.62	0.14	4.10	0.03	0.26
As_2O_5	2.18	1.53	0.31	0.80	0.96	0.03	0.22	0.44
Sb_2O_3	0.05	0.07	0.12	0.05	0.10	0.14	0.11	0.17
Ni	0.01	0.01	0.03	0.12	0.01	0.00	0.01	0.07
S	0.08	0.13	0.07	0.21	0.11	0.06	0.21	0.05

MIL = MILYES; ZOG = ZOGAKI; KYTO = KYTHNOS SLAG HEAP

seems to have been chosen to secure maximum exposure to the north winds. Positive evidence (perhaps from carbon-14 dating of the slag) of the antiquity of these slag heaps remains to be found, but for the Kythnos slag heap such evidence as the discovery of obsidian tools, of primitive granite hammers, of the fine crushing of the slag to extract copper prills and the nature of the associated pottery suggest a date in the Bronze Age. Lead isotope analyses suggest, but do not yet absolutely prove, that some Early Cycladic bronze artefacts from Amorgos may be made of copper from Kythnos.

Bulk chemical analyses of the slags show that, with rare exceptions, they can be classified in Bachmann's System 2; this is consistent with petrographic examination which shows that the dominant phases are fayalite and wüstite. Optical microscope examination together with electron micro-probe analysis of polished sections shows that the copper prills are often surrounded by copper sulphide rims and that mixed aggregations of metallic copper and copper sulphide are not uncommon, even though the ores smelted (proved by scattered ore in the slag heap) were definitely oxidised copper ores of low sulphur content. It is therefore not possible to use such microscopic evidence to deduce that sulphide ores were smelted. Microprobe analyses of copper prills in the Kythnos slags show nickel contents up to 1% and arsenic contents up to 4.5% though many prills contain less than 0.1% of both metals. These high amounts of nickel and arsenic result accidentally from the smelting of oxidised copper ores and iron oxide fluxes, both of which contain variable amounts of arsenic of the order of a few per cent; arsenic was not deliberately added in any form. Accidentally smelted arsenical copper was no doubt quickly recognised as a superior form of copper, having better casting properties and greater cold worked strength.

Determinations of the empirical free-running temperatures of the Kythnos slags show that liquidus temperatures predicted by the SiO_2-FeO-CaO ternary diagram are much too high, often by many hundreds of degrees centigrade. Predictions made by the more appropriate Anorthite-FeO-SiO diagram are much better, but may still be one or two hundred degrees too high. In order to base reliable estimates of furnace temperatures on stuides of ancient slag it seems necessary to make direct measurements of the free-running tempertures, on the slags themselves, although this is a minimum estimate and it is possible that the reaction temperature necessary to produce the slag minerals from the ore/gangue/flux mixture may be higher than the free-running temperature of the slag, once produced.

Acknowledgements

We are grateful to the Institute for Geology and Mineral Exploration, Athens, for encouraging this work. The work was supported by the Science and Engineering Research Council and by NATO, Grant No 574/83.

References

Bachmann, H G 1980. Early copper smelting techniques in Sinai and in the Negev as deduced from slag investigations. In *Scientific studies in early mining and extractive metallurgy*, ed. P T Craddock, 103-134. London

Bachmann, H G & Rothenberg, B 1980. Die Verhuttingsverfahren von Site 30. In *Antikes Kupfer im Timna-Tal, Der Anschnitt, Beiheft 1*, ed. H G Conrad & B Rothenberg, 215-236. Bochum

Branigan, K 1968. Copper and bronze working in early Bronze Age Crete. *Studies in Mediterranean Archaeology*, **XIX**. Lund

Conophagos, C E 1980. *Le Laurium Antique*, 274-302. Athens, Ekdotike Hellados

Craddock, P T 1976. Copper alloys in the classical world, Part 1. *Journal of Archaeological Science*, 3, 93-113

Craddock, P T 1980. The Composition of copper produced at the ancient smelting camps in the Wadi Timna, Israel. In *Scientific studies in early mining and extractive metallurgy*, ed. P T Craddock, 165-173. London

Davies, O 1935. *Roman mines in Europe*, 257-264. Oxford, Clarendon Press

Echard, N (ed.) 1983. *Metallurgies Africaines*. Paris, Mémoire de la Société de Africainistes

Fiedler, K G 1841. *Reise durch alle Theile des Königreiches Griechenland*, ii. Leipzig

Galanos, P 1962. *Seriphos, Part 1*. Athens, privately published

Gale, N H 1978. Lead isotopes and Aegean metallurgy. In *Thera and the Aegean World*, ed. C Doumas, 529-545. London, Aris and Phillips

Gale, N H & Stos-Gale, Z A 1981. Cycladic lead and silver metallurgy. *Annual British School at Athens,* **76**, 169-224

Gale, N H & Stos-Gale, Z A 1982. Bronze Age copper sources in the Mediterranean: a new approach. *Science,* **216**, 11-19

Gale, N H & Stos-Gale, Z A 1985. Cyprus and the Bronze Age metals trade. *Acts of the 2nd Int. Congress of Cypriot Studies, Nicosia 1982.* (In Press)

Honea, K 1975. Early metallurgy on Kythnos Island, Greece. *Acts of the 1st Symposium on Mining History in S.E. Europe.* Varna, Bulgaria (After our visit to Kythnos we received more information from Honea about prehistoric settlement on the island).

Milton, C, Diwornick, E J, Finkelman, R B & Toulmin, P 1976. Slag from an ancient copper smelter at Timna, Israel. *Journal of the Historical Metallurgy Society,* **10**, 24-33

Papastamataki, A 1975. *Investigation of slags of ancient Greek metallurgy for gold and other metals.* Athens, IGME

Stos-Gale, Z A & Gale, N H 1982a. The Sources of Mycenaean silver and lead. *Journal of Field Archaeology.* **9**, 467-485

Stos-Gale, Z A & Gale, N G 1982b. The Minoan Thalassocracy and the Aegean metal trade. Acts of the 3rd Int. Symp. at the Swedish Institute in Athens, *Skrifter utgivna av Svenska Institutet i Athen*, **XXXII**, 59-64

94

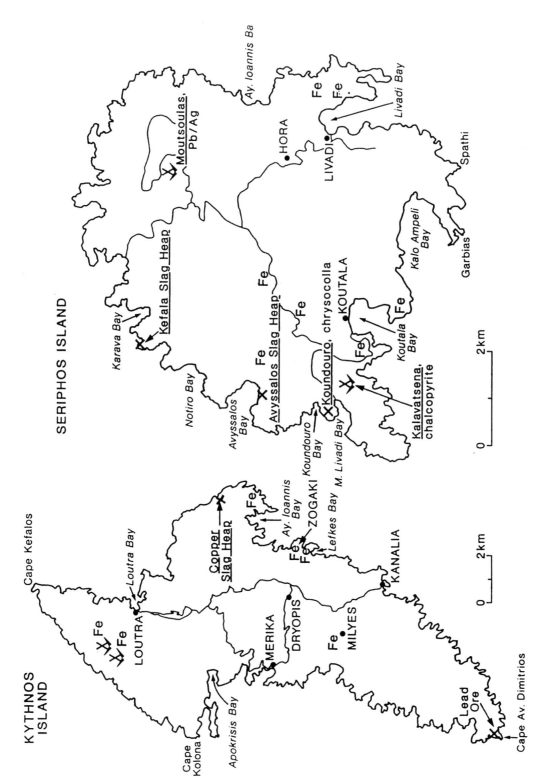

Fig. 1   Sketch map of the Cycladic islands of Kythnos and Seriphos, showing the location of ancient copper slag heaps and of the chief ore deposits

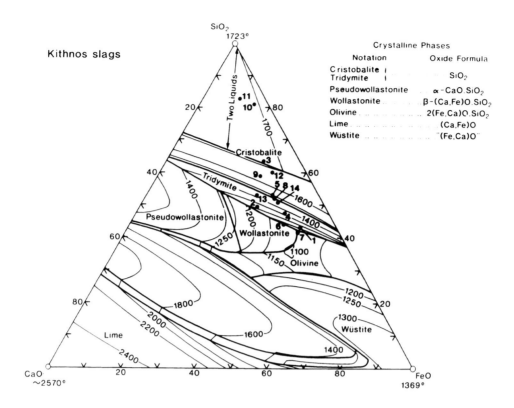

Fig. 2   The plot of Kythnos slags in the simplified SiO₂-FeO-CaO phase
diagram shows that they cluster in the tridymite/cristobalite
fields, and that this diagram predicts high liquidus temperatures

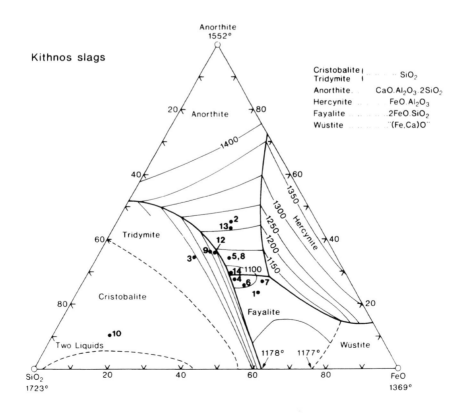

Fig. 3   The plot of Kythnos slags in the more appropriate Anorthite-FeO-
SiO₂ phase diagram shows a clustering in the anorthite/fayalite
fields, with much lower predicted liquidus temperatures

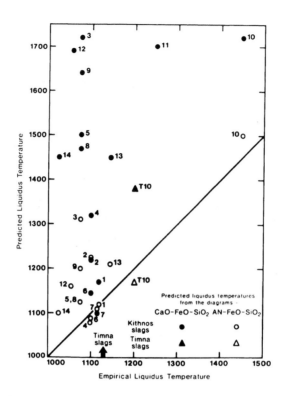

Fig. 4   Plot of empirical free-running temperatures for the Kythnos slags
and one Timna slag against liquidus temperatures predicted by the
SiO_2-FeO-CaO and Anorthite-FeO-SiO phase diagrams. The average
empirical melting point found for Timna copper slags (== 1130°C)
is indicated by a heavy arrow and is quite similar to those found
empirically for the Kythnos slags

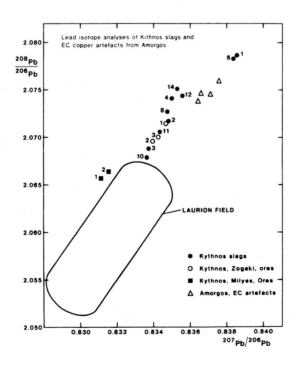

Fig. 5   Lead isotope ratios for Kythnos copper slags and ores compared with
those for Early Cycladic bronze artefacts from Amorgos

Plate 1   Partial view of the Avyssalos copper slag heap on Seriphos
island above Avyssalos Bay

Plate 2   Section of the Avyssalos copper slag heap on Seriphos; the
heap is about 2 m thick at this point

Plate 3   General view of the Kefala copper slag heap on Seriphos island

Plate 4   Kefala slag heap, showing a region where the slag has been
           broken into centimetre-sized fragments to extract the copper
           prills

Plate 5   The Zogaki mining region, Kythnos island. Remains of the ancient
           galleries are to be seen in this plate, which is of a region
           largely blasted out in the Italian exploitation during 1940/41 AD

Plate 6   General view of that part of the Kythnos copper slag heap which
           lies on the steep plunge of the cliff down to the sea

Plate 7   A typical granite hammer found *in situ* in the Kythnos copper slag
heap, having two diametrically opposed hollows to aid in holding
it in the hand when using it to crush slag

Plate 8   Above the lens cap is the largest intact piece of furnace wall
found in the Kythnos slag heap; it reconstructs to a furnace
diameter of about 50 cm

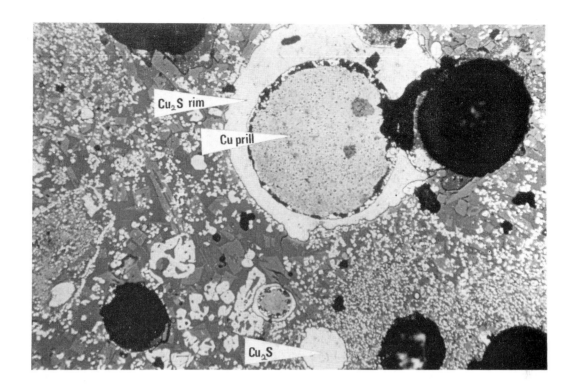

Plate 9   Kythnos slag No 1. Polished section (x125) showing a copper prill
          of about 0.3 mm diameter surrounded by a light-grey rim of copper
          sulphide

Plate 10   Kythnos slag No 3. Polished section (x60) showing darker grey
           copper sulphide (Cu_2S) globules interspersed with copper metal
           (lightest grey). The copper smelting process represented by the
           Kythnos slag heap is uniformly of the smelting of oxidised copper
           ores (carbonates) containing less than 0.5% of sulphur, as is
           proved by ore fragments in the slag heap. The presence of copper
           sulphide in polished sections of slags or copper metal is *not*
           proof that sulphidic copper ores were smelted

SMELTING, REFINING AND ALLOYING OF COPPER AND COPPER ALLOYS IN CRUCIBLE FURNACES DURING PREHISTORIC UP TO ROMAN TIMES

U Zwicker, H Greiner, K-H Hofmann and M Reithinger

Lehrstuhl Werkstoffwissenschaft (Metalle), Universität Erlangen-Nürnberg, Martensstraße 5, 8520 Erlangen, BRD

Abstract

A series of laboratory tests has shown that copper sulphide ores could be smelted in small crucibles of Neolithic type holding about 1 kg of copper using a number of tuyeres for a forced air supply. Late Bronze Age crucibles of much larger size have also been replicated and successful smelting carried out in them. The smelting of mixed ores has also been investigated: copper-antimony, iron-arsenic and cassiterite and copper ores. A study was also made of the formation of brass from zinc ores with either copper ores or copper metal.

Keywords: EXPERIMENTAL ARCHAEOLOGY, SLAG, MICROPROBE
             ANALYSIS, CRUCIBLE, METAL, COPPER, SMELTING
             BRASS, TIN, BRONZE, ARSENIC, BLOW-PIPE,
             CRUCIBLE SMELTING, ALLOYING

Copper ore roasting and smelting

There are only a few metallurgical investigations on dated material, mainly slag and reaction products adherent on crucibles of the Neolithic, the Chalcolithic and of the Early Bronze Age period. From the early site Catal Huyuk in Anatolia (7000-6000 BC), which has shown slaggy material, the absence of iron silicates suggests that it is neither a crucible melting slag nor a smelting slag (Tylecote 1976). Molten copper oxide was observed so that it was proved that the material was heated to more than 1100°C (Neuninger *et al.* 1964). A crucible containing a blowing pipe tip was excavated in Pedra don Ouro, Portugal, dated from Los Millares Culture and shown in Fig. 1 (Leisner & Schubart 1966). Other crucibles from Portugal from that time are similar, 10 cm wide and up to 3 cm deep with a wall thickness of 1-2 cm. The capacity of such a crucible is therefore about 0.2 l, corresponding to 1 kg of liquid copper. One can suggest that these crucibles were heated from the outside and from the inside by charcoal and blowing pipes. Wall paintings in tombs of Egypt of the third millenium BC show that heat was produced by blowpipes in a heap of charcoal in which such small crucibles could be heated. Fig. 2 shows a relief (Capart 1907) in the tomb of Anck-Ma-Hor in Sakkara which was produced during the Fifth Dynasty about 2450-2350 BC. At least three metalworkers are using a blowpipe and one is working in the crucible. The fourth may whirl ore powder which has to be roasted and may smell the concentration of sulphur dioxide gas to find out whether all ore has been roasted. Sulphide type of ores may have been roasted and smelted in such crucibles as could be proved by using three or six blowpipes and a small charcoal heap of 50 cm diameter (Fig. 3). In a crucible of the type mentioned concentrated copper sulphide ore from Bougainville, New Zealand, with the following composition: 29% copper, 27% iron, 31% sulphur, 5% silica, 0.15% zinc, 0.02% arsenic, traces of silver, titanium, molybdenum, manganese, tin, magnesium, calcium and aluminium was roasted at 800°C and smelted to metallic copper at 1100°C. The recovery of metallic copper was more than 50%. If malachite ore was used the recovery was more than 90% and no slag was produced.

Such a reduction of malachite, cuprite or sulphate ore could have been done on a bigger scale in a crucible shown in a larger heap of charcoal in Fig. 4. This wall painting comes from tomb 386 of Thebes and belongs to the Eleventh Dynasty (c. 2000 BC). At least four blowpipes are shown being used to heat the charcoal in which the crucible may have reached a temperature of more than 1100°C so that copper could be smelted and melted. This method was still used in the middle of the second millenium BC in Egypt as can be seen from Fig.5 from a wall relief in the tomb of the vizier Puymrê at Thebes (c. 1500 BC). A metalworker is blowing air from the top into a small furnace or crucible. In another relief (Fig. 6) of that tomb the heating of a crucible in a larger furnace by two tuyeres with two sets of bellows is shown. A casting is produced by tilting a crucible, which is larger than those of the neolithic and chalcolithic periods. The bellows are brought to Egypt by the Hyksos people from the East in the first quarter of the second millenium BC (Zwicker 1969). In the area of the Middle Bronze Age excavation at Kalavasos Ayos Dimetrios, Cyprus, another blowpipe was detected (South 1980). The inner diameter is about 1 cm. It was closed up by a small piece of slag so that it could not be used and was placed on top of a square slag deposit (50 x 50 cm); it is shown in Fig. 7. Therefore one can assume that after the introduction of bellows, blowpipes were still used for special purposes such as heating for welding and soldering. Such a process (Fig. 8) is shown in the tomb of the vizier Rekhmirê of the Eighteenth Dynasty in the reign of the pharaoh Tutmosis III 1500 BC (Davies 1950).

During the excavation of Norsun Tepe in Anatolia in the Early Bronze Age strata (Hauptmann 1979) and in the strata of Late Bronze Age of the excavation of Enkomi (Dikaios 1969) and Kition (Karageorghis 1976) on Cyprus larger crucibles were found which have a hole in the sidewall. The inner diameter of these crucibles is increased to about 25 cm, the wall thickness to about 2.5 cm and the height to about 30 cm or less; the hole is either about in the centre of the crucible wall as shown in Fig. 9 of a crucible from Late Bronze Age Enkomi (Dikaios 1969), or on the bottom as shown in a crucible of the Archaic Period from Kition. The crucible with the hole near the bottom (Fig. 10) was used for the production of tin bronze (Zwicker, forthcoming).

The slag adherent on the hole of the crucible from Enkomi and on the bottom was investigated in detail. Fig. 11 shows the microstructure of a copper prill (P1) with inclusions of copper-sulphide from the slag (P2 and P3) of the bottom of this crucible. Fig. 12 shows another area of this slag (P1-P3) which also shows inclusions which by microprobe analysis (Table) were found to be copper-iron-sulphide in P4. The micrograph of the slag adherent on the hole of the crucible (Fig. 13) shows magnetite (P1) and iron silicates (P2 and P3).

Table: Microprobe analysis Figs. 11-29 (Imp/min x 10³)

	Mica					LiF										Mica
	Al Kα₁₁	Si Kα₁₁	S Kα₁₁	K Kα₁₃	Ca Kα₁₃	Mn Kα₁₁	Fe Kα₁₁	Co Kα₁₁	Ni Kα₁₁	Cu Kα₁₁	Zn Kα₁₁	As Kα₁₁	Pb Lα₁₁	Cr Kα₁₁	V Kα₁₁	Sn Lα₁₃
Fig.11																
P 1	–	–	–	–	–	–	0.24	–	–	80	–	–	–	–	–	–
P 2	1.72	12	–	–	–	–	15.5	2.1	–	0.75	–	–	–	–	–	–
P 3	–	–	–	–	0.60	–	52	2.0	–	0.29	–	–	–	–	–	–
Fig. 12a+b																
P 1	–	–	–	–	–	–	31.5	–	–	–	–	–	–	–	–	–
P 2	1.64	11.8	–	0.70	0.34	0.12	10.1	–	–	–	0.36	–	–	57.5	0.14?	–
P 3	–	–	–	–	–	–	10.7	14	0.36	–	–	–	–	–	–	–
P 4	–	–	4.9	–	–	–	0.53	0.61	–	71	–	–	–	–	–	–
Fig. 13																
P 1	–	–	–	–	–	–	73	–	–	0.66	–	–	–	–	–	–
P 2	0.60	8.8	–	0.46	1.74	–	44	–	–	0.20	–	–	–	–	–	–
P 3	–	8.6	–	0.38	0.64	–	44	–	–	1.8	–	–	–	–	–	–
Fig. 17																
P 1	–	–	–	–	–	–	–	–	–	105	–	–	–	–	–	–
P 2	–	–	1.87	–	–	–	–	–	–	62.5	–	–	–	–	–	–
Fig. 21a+b																
P 1	–	–	17.7	–	–	–	0.54	–	–	96	–	–	–	–	–	–
P 2	–	–	–	–	–	–	–	–	–	103	–	0.79	?	–	–	–
P 3	–	–	–	–	–	–	–	–	–	85	–	–	–	–	–	–
P 4	–	–	–	–	–	–	–	–	–	55	–	0.10	?	–	–	–
P 5	–	–	–	–	–	–	–	–	–	82	–	–	–	–	–	17.3
P 6	–	–	–	–	–	–	0.32	–	–	–	–	–	–	–	–	17.5
P 7	–	–	–	–	–	–	0.50	–	–	–	–	–	–	–	–	0.26
P 8	1.44	14.5	–	–	2.7	0.14?	4.6	–	–	0.21	–	–	2.7	–	–	–
Fig. 26																
P 1	–	–	–	–	–	–	–	–	–	103	9.4	–	–	–	–	–
P 2	–	–	–	–	–	–	–	–	–	90	2.8	–	–	–	–	–
Fig. 27																
P 1	–	–	15	–	–	–	3.3	–	–	82	0.56	–	13.5	–	–	–
P 2	–	–	–	–	–	–	–	–	–	–	1.1	–	–	–	–	–
Fig. 29																
P 1	–	–	–	–	–	–	–	–	–	59	3.9	0.23	–	–	–	2.48
P 2	–	–	10	–	–	–	–	–	–	26	14.4	–	4.3	–	–	–
P 3	–	–	–	–	–	–	–	–	–	55	5.6	0.41	–	–	–	1.67
P 4	–	2.71	–	–	0.47	–	0.17	–	–	19.8	0.75	1.25	–	0.88	–	4.8

Using such a crucible in a laboratory test (Fig. 14) for roasting and smelting concentrated ore from Bougainville the same metallographic structure was observed in the slag if the concentrated ore was roasted at 800°C by heating the crucible within a charcoal fire and blowing air into the crucible through a hole in the wall. The progress of the roasting process can be investigated by smelling the sulphur dioxide content of the air over the crucible or by dissolving the roasted concentrate in water and evaporating the water. If blue copper sulphate is formed the roasting process is complete. After reducing this roasted concentrate with charcoal, which was put into the crucible and heated up to 1100°C, a recovery in excess of 75% copper was achieved if the concentrate of the ore was mixed in pellets with c. 15% of dried cow dung. The crucible (Fig. 14) is shown during the reduction process. The microstructure of this reduction product (Fig. 15) and that of the reduction of copper sulphate ore (Fig. 16) is very similar to that (Fig. 17) of a copper oxhide ingot (Fig. 18) in the Archaeological Museum in Nikosia, probably from the same site and area as the big crucible with the hole in the sidewall from Enkomi. The blister copper of all these samples contains a great amount of sulphides. Therefore, one can assume that in these crucibles with the hole in the wall sulphide ore may have been roasted and afterwards reduced to metallic copper. This could have been done also in Kition where fragments of such crucibles were excavated and where the detailed arrangement of the furnaces was reconstructed. Fig. 19a shows the area of the Bronze Age workshop and Fig. 19b a reconstruction of the metallurgical installation.

Arsenic-bronze production

For producing arsenic bronze there was enough arsenic in the copper-arsenic-antimony-ore of Anatolia. From the ore which was excavated in the Chalcolithic strata of Norsun Tepe a copper arsenic-antimony-alloy could easily be produced by reducing that ore with charcoal in a crucible together with or without liquid copper (Zwicker 1977).

In Cyprus no such copper-arsenic ore was found up till now, but an ore with a high content of arsenic in the form of nickel-iron arsenides is present in the area of Limassol. Such an ore cannot be reduced in a direct reduction by charcoal. But by the addition of 25% calcium oxide it was possible to introduce more than 1% of arsenic into liquid copper, if there was a reducing atmosphere from the presence of charcoal at 1250°C. The hardness and the increase of hardness of such an alloy by cold deformation is the same (Fig. 20) as that of a cast flat axe of arsenic bronze from Cyprus, the microstructure of which has already been investigated (Zwicker et al. 1979).

This figure shows also that the increase in hardness of an axe of tin bronze found in Ugarit, Syria, is much higher than that of the arsenic bronze and therefore the mechanical properties of the tin bronze are superior to that of arsenic bronze (Schaeffer-Forrer et al. 1982).

Tin-bronze production

During the excavation of Kition, crucibles and fragments of crucibles were detected which were in contact with slag containing white spots. The microprobe analysis (P1-P8) of rhomboid inclusions in the slag (Figs. 21a and 21b)

revealed a high tin content. The concentrations of the tin content are as
high as those of cassiterite. The microstructure of the slag of a laboratory reaction of cassiterite with charcoal and copper is the same as that
of the crucible. Therefore one can assume that at Kition during the
Archaic Period cassiterite was used for the production of tin bronze.

Brass production

In an investigation of slag in crucibles (Fig. 22) found in the
Roman town of Nida near Frankfurt, copper, tin, lead and zinc were
detected (Bachmann 1976). The unusual shape of these crucibles suggests
that zinc was introduced via a zinc ore, which can be in the Taunus
mountain nearby. Similar crucibles were excavated in the Roman town of
Ladenburg/Neckar where also in the surroundings a zinc-lead-sulphide
ore was exploited during Roman times (Heukemes 1977). The lid diminished
the evaporation of zinc. Therefore we have investigated at first the reaction of zinc oxide with 0.2 mm copper sheet at 1000°C in open and closed
crucibles. The influence of the reaction time on the zinc content of the
product after reaction at 1000°C are shown in (Fig. 23). The brass produced at that temperature became liquid. After 60 minutes 45.6% zinc was
dissolved in the copper and during cooling some of the zinc was evaporated
as can be seen from Fig. 24. Near the surface an area with (α + β)-grains
with lower zinc content than the interior β-grains was detected. If the
reaction time at 1000°C was increased to more than 60 minutes, the zinc
content in the metallic product decreased, because after the formation of
brass the zinc vapour pressure in the crucible decreased below that of the
copper-zinc alloy and zinc evaporated from the surface of the brass. It
was also possible to produce brass with more than 20% zinc from 3.3 grams
malachite ore and 5 grams zinc carbonate ore from Laurion with only a small
content of lead in a crucible under charcoal at 1000°C after fifteen minutes.
The shape of the metallic piece was still the same as that of the original
malachite piece (Fig. 25). The microstructure of the metal produced by
this method is shown in Fig. 26. In (P1) β brass with eutectoid grain
boundaries (P2) is observed. The intensity of the counts per minute in P2
were lower for copper and zinc than in P1, but no other element could be
detected (Table). Therefore one can assume that the eutectoid or eutectic
structure on the grain boundaries consists of zinc-copper oxides. If 5 grams
of a zinc-lead-sulphide ore from Laurion was smelted together with 5 grams of
copper for fifteen minutes at 1150°C under charcoal in the crucible, α-brass
with a content of about 20% zinc and many inclusions of lead and sulphides
(Fig. 27) was produced. The area of P1 contains copper-iron-zinc sulphides,
P2 lead-zinc oxides, and the matrix about 20% zinc.

In a ring from a Bronze Age stratum at Ugarit (Ras Shamra, Syria)
about 8% zinc and about 5% tin were present. Microprobe analysis showed
zinc-lead sulphides in the microstructure (Schaeffer-Forrer et al. 1982).
Therefore we tried to find out the reaction between 60% malachite, 16.6%
bornite ore, 13.4% zinc-lead sulphide ore from Laurion and 10% cassiterite
(SnO_2) heated up to 1150°C in thirty minutes. The copper alloy which was
produced did contain 8% zinc, about 5% tin and many sulphides (Fig. 28)
of the same type as those of the Bronze Age ring from Ugarit (Ras Shamra,
Syria; see Fig. 29), with copper-lead-zinc sulphide (P2), oxides (P1 and
P3) and silicates (P4).

108

Discussion

It was shown by laboratory tests that copper could be smelted in small
crucibles of the type which were excavated in Neolithic strata and also
from sulphide ore by proper roasting at about 800°C and then smelting at
about 1100°C, using three or six blowing pipes in a charcoal heap of about
50 cm diameter. The capacity of these Neolithic crucibles was about 1 kg
of liquid copper. In Late Bronze Age crucibles with a hole in the side wall
and with a capacity of about 4.5 litres corresponding to about 40 kg of
copper, this roasting and smelting process could also have been performed
as was shown in laboratory tests with such crucibles in crucible furnaces.

Arsenic type bronze could have been produced by using copper-arsenic-
antimony ore found in an Early Bronze Age stratum of the excavation of
Nurson Tepe in Anatolia, by direct reaction with liquid copper. If iron-
arsenic ore, for example, from Cyprus had to be used it was necessary to
add about 25% calcium oxide to introduce more than 1% of arsenic into
liquid copper from that ore. As tin-bronze slag did contain the same
constituents as slag from a laboratory product using cassiterite and liquid
copper, one can assume that at Bronze Age Kition cassiterite ore was used
for the production of tin-bronze in crucibles. Also brass or copper alloys
containing more than 5% zinc could be produced by a reaction of solid copper-
sheet with zinc oxide in an almost closed crucible at 1000°C. By a simul-
taneous reduction of malachite and zinc-carbonate ore from Laurion, brass
with more than 20% zinc can be produced in such crucibles, which were
obviously used in the Roman settlements of Nida and Ladenburg in the Main
and Rhein valley near zinc-containing ore deposits. Using 60% malachite,
16.6% bornite, 13.5% zinc-lead ore from Laurion and 10% cassiterite, a
copper alloy containing about 8% zinc and about 5% tin was produced, which
was of a similar composition and contained similar sulphides as a Bronze
Age ring from Ugarit (Ras Shamra, Syria). Many metallurgical reactions for
the production of blister copper and of copper alloys may have been performed in crucible furnaces from prehistoric to Roman time.

Acknowledgements

Some part of this work was supported by Stiftung Volkswagenwerk, Wolfsburg.
Samples of this investigation were given by Dr Ing K Emicke, Norddeutsche
Affinerie AG, Hamberg, Prof Dr H Hauptmann, University of Heidelberg,
Dr V Karageorghis, Department of Antiquities, Nicosia/Cyprus, H Kaiser,
MA, Karlsruhe, and Prof Dr C F A Schaeffer-Forrer, St Germain-en-Laye/
France. This is gratefully acknowledged. The authors also wish to
thank Dr D Arnold, Vienna, and Prof Dr J Settgast, Berlin, for permis-
sion to photograph in Tomb 386 at Thebes.

References

Bachmann, H G 1976. Crucibles from a Roman settlement in Germany. *Journal
of the Historical Metallurgy Society*, 10, 34-35

Capart, J 1907. *Une Rue de Tombeaux a Sakkara*. Brussel, Uromant et co.

Davies de Garis, N 1950. Paintings from the Tomb of Rechmirê at Thebes,
Egyptian Exploration Society X. New York, Metropolitan Museum of Art

Dikaios, P 1969. *Enkomi, excavations 1984-1958*, 1-438. Mainz, Verlag Philipp von Zabern

Hauptmann, H 1979. Die Entwicklung der frühbronzezeitlichen Siedlung auf dem Norsuntepe in Ostanatolien. *Archäologisches Korrespondenzblatt*, Sonderdruck H. 1, 9-20, pls. 3-12

Heukemes, B 1977. Neue Entdeckungen zum römerzeitlichen und hochmittelalterlichen Silbererzbergbau bei Wiesloch und Nussloch (Rhein-Neckar-Kreis), Disk.-Tagung, Arbeitskreis Archäometrie, 24.-26.2.1977, Heidelberg, 64-65

Karageorghis, V 1976. *Kition, Mycenaean and Phoenician discoveries in Cyprus*. London, Thames and Hudson

Leisner, V & Schubart, H 1966. Die kupferzeitliche Befestigung von Pedra don Ouro, Portugal *Madrider Mitteilungen*, **7**, 9-60

Neuninger, H, Pittioni, R & Siegl, W 1964. Frühkeramikzeitliche Kupfergewinnung in Anatolien. *Archäologia Austriaca*, **35**, 98-110

Schaeffer-Forrer, C F A, Zwicker, U & Nigge, K 1982. Untersuchungen an metallischen Werkstoffen und Schlacken aus dem Bereich von Ugarit (Ras Shamra) Syrien. *Microchimica Acta*, 35-61

South, A K 1980. Kalavasos-Ayios Dhimitrios 1979: A summary report. *Report of the Department of Antiquities Cyprus*, 22-53, pls. vi-ix

Sperl, G 1980. Metallographic examination of Bronze Age copper. *Metals Technology*, **7**, 212-217

Tylecote, R F 1976. *A History of metallurgy*. London, The Metals Society

Zwicker, U 1969. Entwicklung der Schmelz- und Gieß-technik auf den bildlichen Darstellungen in Aegypten zwischen 2500 u. 1500 v. Chr. *Zeitschrift Metall*, **23**, 1-4

Zwicker, U 1977. Investigations on the extractive metallurgy of Cu/Sb/As ore and excavated smelting products from Norsuntepe (Kebau) on the upper Euphrates (3500-2800 BC). In *Aspects of Early Metallurgy*, ed. W A Oddy, Occasional Paper No. 17, 13-26. London, British Museum

Zwicker, U (forthcoming). Excavations at Kition metallurgical workshops. *Kition* **V**, 1984

Zwicker, U, Nigge, K & Urbon, B 1979. Verteilung metallischer Elemente in Patinaschichten. *Microchimica Acta, Suppl.* **8**, 393-419

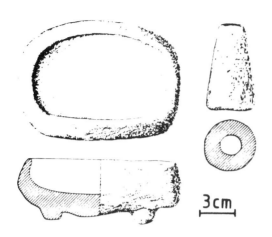

Fig. 1   Neolithic crucible and
          blowing tube from Pedra
          don Ouro, Portugal

Fig. 2   Smelting or melting procedure
          on relief of tomb of Anck-Ma-
          Hur, Sakkara Egypt, 2450-2350 BC

Fig. 3   Smelting of copper sulphide
          ore in a small crucible with
          blowpipes and charcoal

Fig. 4   Wallpainting in tomb 386 of
          Thebes with crucible in
          furnace (~2000 BC)

Fig. 5   Fig. 6

Figs. 5 and 6   Relief from the tomb of Puymrê Thebes, with metalworkers
                using blowing pipe (Fig. 5) and bellows (Fig. 6) Eighteenth
                Dynasty ~1500 BC

Fig. 7 Late Bronze Age (~1250 BC)
blowing tube from excavation
Ayos Dhimetrios (Kalavasos)
Cyprus

Fig. 8 Metalworker using blowing
pipe, wallpainting in the
tomb of Rechmirè Thebes Egypt,
Eighteenth Dynasty ~1500 BC

Fig. 9 Big crucible with a hole in
the middle area of the sidewall with a capacity of about
3,2 l corresponding to 28 kg
liquid copper from B.A. Enkomi,
Cyprus

Fig. 10 Crucible with a hole in the
bottom area of the sidewall for
production of tinbronze from
Archaic stratum of Kition,
Cyprus

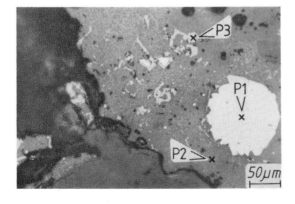

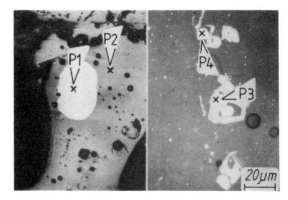

Fig. 11

Fig. 12

Figs. 11 and 12 Micrographs of slag from the bottom of the crucible (Fig. 9)
from Enkomi and areas of microprobe analysis

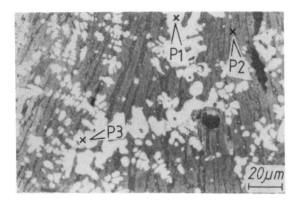

Fig. 13 Micrograph of slag from the area of the hole of the crucible (Fig. 9) from Enkomi and areas of microprobe analysis

Fig. 14 Roasting and smelting process in a crucible with hole in the sidewall during laboratory tests with copper sulfide ore

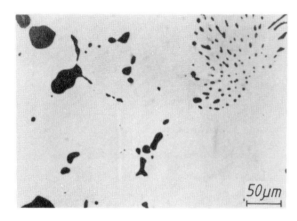

Fig. 15 Micrograph of reduction-product after roasting and smelting of sulphide ore in crucible of Fig. 14

Fig. 16 Microstructure of blister copper smelted from copper sulphate ore of Troullimine, Cyprus

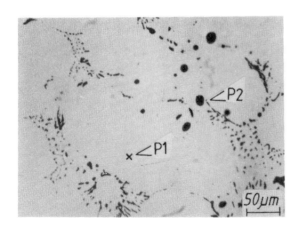

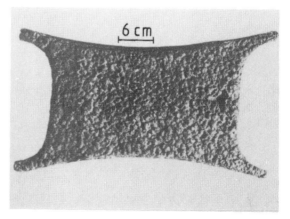

Fig. 17 Micrograph of blister copper from oxhide ingot Museum Nikosia (Fig. 18)

Fig. 18 Oxhide ingot probably from L.B.A. Enkomi, Museum Nikosia

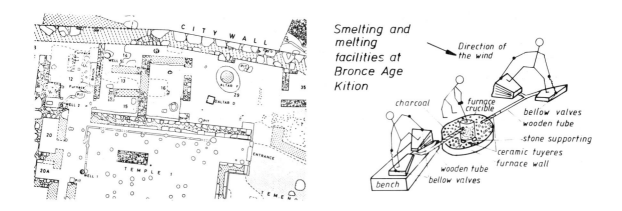

Fig. 19a   Fig. 19b

Figs. 19a and 19b Arrangement of furnaces (Fig. 19a) and reconstruction of facilities (Fig. 19b) of L.B.A. copper workshop of Kition

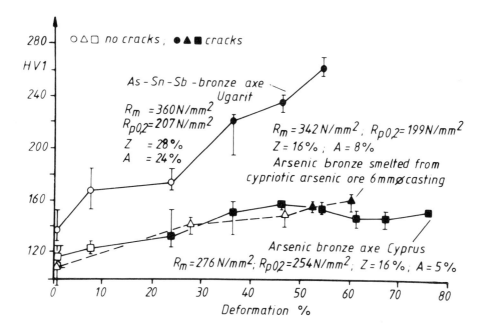

Fig. 20 Increase in hardness of different copper alloys by cold deformation

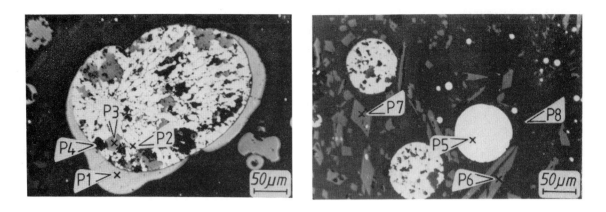

Fig. 21a   Fig. 21b

Figs. 21a and 21b Micrographs of slag from archaic crucible with hole near
the bottom of the sidewall and areas of microprobe analysis

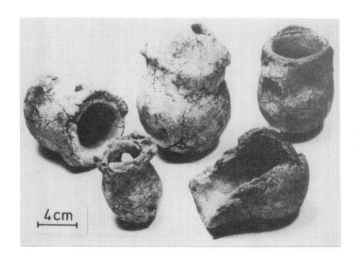

Fig. 22 Crucibles with lids from the Roman settlement Nida near Frankfurt
Main

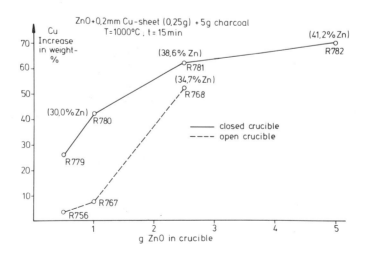

Fig. 23 Influence of reaction time on the zinc content of copper after
reaction with ZnO at 1000°C

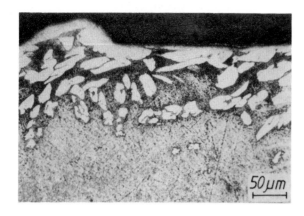

Fig. 24 Micrograph of surface area
(α+β) and central area (β)
of reaction product ZnO+Cu+C,
1100°C, 60 min

Fig. 25 Brass ingot in the shape of
malachite as a reaction product
between zinc-carbonate-ore and
malachite (Laurion), at 1000°C,
5 min

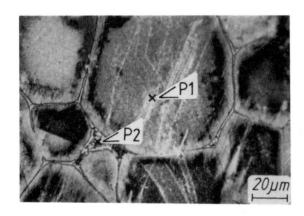

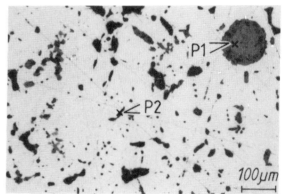

Fig. 26 Micrograph of the brass of
Fig. 25 and areas of microprobe analysis

Fig. 27 Micrograph of a brass produced
by reaction of lead-zinc-ore
from Laurion with copper at
1150°C for 15 min and areas of
microprobe analysis

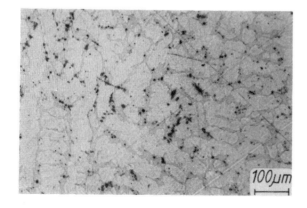

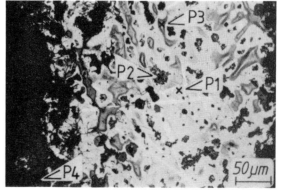

Fig. 28 Micrograph of copper-zinc-
tin alloy produced by
reaction of SnO$_2$ + malachite +
zinc-lead-sulfide-ore from
Laurion with copper + carbon,
1120°C, 30 min

Fig. 29 Micrograph of B.A.-ring from
Ugarit (Ras Shamra) Syria of
copper-zinc-tin alloy and
areas of microprobe analysis

SMELTING OF COPPER IN THE ENEOLITHIC PERIOD OF THE BALKANS

Borislav Jovanović

Institute of Archaeology, Knez Mihajlova 35/II 11000 Beograd, Yugoslavia

Abstract

Smelting of copper in the primary metallurgy of the Balkans had been most likely carried out in the settlements. This has been confirmed by the discovery of traces of copper slag in the Late Vinca group (Vinca, Divostin, Selevac). The rich deposits of oxide ores were exhausted already in the Eneolithic (Ai Bunar, South Bulgaria) or even in the Early Eneolithic (Rudna Glava, East Serbia, Yugoslavia). This indirectly points to the rather developed technology of smelting copper at the very beginning of the use of this metal in the Balkans and Carpathian Basin. The fall in the copper production during the Late Eneolithic is therefore not a decline but just a transition period to the new technology of smelting sulphide ores. It is possible that the significant cultural and population processes during the Late Eneolithic (third millenium BC) in the Balkans and Carpathian Basin were also the consequence of the important technological changes in the metallurgy and industry of copper.

Keywords: LATE VINCA CULTURE, PRIMARY METALLURGY, CRUCIBLE, PLOCNIK, ADMIXTURE, COPPER MINING, DEPOSIT, COPPER TOOLS, POPULATION MOVEMENT, ALLOYING, COPPER ORES

Introduction

Direct archaeological evidence for the smelting of copper in the Early Eneolithic of the Central Balkans does not exist. That is to say at present the necessary data on furnaces, moulds and crucibles is missing. Such data are available only for the Late Eneolithic and beginning of the Early Bronze Age. Smelting is suggested by the presence of the copper carbonate minerals malachite and azurite at some sites of the Late Vinca culture group, for example at Divostin (McPherron and Srejović 1971), Fafos, Grivac, or Vinca itself (Jovanović and Ottaway 1976). Slag remains of the smelting of carbonate or oxide ores have been discovered at the Late Vinca sites Gornja Tuzla (Čović 1973) and, recently, at Selevac (Glumac 1982).

The very active copper mining operations in the metalliferous zone of East Serbia is another proof for smelting of copper, at least in the southern variant of the Vinca group. An experiment with smelting of oxide copper ores from the shaft No. 5c from the Early Eneolithic mine at Rudna Glava near Majdanpek has confirmed the ease of processing this type of ore by primitive technology (Tylecote 1982, Craddock 1982). The well-known hoards of massive copper tools from Plocnik (South Serbia), the site of the

Late Vinca group, illustrate very clearly the final production of the
copper metallurgy of the south Morava variant of the Vinca group (Jovanović
and Ottaway 1976).

The absence of separate smelting places in the Early Eneolithic of the
Balkans could be a sign of the processing of copper exclusively in the
contemporaneous sites. But smelting was carried out at Chinflon, a copper
mine in southern Spain, exploited also in the Chalcolithic and Early Copper
Age (Rothenberg and Blanco-Freijero 1981). Present evidence for the Balkans,
as it has just been seen, fits well with the first conclusion. One should
also mention small cylindrical crucibles with thick walls, usually filled
with malachite and azurite, ground into powder. Some of them showed traces
of smelting, which is also an argument for their metallurgical use (Novotna
1976). Such small vessels exist in the hoard No. 4 of the massive copper
tools for Plocnik and hoard No. 3 also contains damaged copper tools and
ingots, prepared, obviously, for re-melting (Stalio 1964, 1973). It seems
that production of new tools from scrap material was a method introduced
at the very beginning of the copper metallurgy. It is understandable that
one ought to think that a very small number of objects were made of copper
ores or of native copper from a single source. Spectrographic analyses
confirm such facts for the copper objects from the Vinca group; it indicates the beginning of the production of this metal in the Balkans.

Small tools from the site of Gornja Tuzla consist of very pure
copper with insignificant traces of iron and gold (Čović 1973). But
the beads from the Vinca layers from Gomolava already show some admixture
of arsenic and their copper was not of high purity (Ottaway 1979).
Geographically, Gomolava already belongs to the Panonnian plain, so the
differences in composition of the copper compared with Gornja Tuzla could
be explained by the use of different sources of ores. But one of them
has a rather high percentage of tin (6.6%), so that it could belong to one
of the later periods at Gomolava (Ottaway 1979).

Summing up all the evidence, it would be reasonable to consider the
local processing of copper in the Early Eneolithic sites in the metalliferous regions of the Balkans and the Carpathian Basin.

It is also noticeable that grouping of the general alloys of copper
is evident during the Eneolithic period in this region which is one of the
earliest centres of copper metallurgy in Europe. Furthermore those categories of processed copper correspond to the established chronological
and cultural framework. In general, copper of high purity belonged to the
flourishing copper metallurgy of the Early Eneolithic of the Balkans and
Danube Basin, while arsenical copper is characteristic of the Late
Eneolithic only. Finally, alloying copper with tin took place in the
Early and Middle Bronze Ages. So even though the copper was permanently
mixed, nevertheless it has been possible to determine the main composition
of the metal used in the Eneolithic and Bronze Age.

The quantitative change in the production of copper has also been
recognised: copper of high purity was processed in large quantity, while
arsenical copper corresponded to a marked fall in the production. The
suggested reasons for that remarkable decline of the Late Eneolithic
copper metallurgy of the Balkans and Carpathian Basin have already been
discussed, especially relative to the previous rapid progress during the
Early Eneolithic (Vulpe 1976, Kuna 1981). The answer to this question has
usually been looked for in the strong cultural and population movements
which spread across the Balkans in the third millenium BC.

Some of the former Early Eneolithic groups, as they were in the Central and West Balkans area Vinca or Butmir, disappeared, while the new cultural groups of the Late Eneolithic, as they were in Baden, Kostolac or Cotofeni, did not reach the level of production of copper of the previous period. Perhaps such negative evidence is just the question of the lack of excavated settlements, cemeteries and mines, but in this case it seems that two other possibilities could be mentioned: a change of technology or a specific cultural development. In other words, one should see in the Late Eneolithic of the Balkans a period when already acquired interest for production and use of copper were lost and when the developed metallurgical knowledge of the Early Eneolithic was forgotten.

The exhaustion of the richest deposits of the oxide and carbonate ores in the Early Eneolithic is clearly proved by the investigated mines, such as Rudna Glava (Jovanovic 1982) and, for the Late Eneolithic, Ai Bunar (South Bulgaria). The size of that exploitation is really surprising. For example, for Ai Bunar it is proposed that there are about 20,000-30,000 tons of excavated material, which have produced about 2000-3000 tons of copper ores or 500-1000 tons of copper (Cernych 1982). If one takes into consideration the presently-known number of massive copper tools from the Eneolithic period of Bulgaria - amounting to nearly 488 (with the weight of about 400-450 kg: Cernych 1982), it is clear that just a small proportion of the produced Eneolithic copper tools have been collected. Such a relation between the excavated ores and processed copper is most probably the same as that between the Rudna Glava mine and the metallurgy of the Vinca group.

The exhaustion of the oxide ore beds must have led to the poverty of metal in the evolved eneolithic metallurgy of the Balkans and Danube Basin. Replacement of the suitable and rich sources of the raw material was not easy to provide. Processing of other ores, for example those with an arsenic component, was not enough to wholly replace the use of copper carbonate minerals. Experiments with processing of arsenic-copper ores were made at the beginning of the copper metallurgy in the east part of the Carpathian Basin - namely in the Tiszapolgàr group (Novotna 1976). But the Late Eneolithic was the period when arsenic-copper appeared in larger quantity in the Balkans and the Carpathian Basin. Tools made of that alloy called 'arsenic bronze' belonged also, according to their chronological and typological determination, to the Late Eneolithic.

The fall in the copper production in the Late Eneolithic is therefore the result of the substitution of the older technology of smelting of oxide ores with the new one, orientated to the smelting of arsenic and sulphide ores. Thus the decline of copper metallurgy in this period is just illusory. It is an intermediate stage caused by the replacement of one technology of copper smelting with another. At the end of that process the mass smelting of sulphide ores began. Later the use of tin caused arsenical copper to gradually disappear. This advance in the smelting of copper finally provided sufficient quantities of metal for the Late Eneolithic and Early Bronze Age metallurgy in the Danube Basin and Carpathians. The source of the new raw materials now moved north and west of the Carpathians to the Alps and Czechoslovakian ore mountains, where deposits of sulphide ores existed.

The disappearance of the massive tools and weapons of the Eneolithic period was caused by their replacement with new improved types, (Fig.) and by the shortage of copper. The efficiency of those older types were, of course one of the most important factors in the evolution of the tools, but this time the shortage of carbonate copper minerals was responsible for the disappearance of these copper objects.

Comparing parallel metallurgical developments with the cultural evolution of the Late Eneolithic and the Early Bronze Age of the Balkans and Carpathian Basin, one could conclude that technological advance played a very important role. The innovations in the technology of processing the copper were not the main or single cause for those large cultural and population movements, but still played a much more important role than is usually recognised.

References

Craddock, P T 1982. Analytical techniques. In *Rudna Glava, najstarije rudarstvo bakra n Centralnom Balkanu* (Rudna Glava, der älteste Kupferbergbau in Zentralbalkan), B Jovanovic, p.116. Bor-Beograd

Cernych, N E 1982. Die ältesten Bergleute und Metallurgen Europas. *Das Altertum*, **28** /1, 5-15

Čović, B 1973. Praistorijsko rudarstvo i metalurgija u Bosni i Hercegovini, *Materijali Simpozijuma "Rudarstvo i metalurgija BiH od praistorije do početaka XX vijeka"*, Zenica (manuscript), 1-40

Glumac, P 1982. *Arheometalurška ispitivanja materijala sa lokaliteta Selevac* (Archaeometallurgical examination of the samples from the site of Selevac). *Zbornik Narodnog muze ja* (In Press)

Jovanović, B & Ottaway, B S 1976. Copper mining and metallurgy in the Vinca group. *Antiquity*, **198**, 104-113

Jovanović, B 1982. *Rudna Glava, najstarije rudarstvo bakra na Centralnom Balkanu* (Rudna Glava, Der älteste Kupferbergbau im Zentralbalkan). Bor-Beograd, Arheoloski Institut, Muzej rudarstva i metalurgije

Kuna, M 1981. Zur neolitischen und äneolitischen Kupferverarbeitung im Gebiet Jugoslawiens. *Godišnjak*, **XIX**, 13-81. Centar za balkanološka istraživanja Sarajevo

McPherron, A & Srejović, D 1971. *Early farming cultures in Central Serbia* (Eastern Yugoslavia). Kragujevac, Narodni muzej

Novotna, M 1976. Beginn der Metallverwendung und verarbeitung in östlichen Mitteleurope. In *Les débuts de la metallurgie*, ed. H Müller-Karpe, 118-129. Nice, Union international des sciences prehistoriques et protohistoriques, IX Congres

Ottaway, B 1979. Analysis of the earliest metal finds from Gomolava. *Rad vojvodjanskih muzeja*, **25**, 53-56

Rothenberg, B & Blanco-Freijeiro, A 1981. *Studies in Ancient Mining and Metallurgy in South-West Spain*, Metal in History: 1. London, Institute for Archaeo-Metallurgical Studies, Institute of Archaeology, University of London

Stalio, B 1964. Novi metalni nalaz iz Pločnika kod Prokuplja (Dépôt d'objets metaliques nouvellement mis au jour à Pločnik près du Prokuplje). *Zbornik Narodnog muzeja*, **IV**, 35-41

Stalio, B 1973. Četvrti nalaz bakarnog i kamenog orudja sa Pločnika kod Prokuplja (La quatrième decouvèrte d'outils en cuivre et en pierre a Pločnik pres de Propkuplje). *Zbornik Narodnog muzeja*, **VII**, 157-161

Tylecote, R F 1982. Smelting copper ore from Rudna Glava, Yugoslavia. In *Rudna Glava, najstarije rudarstvo bakra na Centralnom Balkanu* (Rudna Glava, Der älteste Kupferbergbau in Zentralbalkan), B Jovanović, 115-116. Bor-Beograd

Vulpe, A 1976. Zu den Anfängen der Kupfer-und Bronzemetallurgie in Rumänien. In *Les débuts de la métallurgie*, ed. H Müller-Karpe, 134-175. Nice, Union international des sciences préhistoriques et protohistoriques, IX Congrès

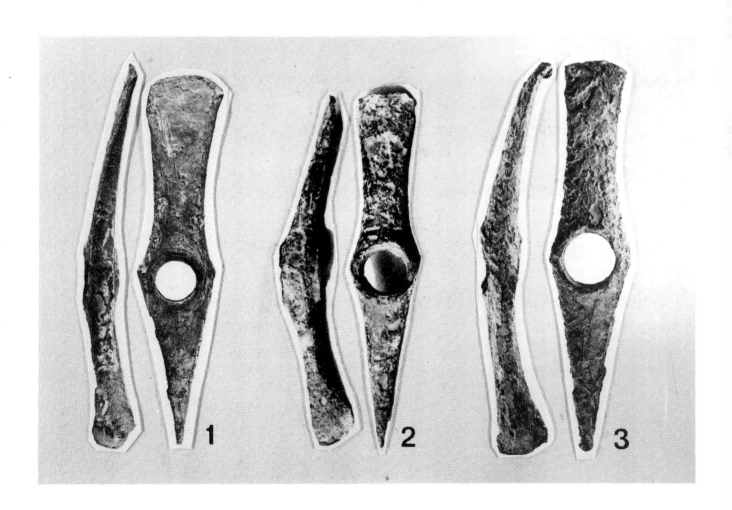

Fig. Cast Late Enolithic copper axe - adzes from the Central Balkans:
1. Bela Crkva (scale ½); 2. Miroc (scale ⅔); 3. Mramorak (scale ½) Yugoslavia

COPPER SMELTING FURNACES IN THE ARABAH, ISRAEL: THE ARCHAEOLOGICAL EVIDENCE

Beno Rothenberg

Institute of Mining and Metals in the Biblical World,
Tel Aviv
Institute for Archaeo-Metallurgical Studies, Institute of
Archaeology, University of London

Abstract

In 1972 a series of copper smelting furnaces was published (Rothenberg 1972), which had been excavated in
1964-1969 in the area of the Timna Valley, South Israel,
(Fig. 1) and dated to the Chalcolithic Period (fourth
millennium BC), the Late Bronze Age (fourteenth-twelfth
centuries BC) and to Imperial Roman times (second century AD). Subsequent systematic excavations in Timna
and the Arabah in 1974-76 (Conrad & Rothenberg 1980),
more fieldwork (so far unpublished) in 1979-1982, and
copper smelting experiences by Bamberger and Merkel
based largely on the archaeological evidence from Timna,
have led to a revised interpretation of the copper smelting installations found at Timna and of ancient copper
smelting furnaces in general.

Keywords: FURNACE, SMELTING, COPPER, METALLURGY,
ARABAH, BRONZE AGE, TUYERE

Introduction

In the light of our recent reinvestigation of the copper smelting installations and products excavated in the Timna Valley in 1964-69, as well as
copper smelting experiments in Timna-type furnaces by Bamberger and Merkel
(Bamberger MS, Merkel 1982), a number of questions had to be asked concerning
the interpretation of the Timna furnace remains and their reconstruction:

1. How far are the furnace remains as found *in situ* truly representative of
   the copper smelting furnaces actually used; i.e. what is the factual
   field evidence for the reconstruction of furnace geometry and function?
   (Tylecote 1962,25-39; Rothenberg 1972,235-239; Tylecote 1976,5-37;
   Bachmann & Rothenberg 1980).

2. Was the use of furnace lining really common practice in all periods and
   for all types of furnaces?

3. What is the available evidence for the use of tuyeres, their shape,
   number and position?

4. Is there archaeological evidence for the generally accepted furnace
   working model: slag on top and bun-shaped, plano-convex ingot on the
   bottom of the smelting furnace?

In the excavations at the smelting sites in the Arabah a large number of fragmentary furnace installations were uncovered, but we shall present here only furnaces found in a reasonable state of preservation. Because of the rather damaged and eroded state of most of the furnace walls and bottoms, only approximate measurements could be obtained.

In the following the analytical and purely metallurgical aspects of the excavated installations and their products have been omitted since this aspect has lately been dealt with elsewhere (Bachmann 1980).

A Chalcolithic furnace (fourth millennium BC). (Figs. 2, 3 and Pl. 1)

A copper smelting furnaces was excavated at Timna Site 39 and dated to the Chalcolithic Period (second part of fourth millennium BC) by pottery and flint tools (Rothenberg 1978,7-15; Berkovici 1978,16-20). It was a hole-in-the-ground, bowl-shaped smelting hearth with a low superstructure of small rocks around its rim. A large rock was placed behind the furnace, probably as a base for bellows (Pl. 1). The Nubian sandstone, used here as building material, had to be 'imported' to the furnace site from further up the wadi. No lining was found in situ inside the furnace. The inner furnace diameter was about 45 cm, its depth 45-50 cm (measured from the present surface and without the superstructure the height of which could not be established). No tuyeres were found at Site 39. The furnace bottom was solid bedrock.

Small, crushed pieces of rather viscous slag were found dispersed around the furnace and over much of the hillside. It was obvious that a number of furnaces had been operating at the site. This was non-tapped slag which must have been removed from the furnace at the end of the smelting operation and crushed to small fragments in order to extract the entrapped copper prills.

Among the dispersed slag were pieces of slagged, hard-burned soil lumps and also small slagged rocks, which appeared to be fragments of a smelting hearth. The appearance of the furnace remains and the slag of Site 39 indicated that the whole of the furnace contents was raked out at the end of the smelting operation, removing also part of the slagged furnace walls. This obviously means that the dimensions of the excavated furnace were much larger than the actual Chalcolithic hole-in-the-ground smelting hearth at the time of its actual operation. No slagged furnace lining was found at the site and the slagged lumps of very sandy soil, found near the furnace and among the dispersed slag, were sintered parts of the unlined sandy sides of the hole in the ground raked out together with the slag.

We therefore propose a new reconstruction of the Chalcolithic furnace, with a diameter of about 20 cm and a height of 40-50 cm, including the superstructure (Fig. 3).

Late Bronze Age furnaces (fourteenth-twelfth centuries BC)

At Site 30, excavated in 1974-76 (Rothenberg 1980,187-213), three archaeological strata produced copper smelting installations. The two lower strata (Layers III and II) could be dated to the Nineteenth and Twentieth Dynasties of Egypt's New Kingdom, from the late fourteenth to the middle of the twelfth century BC. A smelting installation of this phase of the Late Bronze Age would consist of a small, clay-lined bowl furnace standing at the edge of a stone-paved working floor. Most of these installations would be contained by a roughly built stone fence which served as a retaining wall for the ever growing slag heaps around the smelter.

Locus 50 (Fig. 4, Pl. 2)

Locus 50 was a typical copper smelting installation. The furnace was built of stone and sand, lined with a thick layer of clay mortar, its slightly concave bottom had a diameter of *c*. 40 cm and it had tapering sides. We do not have factual evidence for its height but the preserved walls would suggest a total height of about 50 cm.

Locus 219 (Fig. 5, Pl. 3)

Similar to Locus 50, this smelting installation consisted of a paved stone floor and a clay-lined, bowl-shaped smelting hearth with tapering sides, all contained by a retaining wall. After having served for smelting (in Layer II), this installation was rebuilt to serve as a potter's workshop consisting of several stone basins for clay preparation and a small kiln with attached charcoal storage compartment.

A large stone basin, constructed of several medium-sized rocks, was placed onto the disused smelting hearth (lower left corner of Fig. 5) thereby obliterating about half the furnace. However, the remaining half indicated the shape of a large bowl, *c*. 35 cm in diameter, with tapering sides and a slightly concave bottom. The clay lining was sintered to light red. The soil around the hearth showed heat-discolouration for some distance from the furnace, which clearly indicated that at least the lower part of the furnace was dug into the ground. The uppermost part of the hearth would have stood above the floor level.

The furnace lining found *in situ* had three superimposed layers of clay mortar, with imprints of fettling hands still clearly visible on the inside of the furnace walls (Tite *et al*. MS).

Site 185 (Fig. 6)

Site 185 is a smelting site in the Timna Valley near the Egyptian mining sanctuary, so far unpublished. A furnace fragment was observed sticking out of a badly eroded slope at the edge of the site and on excavation proved to be a fragmentary smelting furncace *in situ* (Fig. 6). Its shape was similar to the furnaces of Timna Site 30, Strata III-II: the same bowl-shape with tapering sides, a slightly concave bottom and clay mortar lining. There were two layers of clay lining indicating refettling of the hearth after its first operation (Tite *et al*. MS).

Other Late Bronze Age furnace fragments

Several more fragmentary copper smelting furnaces of the same type were found in the smelting camps of Timna but often only the furnace bottoms remained *in situ*. All these fragments indicated a furnace diameter of 30-40 cm.

Wherever furnace walls were found *in situ*, their lowermost parts near the bottom were never slagged; the same applied to the furnace bottom whose typical appearance would be that of a rather eroded, slightly concave or flat surface covered by a very fine, light-grey, dusty layer of burned clay, often mixed with very fine charcoal dust. However, contrary to the furnace bottom, the lining of the lower part of the furnace wall was usually missing, apparently forcibly removed together with the contents of the smelting hearth. Although parts of furnace walls were found *in situ* in a number of furnaces, we do not have direct factual evidence for the construction of the top or the height of the smelting hearth.

No tuyeres were found *in situ* in any of the excavated furnaces of this Late Bronze Age bowl-furnace type and we have therefore no direct archaeological evidence for the number or the precise position of the tuyeres of this furnace type. However, a very large number of small, hemispherical clay tuyeres, 6-7.5 cm wide, 4-7 cm long with a central aperture of 2 cm, were found on working floors and slag heap stratigraphically belonging to this phase of the Late Bronze Age (Pl. 4). All these tuyeres were prefabricated by a potter's workshop (e.g. Site 30, Locus 219), apparently made in clay and reed to standard sizes. The tuyeres found in all of the Egyptian New Kingdom smelting camps of the Arabah (and Sinai: Rothenberg 1979,164-166) were of uniform shape, but the slagging on their outside indicated two different positions in the furnace walls: most of the tuyeres protruded into the smelting hearth at an angle of 25°-30° to the horizontal, but there were also many tuyeres which must have protruded into the furnace horizontally (Fig. 7). The vertically inclined tuyeres could have been located anywhere in the upper part of the furnace with its outer end most likely at the level of the working surface above ground, but the horizontal tuyeres could only have been introduced into the furnace through the furnace front, unfortunately always found missing by the excavator.

The slag produced in these Late Bronze Age - New Kingdom furnaces was basically of two types; both were always found together and it seems obvious that they were produced by one and the same smelting process:

1. Solid, black plate slag, *c.* 2-3 cm thick, which was formed by tapping the slag onto a flat surface outside the furnace and then breaking it up into small pieces, probably in order to extract any entrapped copper (Pl. 5).

2. Non-tapped furnace slag of rather viscous appearance, full of gas holes, charcoal inclusions, semi-molten gangue and some copper prills. This slag must have originally remained inside the furnace after most of the slag was tapped out. It was removed before the hearth was refettled for further use.

All of the Egyptian New Kingdom smelting enterprises in the Arabah and Sinai used this type of furnace and it may well be considered the standard equipment and technology of this period.

Later Late Bronze Age furnaces (*c.* twelfth century BC)

Site 2, a large New Kingdom copper smelting camp in the Timna Valley, was partly excavated in 1964 and 1966 (Rothenberg 1972,67-111). There were essentially two main phases of copper smelting, the earlier (Layer II) could be dated to the Nineteenth-Twentieth Egyptian Dynasties (fourteenth-twelfth centuries BC) and its smelting furnace technology was the same as that of Layers III-II of Site 30, described above. The later and final phase of the main era of copper smelting at this site (Layer I) was dated to the twelfth century BC and we shall deal in the following section with the furnaces of this final phase of Site 2. Very recent excavations have shown some copper smelting activity as late as the seventh century AD; on site 2 see below p. 128.

Furnace II - Area G (Figs. 8,9 and Pl. 6)

Furnace II (Pl. 6) was built into a shallow pit, dug through several working levels of earlier metallurgical activities in Layer II. In this earlier layer remains of furnaces (V-VI), broken slag, tuyeres and a large number of

rock-cut pits were found. Furnace II was a semi-circular low structure built
of dolomite rocks, its straight sides and flat bottom lined with a layer of
clay mortar 2-3 cm thick. The stone walling was left open at the front and
must have been closed by at thick layer of clay mortar. This arrangement
facilitated the proper servicing of the furnace: tapping,removal of smelting
products which remained in the furnace after tapping, and refettling for
further use. A stone-paved working floor was laid behind and beside the
smelting hearth.

In front of the hearth two 80-100 cm long stone slabs standing on edge
flanked a shallow slag tapping pit, apparently for the protection of the men
at work at the furnace. The front part of the hearth was only partly preserved near the furnace bottom and had the shape of a low ridge of hard-burned
clay, separating the higher furnace bottom from the lower slag pit. Even the
lower half of the actual tap hole was still preserved in Furnace II.

The smelting hearth had an inner diameter of $c.$ 40 cm and was preserved
to the height of $c.$ 35 cm. Both sides and the back wall of the hearth were
preserved up to present ground level and were heavily slagged with a conspicuously thick slag layer adhering to the upper half of the back wall. The
bottom was flat, somewhat eroded, and showed no signs of any slagging. As
in the earlier furnaces described above the lining and any slag adhering to
the lower part of the furnace walls was missing. It had obviously been forcibly removed at the end of the smelting operation.

About 30 cm from the bottom several fragments of one tuyere were found
in situ (Pl. 7), its original shape still clearly discernible: a clay tube
of $c.$ 12 cm diameter and 20 cm long, which penetrated the furnace wall at an
angle of 25-30° to the horizontal; i.e. its aperture into the furnace was
at height of $c.$ 20 cm from the furnace bottom. There was no further sign
of any additional tuyeres in the furnace walls and apart from the missing
front and/or the open top of the hearth, there simply was no way any additional tuyere could have penetrated through the furnace walls into the
hearth.

In previous publications (Tylecote et al. 1967,240; Rothenberg & Lupu
1967, pl. VII; Rothenberg 1972,75-76; Tylecote 1976,30) the tubular tuyere
found in situ in Furnace II had been reconstructed as part of a complex
tuyere system consisting of the tubular tuyere, which penetrated the furnace
wall, the actual bellows tube, which was introduced into the furnace through
this tubular tuyere, and the small semi-spherical tuyere, which was fitted
into the furnace end of the tubular tuyere in order to protect the bellows
tube against the intense heat of the furnace.

Subsequent stratigraphic investigations at Site 2 and other smelting
sites in the Arabah convinced us that the small semi-spherical tuyeres belong
exclusively to Layer II of Site 2 (III-II of Site 30) and the tubular tuyeres
to the later furnace type of Layer I. This has been further confirmed by the
discovery in January 1983 of a rock-cut smelting furnace with a tubular tuyere
in its back wall (Rothenberg 1983). This furnace belonged to the later phase
(Layer I) of Site 2. There were no small tuyeres with the furnace or in the
nearby heap of slag.

Furnace II was located right next to a heap of ring-shaped, tapped slag
cakes, each with a cast-in hole in its centre (Pl. 8). Wherever slag of this
phase of Late Bronze Age copper smelting was found in the Arabah it was of
this peculiar shape. This appears to have been a local innovation and became
the local 'traditional' tapped slag shape in the Arabah up to Early Islamic
times (for Roman slag see Rothenberg 1972,212,pl.120 - Early Islamic slag at
Site 64 in the Arabah, unpublished). The weight of these Late Bronze Age
slag rings was 15-20 kg.

A rock-cut smelting furnace with a tubular tuyere at the back excavated in 1983 at Site 2, area Z (Rothenberg 1983) produced ring-shaped slag cakes in an attached slag tapping pit also cut into the rock. Although the pottery around this furnace was exclusively New Kingdom, charcoal found on the furnace bottom gave a date of 1210 ± 100 (BM 2242). Thus the Late Bronze Age date for Layer I type furnace of Site 2 may have to be revised after further investigations (added June 1984).

Furnace I - Area E (Fig. 10, Pl. 9)

Furnace I was built on undisturbed ground somewhat outside the main area of smelting activities at Site 2. As only Layer I material appeared in its context (twelfth century BC), this discovery was of considerable stratigraphic importance.

Right next to Furnace I was a slag heap of the same ring-shaped slag with a central cast-in hole obviously dumped from the furnace site down the lower slope and into the shallow riverbed.

Furnace I was very similar to Furnace II and equally fairly well preserved. It was also stone-built and clay-lined and was heavily slagged on the upper part of the walls, especially on the back wall. Furnace I had a flat bottom but its front wall and one of the flanking stones of the slag pit were found missing. There was no sign of any tuyere but, as in Furnace II, heavy slagging indicated the possible position of a tuyere in the back wall of the hearth.

Furnace IV - Area C (Fig. 11, Pl. 10)

Furnace IV was in principle of the same type as Furnaces I and II. However, it was not stone-built but was essentially a hole-in-the ground bowl-furnace, its walls and concave bottom lined with a thick layer of clay mortar. Its tapping pit, protected by long flanking stones, was located next to the (missing) furnace front. The smelting hearth as found had a maximum diameter of 45 cm and was c. 40 cm high. However, the actual furnace diameter must have been considerably smaller, as the furnace lining was missing on the lower part of the walls. This gave the furnace, which had no stone walling behind the clay lining, a globular rather than a tubular appearance. We must of course also take in account the rather abrasive character of the reaction between the molten slag and the clay lining; i.e. the furnace walls were heavily attacked and damaged by the smelting process, mainly in the lower part of the smelting hearth between the tuyere(s) and the tap hole.

As with Furnaces I and II, the uppermost part of Furnace IV protruding originally above ground was not preserved. In fact the top of the furnace, from the level of the working floor was missing. Contrary to Furnaces I and II, the walls of which showed heavy slagging only at the back wall opposite the furnace front, Furnace IV was very heavily slagged on the upper half of at least three of its walls, indicating the possible position of tuyeres. The front wall was missing. This is the only Late Bronze Age furnace found in Timna which may have had more than one tuyere, perhaps even three. This assumption is based on the observation that a heavy slag build-up is normally formed on the furnace wall right above and on both sides of a tuyere - an observation made on excavated furnaces and during the smelting experiments of Bamberger and Merkel.

As there was no trace whatsoever of any penetration of tuyeres through the well-preserved, slag-covered furnace walls up to the height of 40 cm, the tuyeres must have penetrated the smelting hearth at the level of the stone-paved working floor or above. However, only one fragment of a clay tuyere was found *in situ* in the back wall of Furnace IV sticking to heavy slag incrustation *c.* 26 cm above the furnace bottom. It was too small to indicate the dimensions of the tuyere, but was similar to the tubular tuyere fragment of Furnace II.

The slag heap next to Furnace IV contained the same ring-shaped tapped slag (15-20 kg), as found next to Furnaces I and II. In spite of the differences in the building methods of these furnaces, their operational principles were obviously the same and there is archaeological evidence for their identical date.

Iron Age furnaces - problems and reconstruction

Site 30 Layer I

Like most of the other New Kingdom smelting camps of the Arabah, Site 30 was abandoned by the Egyptians in the middle of the twelfth century BC. During the excavations at Site 30 (Rothenberg 1980,187-213) a further period of smelting activities (Layer I) could be identified, dated by Egyptian pottery and carbon-14 to the Twenty-second Dynasty (tenth century BC), probably during the short Asian campaign of Sheshonk I.

No furnaces were found *in situ* in this layer, yet the furnace fragments, tuyeres and slag, only found in this uppermost layer of activities at Site 30, represented a much more sophisticated smelting technology than any yet encountered in the Arabah. The furnace fragments were made of clay heavily tempered with tiny pieces of crushed slag (Bachmann & Rothenberg 1980,218-221) between 5 and 10 cm thick. Their inside, i.e. the face facing the smelting hearth, was sintered to a hard and smooth surface often slagged. The outsides of these fragments were extremely brittle and in most cases had no proper surface, though sometimes fingerprints of fettling hands were still preserved. There were also fragments, *c.* 4-5 cm thick, with fingerprints on both sides which must have been rims of the free-standing uppermost part of the shaft-like furnace.

Taking into account the curvature of a number of furnace fragments (Pl. 11), Bachmann and Rothenberg (1980,218-223) proposed a rather round-bellied, pear-shaped smelting furnace with a short shaft, an inner diameter of *c.* 54 cm and a shaft diameter of *c.* 24 cm (Fig. 12).

Among the smelting debris of Layer I a number of tuyeres were found made of the same heavily slag-tempered clay as the furnace fragments. These tuyeres were quite different from the New Kingdom tuyeres of Site 30 Layers III-II and the other New Kingdom smelting camps of that period in the Arabah (Pl. 12). Instead of the small, hemispherical New Kingdom tuyeres, the tuyeres of Layer I were very large, 12.5-16 cm wide, with a central aperture of 2-5 cm. These tuyeres protruded into the furnace for 2-5 cm, either horizontally or at an angle of 20°-25° to the horizontal. According to the slag deposit on these tuyeres, which was often several centimeters thick, the tuyeres must have been positioned inside the shoulder-like curved upper part of the furnace wall. One almost S-shaped fragment of this part of the furnace still showed the imprint of a broken-off tuyere.

Further meticulous investigations and measurements of a large number of furnace fragments and tuyeres from Site 30 and more fieldwork in 1981/3 led to a revised reconstruction of the Iron Age furnace of Timna and its building method (Fig. 13). The furnace was built of heavily slag-tempered clay and the same material was packed as a compact mass around the smelting hearth to form a solid platform with the furnace in its centre. This platform was partly stone-paved, probably to facilitate the workings of the bellows. The furnace was in fact almost tubular, its diameter c. 40 cm. The furnace top curved inside and formed a shaft of c. 20 cm and a height of probably 30 cm. Only this shaft protruded above ground, whilst the actual smelting hearth was completely 'underground'.

The tuyeres were inserted into the curved upper part of the wall and protruded several centimeters into the furnace. The position of the tuyere(s) was indicated by the border of heavy sintering and slagging separating the protruding tip from the hind part which remained inside the wall and was never slagged (Pl. 12).

The hard crust found on the furnace walls was formed by the sintering of the clay surfaces, due to the high temperature. This explains why many fragments of hard-burnt 'lining' found at Site 30, Layer I, with the exception of the fragments of the free-standing shaft, showed only one solid and smooth side (the inside) and appeared to be broken off at the opposite side (the outside).

A diameter of c. 40 cm for the smelting hearth, c. 20 cm for the shaft and a total height of c. 60-70 cm would best fit the measurements and slag incrustations of the furnace fragments found at Site 30 Layer I. This revised reconstruction would also explain the shaft as a functional necessity to obtain the furnace height required above the tuyeres. The actual reducing centre would be in the middle of the hearth, above the airstream issuing from the tuyere nozzles, just slightly below the beginning of the shaft-like top part of the furnace. It is exactly here that heavy slagging was observed on the almost S-shaped furnace fragments.

Timna Site 30 Locus 10 (Fig. 14, Pl. 13)

Important archaeological evidence for the construction methods of the Iron Age furnaces of Site 30, Layer I, though not quite conclusive, is available from an installation, Locus 10, found *in situ* in Layer I (Rothenberg 1980, 198-203). Clearing layers of debris and soil, there appeared a flat area of red clay, heavily tempered with crushed slag, and in its centre what looked like an almost complete circle of heat-discoloration with a well-defined inner diameter of c. 50 cm. After further excavation this inner circle turned into a hard-burnt, round opening, unfortunately not completely preserved, whilst the area of heat-discoloration became the hard-burnt outside of a low dome-shaped structure. Soon it became evident that we had uncovered a furnace, made of the same slag-tempered clay as the furnace fragments and tuyeres found previously in the slag heap of Layer I.

Locus 10 was a compact mass of clay with a dome-shaped furnace cavity in its centre. At the opening on top the curved uppermost furnace wall turned upwards, but this part, apparently a shaft, was unfortunately missing. The outside diameter of this shaft at its base was c. 30 cm.

The front wall of Locus 10 and part of its side walls were missing. There were no tuyeres in the preserved parts of the furnace, though the sintering of the walls and of course the heat-discoloration on top indicated clearly that this installation was indeed used at a high temperature. The furnace dimensions, as found in the excavation, were as follows: the hearth diameter was c. 90 cm, its height c. 28 cm. We have no clear evidence for the height of the shaft, though a number of rimmed fragments indicated a height of 20 - 30 cm.

When found, Locus 10 contained a 10 cm thick layer of tiny slag fragments (0.3-0.5 cm), perhaps tempering material. Because of this and even more because of the large diameter of the installation, we are hesitant to describe this as a smelting furnace, though we have no other interpretation to offer. It is of course possible that Locus 10 was indeed originally a smelting furnace of smaller dimensions which became deformed and damaged beyond repair by continuous use and was thereafter turned into a container for slag temper. Similar, secondary use of other installations was observed in the same context. In any case Locus 10 can serve as evidence for the construction methods of Iron Age furnaces at Site 30.

The smelting slag of Site 30 Layer I (Pl. 14)

The slag from Layer I was quite different from the New Kingdom slag of Layers III-II and the slag rings of Site 2 Layer I: it was tapped out of the furnace and formed large, mostly oval-shaped plates 40 x 60 cm, 5-10 cm thick and weighing 15-25 kg. These slag cakes were dumped without any further use onto the slag heap. Together with this tapped slag, there was also some non-tapped furnace slag. It should also be mentioned here that this slag was fluxed with manganese oxide (MnO_2) instead of the usual iron oxide flux of the earlier and later periods in the Arabah.

Roman furnaces at Beer Ora (Site 28)

Just south of the Timna Valley near an ancient well still in use by the nearby settlement of the same name - Beer Ora - several large heaps of heavy, black, circular slag and slag-built houses, together with second-century AD Roman pottery, witnessed the existence in the Arabah of a Roman copper industry. Two copper smelting furnaces were excavated near these slag heaps (Rothenberg 1972,210-223).

Roman Furnace I (Fig. 15, Pl. 15)

Roman Furnace I (in Area A) was a hole-in-the-ground bowl hearth, its diameter, as found in the excavation, *c.* 55 cm. Its walls were carefully lined with clay mortar, but much of the lining was found missing. A slag tapping pit was located in front of the furnace.

Only the lower part of the hearth, *c.* 30 cm deep, was preserved. It was clay-lined and its back wall heavily slagged. The originally flat furnace bottom was found somehow out of its original horizontal position and tilted towards the furnace front (Rothenberg 1972,216). Part of a superstructure built of small and medium sized rocks was preserved *in situ* and provided enough construction details to allow the reconstruction of this furnace. The furnace lining, *c.* 3 cm thick, of the lower part also continued on the inside of this superstructure. The furnace front above the tapping pit had been broken open, but was subsequently repaired by a compact wall of small stones and clay and refettled with a 3 cm thick clay mortar lining, found *in situ*. There was no sign of any tuyere in the walls of the lower part of the hearth, including the refettled front wall. However, a slag indentation in the back wall at the height of *c.* 28 cm may well indicate the position of a tuyere. As bellows must have been used, this would be placed on the ground next to

the furnace and its tube(s) would penetrate into its hearth almost at ground
level, somewhere between the superstructure and the underground part, as
indeed indicated by the indentation in the back wall. Heavily burnt clay lumps,
found on the slag heaps of Beer Ora, could well be part of tubular tuyeres. No
other types of tuyere were found at Beer Ora or at any of the other smaller
Roman smelting sites in the Arabah.

Roman Furnace IV (Fig. 16)

A second copper smelting furnace, Roman Furnace IV (in Area F), was similar
to Roman Furnace I. However, its front wall was missing and its bottom badly
eroded. Although the upper half of its side walls was also slagged, the back
wall had conspicuously more slag adhering to it, indicating the position of a
tuyere.

A most interesting detail was found in the bottom of the slag-tapping
pit. The actual slag pit of the Roman furnace was located inside a shallow
hollow in the ground; in fact it was a kind of ring-shaped mould for the slag
tapped out of the furnace. In its centre a round patch of hard-burnt, baked
sand was found *in situ*, which must have served as the core needed to make the
cast-in centre hole of the circular Roman slag cake (Pl. 16). Although such
centre holes were already known in the late New Kingdom tapped slag of Timna
Site 2 and similar sites in the Arabah and also in much later slag dated
to the Islamic Period (*c.* seventh century AD) found at Site 64 next to Beer
Ora, this is the first archaeological evidence for the 'casting' method of
this centre hole in the slag.

The Roman furnace was technologically a continuation of the Late Bronze
Age metallurgical traditions and represents a well-established, probably
rather universal standard practice. The cast-in hole in the slag, however,
seems to have been a locally developed metallurgical tradition of the Arabah.

Discussion and summary

1. The fragmentary remains of ancient smelting furnaces found in excavations
do not usually represent in shape or dimensions the furnaces as used in the
actual smelting operation. The smelting process itself always causes altera-
tions of furnace dimensions and shape and usually destroys essential parts of
the evidence. The uppermost parts of the furnace, including the working level
of the tuyere(s), have not yet been found *in situ* in any furnace, mainly
because these rather fragile parts protruded above ground and would be the
first to be destroyed or disintegrate. However, it is only through the
evidence of excavated furnaces that reconstructions of ancient process models
may be proposed. Furthermore, only by mathematical and experimental
technological research can the technological validity of such models be
established and through this its historicity.

2. After the primitive Chalcolithic-Early Bronze Age beginnings of extractive
metallurgy in simple pits dug into the ground and without any lining, especially selected and prepared refractory materials began to be used. Sandstone
and dolomite rocks were known to have been 'imported' to smelting sites and clay
mortar was used for furnace lining. However, there is now evidence that a
hard-burnt, heavily sintered inner surface layer of a sand- or clay-built furnace may misleadingly look like intentional lining.

3. We do not yet have definitive archaeological evidence for the number or
the exact position of the tuyere(s). However, we do have evidence for the
fact that tuyeres - one to three tuyeres at the most for Timna-type furnaces

of any period - were introduced into the smelting hearth at the juncture between the underground part of the hearth and its superstructure which protruded
above ground. There is further evidence for an inclination of 20°-30° to the
horizontal of most of the tuyeres vertically introduced at this juncture, but
we do not yet have any clear indication for the position of horizontal tuyeres
found in considerable quantities in Late Bronze Age and also in Early Iron
Age context.

4. No mould-like, crucible-shaped depressions or indentations were found in
the furnace bottoms to serve as receptables for metallic copper and none of
the furnace bottoms found in the Timna furnaces could have produced a bun-
shaped ingot or an ingot of similar shape. The few ingots found in Timna
were irregular runs of copper, often still sticking to slag. As this was
solid tapped slag, there exists of course the possibility that the copper
had run out of the furnace accidentally together with the tapped slag and
settled at the bottom of the slag.

Some of the ingots found in Timna and at Bir Nasib in Sinai appear to
have formed inside a smelting hearth, but these are very small pieces mostly
of rather irregular and mainly plate-like shape. We shall list here several
examples: ingots from Timna Site 2 (Late Bronze Age) i) 6.5 x 5 cm, 1 cm
thick, ii) 18 x 2-6 cm, 1-1.3 cm thick (very irregular flat piece); ingot
from Beer Ora (Roman) 8 x 7.2 cm, 0.5-1.5 cm thick (sticking to tapped slag);
ingot from Bir Nasib (New Kingdom) 9 x 11 cm, 0.8-1.2 cm thick (nearly plano-
convex with very much metallic iron). The bun-shaped copper ingot of *c.* 7 kg
found in the Arabah out of any context (Rothenberg 1972,69) would not have
fitted any of the furnace bottoms of the Timna furnaces. Its shape, especially its completely flat top, indicated that it was a cast and not a primary
smelting product.

If the copper had been intentionally tapped out of the furnace together
with the slag, there would of course be clear evidence for it on the bottom
of the tapped slag cakes. A very good sample of such slag was recently published by G. Weisgerber (Weisgerber 1978, figs. 3-4) though Weisgerber's interpretation of these slag pieces as having solidified inside a smelting hearth
as a primary smelting product seems unlikely. They are probably tapped slag
solidified in a crucible-shaped slag pit outside the smelting hearth or a
product of a secondary process not involving primary smelting. Nothing like
these slag cakes have ever been found in the Arabah or Sinai.

Summing up the archaeological evidence from Timna it appears that the
previously proposed slag-on-top-with-plano-convex ingot-at-the-bottom model
is indeed an oversimplification of a much more complicated process. It now
seems rather doubtful that the bun-shaped, plano-convex or even the very
regular disc-like copper ingots found in many hoards from the sea or from
excavations, are in fact primary smelting products. This conclusion is
strengthened by numerous ingot-shaped clay mould fragments lately identified
as such among the furnace parts from Site 30 Layer I and especially by recent
experiments in Bronze Age copper smelting (Bamberger MS, Merkel 1982).

Acknowledgements

The original fieldwork in the Arabah was carried out by the author in the
years 1959-70 on behalf of the Institute of Mining and Metals in the Biblical
World, The Arabah Expedition, Tel Aviv, and from 1974 as part of the New
Arabah Project sponsored by the Volkswagen Foundation, Hannover. It is thanks
to this support by the Volkswagen Foundation and the trustees and sponsors of
the Institute for Archaeo-Metallurgical Studies, Institute of Archaeology,

University of London, that this long-term Arabah Project, including the experimental research by M. Bamberger and J. Merkel, could be carried out. Amongst the many people whose active participation, advice and steady support were of decisive importance for this work I would like to mention here my friends R F Tylecote, H G Bachmann and P Wincierz. Many thanks are due to the General Director and trustees, past and present, of Museum Haaretz, Tel Aviv, who for over twenty years provided a home for our research and finds and have now set up a permanent exhibition of Timna furnaces in its Nehushtan Pavilion.

Although the problems of the Timna furnaces and metallurgy were continuously discussed with many of my colleagues, the responsiblity for the above interpretations and views is entirely my own.

References

Bachmann, H G 1980. Early copper smelting techniques in Sinai and in the Negev as deduced from slag investigations. In *Scientific studies in early mining and extractive metallurgy*, ed. P T Craddock, Occasional Paper No. 20, 103-134. London

Bachmann, H G & Rothenberg, B 1980. Die Verhüttungsverfahren von Site 30. In *Antikes Kupfer*, eds. Conrad & Rothenberg, 215-236

Bamberger, M (In preparation). 'Bronze Age copper smelting'. In *The Bronze Age copper metallurgy in the Arabah*, eds. Bachmann & Rothenberg, Metal in History, vol. 3

Bercovici, A 1978. Flint implements from Timna Site 90. In *Chalcolithic copper smelting*, eds. Rothenberg, Tylecote & Boydell, 16-20

Conrad, H G & Rothenberg, B 1980. *Antikes Kupfer im Timna-Tal, Bochum*, Beiheft 1. Deutsches Bergbau Museum

Merkel, J 1982. 'Late Bronze Age copper smelting based on furnaces excavated in the Timna Valley'. Unpublished Ph.D. thesis, Institute of Archaeology, London University, (to be published in Metal in History, vol. 3)

Rothenberg, B 1972. *Timna*. London, Thames and Hudson

Rothenberg, B 1978. Excavations at Site 39. In *Chalcolithic copper smelting*, eds. Rothenberg, Tylecote & Boydell, 1-23

Rothenberg, B 1979. *Sinai - Pharaohs, Miners, Pilgrims and Soldiers*. Bern, Kummerly and Frei

Rothenberg, B 1980. Die Archäologie des Verhüttungslagers Site 30. In *Antikes Kupfer*, eds. Conrad & Rothenberg

Rothenberg, B 1983. A rock-cut copper smelting furnace in the Timna Valley. *Journal of the Historical Metallurgy Society*, 17/2, 116-118

Rothenberg, B & Lupu, A 1967. Excavations at Timna. *Bulletin Museum Harretz, Tel Aviv*, 9, 53-70, pls. 5-10

Rothenberg, B, Tylecote, R F & Boydell, P J 1978. *Chalcolithic copper smelting*, Monograph No. 1. London, IAMS

Tite, M S, Hughes, M J, Freestone, I C, Meeks, N D, Bimson, M (In preparation). 'Technological characterization of Timna refractory ceramics', (to be published in *Metal in History* vol. 3)

Tylecote, R F 1962. *Metallurgy in archaeology*. London, Edward Arnold

Tylecote, R F 1976. *A History of metallurgy*. London, The Metals Society

Tylecote, R F, Lupu, A & Rothenberg, B 1967. A study of early copper smelting and working sites in Israel. *Journal of the Institute of Metals*, **95**, 235-243

Weisgerber, G 1978. A new kind of copper slag from Tawi Aarja, Oman. *Journal of the Historical Metallurgical Society*, **12**, 40-43

136

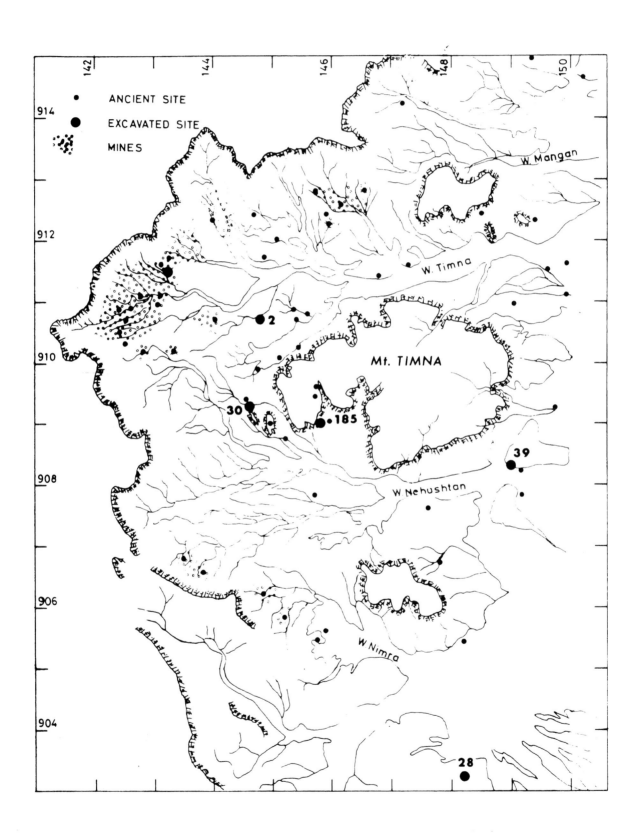

Fig. 1 Map of the Timna Valley and its mining and smelting sites

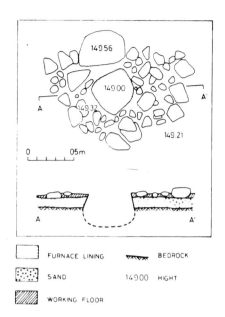

Fig. 2 Plan and section of excavated
furnace at Site 39 (Chalcolithic)

Fig. 3 Reconstruction of Chalcolithic
bowl-furnace

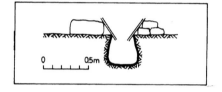

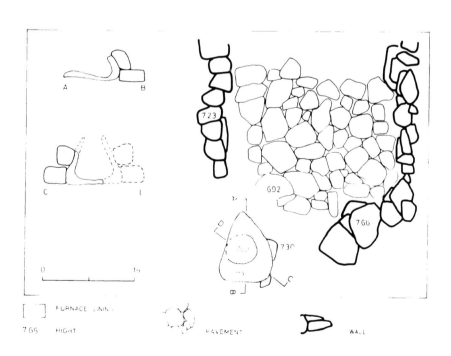

Fig. 4 A Late Bronze Age copper smelting installation: small bowl-furnace
next to stone pavement contained by retaining walls - Site 30,
Locus 50

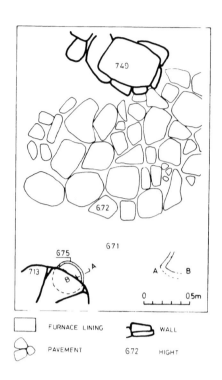

Fig. 5   Late Bronze Age installation -
Site 30, Locus 219. Smelting
furnace underneath large stone
basin (bottom left)

Fig. 6   Late Bronze Age smelting furnace
fragment found *in situ* - Timna,
Site 185

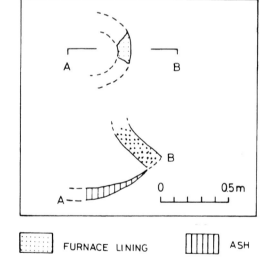

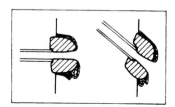

Fig. 7   Reconstructed position of the
small tuyeres found in all
Egyptian New Kingdom (Late
Bronze Age) smelting camps of
the Arabah and Sinai

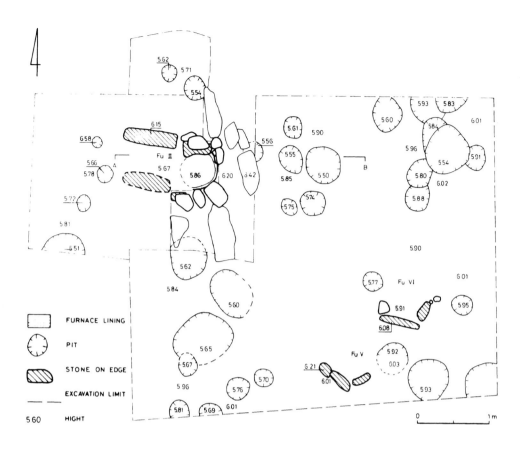

Fig. 8 Timna, Site 2, Area G - Furnace II of Layer I and rock-cut pits and
Furnace V and VI of Layer II

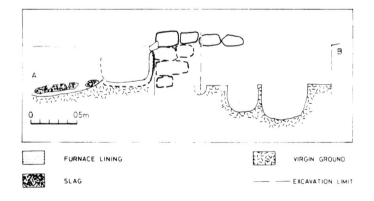

Fig. 9 Schematic section of Furnace II of Layer I, showing stone-built, clay-
lined hearth with slag tapping pit in front. Behind Furnace II two
rock-cut pits of earlier (Layer II) activities.

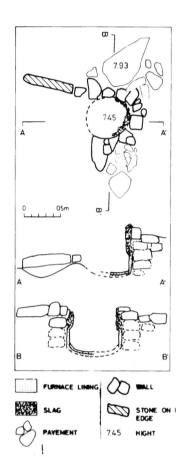

Fig. 10   Stone-built and clay-lined
           Late Bronze Age smelting
           furnace - Site 2, Area E,
           Furnace I

Fig. 11   Furnace IV - Site 2,
           Area C - was a hole-
           in-the-ground bowl-
           type furnace of the
           Late Bronze Age

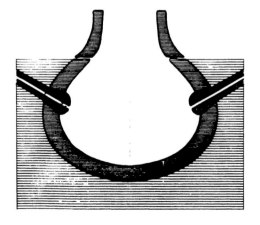

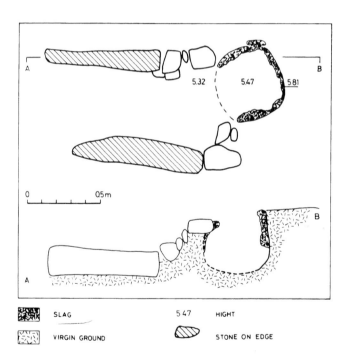

Fig. 12   First reconstruction (1980)
           of Iron Age furnace from
           Timna, Site 30, Layer I

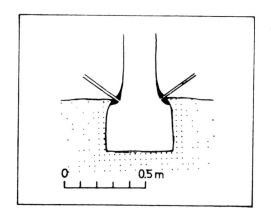

Fig. 13 Revised proposal for reconstruction of Iron Age furnace -
Site 30, Layer I

SLAG TEMPERED CLAY

SINTERED CLAY

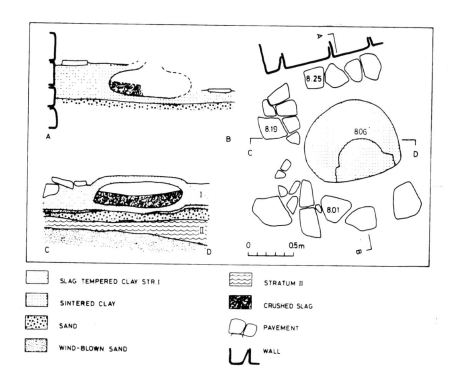

Fig. 14 Timna, Site 30, Locus 10. Furnace IV - Early Iron Age

142

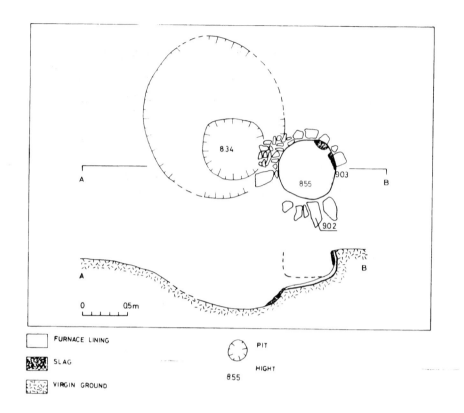

FURNACE LINING

SLAG

VIRGIN GROUND

PIT

HIGHT

855

Fig. 15 Roman Furnace I from Beer Ora (Site 28), second century AD

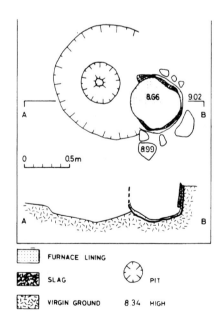

FURNACE LINING

SLAG

VIRGIN GROUND

PIT

8 34 HIGH

Fig. 16 Roman Furnace IV from Beer Ora (Site 28). In the centre of the
        slag pit the core of the cast-in hole found *in situ*

Plate 1   Chalcolithic copper smelting furnace - Timna, Site 39

Plate 2   Late Bronze Age copper smelting furnace - Timna, Site 30, Locus 50

Plate 3   Late Bronze Age copper smelting furnace found underneath a large
          stone basin of a Late Bronze Age potter's workshop

Plate 4   Typical small tuyere found at all Late Bronze Age - Egyptian New
          Kingdom copper smelting sites in Timna, the Arabah and Sinai. Centre:
          slagged tuyere tip; right: side view, showing typical 'slag beard';
          left: slag-free back of the tuyere, showing the ring-shaped socket
          for the bellows tube

Plate 5   Broken Late Bronze Age plate slag from Timna

Plate 6   Later Late Bronze Age copper smelting furnace

Plate 7 Close up of Furnace II, showing tubular tuyere fragments *in situ*
(the lower piece slipped slightly out of its original location)

Plate 8 Heap of broken ring-shaped tapped slag cakes from Timna, Site 2,
Layer I (Later Late Bronze Age)

Plate 9   Stone-built Late Bronze Age smelting furnace,   Timna, Site 2,
          Furnace I (partly excavated)

Plate 10   Furnace IV, Timna, Site 2, Later Late Bronze Age

Plate 11   Curved furnace fragment from Timna, Site 20, Layer I (Early Iron
           Age I)

Plate 12   Large tuyere from Timna, Site 30, Layer I (right) shown next to
           small Late Bronze Age tuyere from same site, Layer II

Plate 13   Early Iron Age furnace,   Timna, Site 30, Layer I, Locus 10.   Stone-
           paved working floor behind and in front of the furnace

Plate 14   Complete tapped slag cake from Timna, Site 30, Layer I (Early
           Iron Age I)

150

Plate 15   Roman copper smelting furnace from the Arabah (Beer Ora, Site 28)

Plate 16   Roman tapped slag from Beer Ora - most have cast-in hole in the
           centre

THE WORKING CONDITIONS OF THE ANCIENT COPPER SMELTING PROCESS

M Bamberger

Israel Institute of Metals, Technion, Haifa, Israel

Abstract

The smelting of copper from oxide ores is a thermo-chemical process. This is carried out by the burning of charcoal, which supplies the heat and carbon monoxide required for the reduction of the ore. During the course of the research the working conditions of the copper smelting were determined. The airflow in a wooden chip heap was measured using a hot-wire anemometer. The experiments indicated that an inclined nozzle, rather than a horizontal one, will ensure higher air supply towards pile bottom. In every case the penetration depth is 10-20 cm which indicates a furnace diameter of 20-40 cm. Extraction experiments were carried out in a 40 cm diameter furnace, using a synthetic ore containing SiO_2, haematite and brass chips as a source of copper. The parameters changed during the experiments were airflow, pre-heating time and ore-to-fuel ratio. The working conditions were found to be as follows: airflow, using six tuyeres with at least 200 l/min each; pre-heating time 1½ hr is sufficient to prevent solidification of slag on furnace bottom; ore-to-fuel ratio up to 2:1.

Keywords: COPPER SMELTING, AIRFLOW, ORE-TO-FUEL RATIO, PRE-HEATING, FURNACE, EXPERIMENTAL ARCHAEOLOGY, METALLURGY

Introduction

The extraction of copper from its oxide ores is done by reducing the oxides using carbon monoxide at high temperatures and creating slag to remove the silica by using a flux. The source of the carbon monoxide and the required temperature is charcoal and iron oxide is used as flux. An essential prerequisite for the success of the process is a high enough temperature in the furnace.

To obtain such conditions optimal air supply should be secured as well as the right quantity of air, rate of ore loading and the ratio of ore to fuel. This paper deals with the experiments that were conducted to study these parameters.

Airflow experiments

The airflow distribution in the furnace is a factor of prime importance for the success of the smelting because places where air does not reach remain cool. Therefore sufficient air penetration should be assured to the bottom and centre of the furnace so as to heat the bottom and obtain an even

combustion throughout the furnace cross section. The measurement of airflow during the combustion process is very complicated and therefore simulation was carried out in a cold state. For the purpose of the experiment
a 30 cm diameter barrel was used. A tuyere, 20 cm from the bottom, was
installed and the airflow distribution in a pile of wood chips (chip size
10-40 mm) 50 cm high was measured.

The experiments were conducted using different air intakes and velocities, through tuyeres ranging in diameter from 15-25 mm. A horizontal
tuyere and a tuyere inclined towards the centre of the bottom of the barrel
were used.

A hot-wire anemometer was used to obtain the air velocity at different
planes above and below the plane of the tuyere.

In Figs. 1-3 examples of the airflow distribution can be seen in the
wood chips pile, when the air supply was rated at 220 l/min. Fig. 1 shows
results for a 25 mm diameter tuyere, placed horizontally. In Fig. 2 the
results for a 15 mm horizontal tuyere and in Fig. 3 an inclined tuyere, 15 mm
in diameter, are shown. The following observations were made:

In all cases the airflow on a plane 10 cm above the tuyere and 10-20 cm
away from the wall was stronger than at a greater distance. This flow was
usually quite uniform across the whole of the cross section examined. The
area where the strongest flow occurs is called the 'turbulence zone' and the
distance over which the flow is reduced is defined as 'depth of penetration'.

The flow in the plane 10 cm below the horizontal tuyere is almost uniform across the entire cross section.

When an inclined tuyere is used then an area where the flow is turbu-
lent before stabilizing is apparent.

The flow in this unstable area is stronger than the same area when a
horizontal tuyere is used.

At the bottom of the furnace (20 cm away from the tuyere) an air movement was detected when using an inclined tuyere but not when a horizontal
tuyere was used.

By increasing the air supply rate at the same tuyere the depth of penetration increased. The flow in the turbulence area increased with an
increased air supply rate, but beyond it no such effect was measured. The
depth of penetration remains fairly constant at different flow velocities.
The average air velocity 20 cm below the tuyere as a function of the air
supply rate is depicted in Fig. 4. From the graph we can see that changing
the air supply rate from 150 l/min to 250 l/min caused a change of 80% in
the air velocity at the bottom of the pile.

The following conclusions can be drawn from the experiments:

A. To ensure an adequate air supply to the burning charcoal the furnace
   radius should be no bigger than the depth of penetration, i.e. 10-20 cm.

B. A tuyere inclined towards the centre of the furnace bottom ensures a
   more substantial air supply to the bottom than a horizontal tuyere.

C. At a fixed air supply rate the tuyere's diameter has no effect because
   it does not change the depth of penetration.

The results of these measurements were used to construct a cylindrical
furnace 40 cm in diameter, 70 cm high, with three 12.5 mm diameter tuyeres
20 cm above the furnace floor, inclined towards the centre of the bottom.

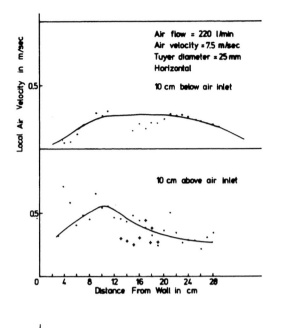

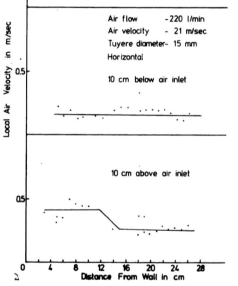

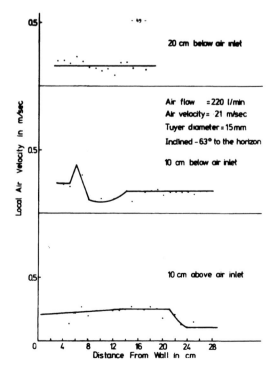

Fig. 1   Local air velocity in medium
         of wood chippings (horizontal
         tuyere 25 mm diameter)

Fig. 2   Local air velocity in medium
         of wood chippings (horizontal
         tuyere 15 mm diameter)

Fig. 3   Local air velocity in medium
         of wood chippings (inclined
         tuyere 15 mm diameter)

Inclined Tuyere

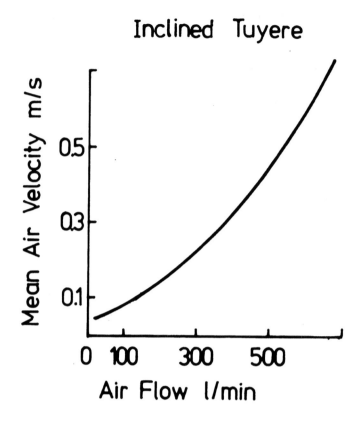

Fig. 4   Average air velocity 20 cm below an inclined tuyere

Description of the smelting experiments

The copper smelting experiments were conducted using synthetic ore containing haematite (10-15% SiO_2 - 70% Fe_2O_3), clean quartz sand, and brass swarf as a copper source. The composition of the synthetic ore was fixed such that the Fe_2O_3: SiO_2 ratio was 2:3. The copper concentration was 25%. Each experiment included the following stages:

1. Preheating, using charcoal

2. Charging the ore and charcoal

3. Heating before tapping

4. Tapping

5. Cooling and dismantling the furnace.

The various stages of the experiments are depicted in the table (p. 155).

Table: Conditions of the smelting experiments

No.	Number of tuyeres	Airflow in tuyere l/min	Rate of charcoal loading kg/hr	Preheat time hr	Ratio of ore to fuel	Time of ore+fuel loading hr	Air pressure on entry mm H2O	Average rate of furnace wall temp.increase °C/hr
1	3	400	21	3.5	1:1	1	–	40
2	6	250	23	3	2:3	2	110	74
3	6	150	13	3	2:3	2.5	40	50
4	6	200	18	3	2:3	2	60	73
5	6	250	23	1.5	2:3	1.5	130	162
6	6	250	23	1.5	2:1	1.5	–	88
7	6	250	23	1.5	3:1	2/3	–	138

The array of experiments was characterized by the fact that each experiment was based on the results of the previous ones and was made in order to examine a certain parameter. Therefore the results of each experiment included the conclusions which determined the conditions of the next experiments.

Results of smelting experiments

The chemical composition of the slag in experiment No. 1 was:

	SiO_2	FeO	Al_2O_3	CaO	Cu
min.	35.9	27.4	0.9	3.4	0.2
max.	46.4	45.3	3.8	9.4	1.2

In all cases the slag is fayalite. The composition of the synthethic ore ensures an excess of iron over what is required for stoichiometry to create fayalite, but silica was also introduced from the furnace walls to the amount required by the composition of fayalite. In experiment No. 1 slag of low viscosity was tapped and at the bottom of the furnace a lump was found containing slag, ore and copper. This slag had solidified on the furnace bottom as well as on the walls (Plate 1). The location of this lump indicates that the slag solidified between the nozzles, this in turn shows that the combustion in the furnace was not uniform.

As a result, all subsequent experiments were conducted in a furnace with six tuyeres.

In experiment No. 2 very liquid slag was tapped into a metal mould. The slag contained copper which sank to the bottom of the slag pool before the slag solidified.

156

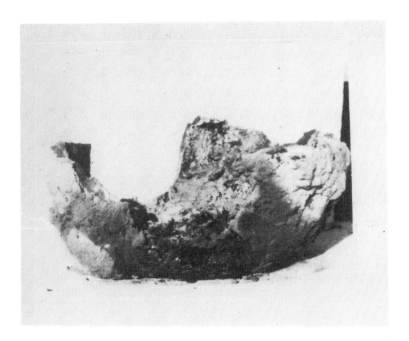

Plate 1   The lower part of the furnace contains charcoal, ore
          and slag on bottom and walls

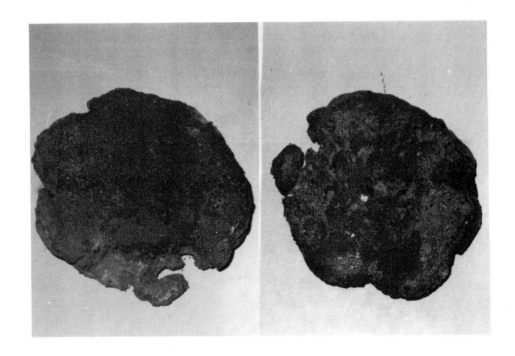

Plate 2   Slag and copper over whole furnace cross section (left:
          top side; right: underside)

In experiments 3 and 4 the effect of the rate of airflow on the smelting was examined. In experiment No. 3 the slag was too viscous and could not be tapped. Despite this no slag solidified on the wall, a fact which indicates the advantages of using six tuyeres as against three.

In experiment No. 4 copper and slag were tapped, but charcoal was found on the bottom indicating that the liquid slag did not reach the bottom. The conclusion was that an airflow rate of 200 l/min per tuyere is a borderline and all subsequent experiments were conducted using 250 l/min flow rate.

Experiment No. 5 showed that preheating time can be shortened to 1½ hours. Experiments 6 and 7 examined the influence of the ore-to-fuel ratio on loading. In experiment No. 6 very liquid slag was tapped. The furnace yielded a 4 cm thick slag 'cake' below which was a 1.5 cm thick copper plate, 30 cm in diameter (Plate 2).

In contrast in experiment No. 7 the slag viscosity was lower and the slag solidified outside the furnace at a faster rate. These facts indicate that the slag temperature in experiment No. 7 was lower than in experiment No. 6. Apart from that no separation between charcoal and slag occurred. This indicates that the 3:1 ore-to-fuel ratio is too high.

The air pressure at entry to the tuyere is very low and can be obtained by manually operated bellows. This indicates that the furnace can easily be operated using manual bellows.

Conclusions

The experiments conducted suggest optimum conditions for smelting copper from its oxide ores by reduction using carbon monoxide and heat. These are:

> Diameter of furnace 20-40 cm;
>
> Up to six tuyeres, inclined towards the bottom;
>
> Airflow rate of 250 l/min per tuyere;
>
> Preheat of 1½ hr;
>
> Ore-to-fuel ratio of 2:1;
>
> Height of furnace 50 cm. The distance between the furnace bottom and the tuyeres' plane was no more than 15 cm.

This data fits the archaeological discoveries in the Timna Valley (Rothenberg 1972 and elsewhere in this volume, page 124) as far as furnace diameter, furnace bottom and slag composition are concerned.

It can therefore be concluded that the ancients used similar methods.

Reference

Rothenberg, B 1972. *Timna, Valley of the biblical copper mines*. London, Thames and Hudson

A FIELDWORK STUDY OF THE ROMANO-BRITISH IRON INDUSTRY IN THE WEALD OF SOUTHERN ENGLAND

J S Hodgkinson[1] and C F Tebbutt[2]

1   20, Spinney Close, Crawley Down, West Sussex and
2   The Pheasantry, Wych Cross, Forest Row, East Sussex
on behalf of the Wealden Iron Research Group

Abstract

A field walking project to assess the situation in relation to geography, geology and density of bloomery furnaces in a given study area of the Weald of southern England is described. This was followed by a number of simple excavations of selected bloomery slag heaps in order to recover pottery for dating purposes. The majority of these sites proved to be Romano-British. Two sites were completely excavated to ascertain furnace types and smelting methods.

Keywords: IRON, SLAG, ARCHAEOLOGY, SMELTING, ROMANO-BRITISH

Introduction

The Wealden Iron Research Group (WIRG) was founded in 1968. Its aim was to continue the pioneer work of Ernest Straker contained in his book *Wealden Iron* published in 1931. For several years the field group members, all amateur archaeologists, concentrated on visiting and surveying all the post-medieval water-powered sites and some of the bloomeries recorded by Straker. In the course of this work a number of new discoveries were made in both categories. Most of the water-powered sites had documentary evidence, but the bloomeries, whether prehistoric, Roman or medieval, were almost without exception evinced only by their waste heaps of characteristic tap slag which is indistinguishable as to date, and by the occasional place name.

On the completion of this survey it was decided to devote several seasons to the study of bloomery furnace sites in their relationship with the geography and geology of the Weald, and to attempt some measure of their density and date. The Weald is well wooded country and field walking was confined to the autumn, winter and early spring when vegetation density would be low. The area of study was defined as 182 km^2 of the central Weald (Fig. 1) which is formed of the sandstones and clays of the Cretaceous Hastings Beds (Fig. 2), (Tebbutt 1981).

Initially the field walking was based on streams near which it was believed all bloomeries were to be found. This assumption proved to be generally but not completely true, and a number were recorded in the course of field walking on hillsides well away from present day streams. We were often indebted to friendly farmers who had noticed slag when ploughing such sites. It became evident that the proximity of iron ore was probably a

160

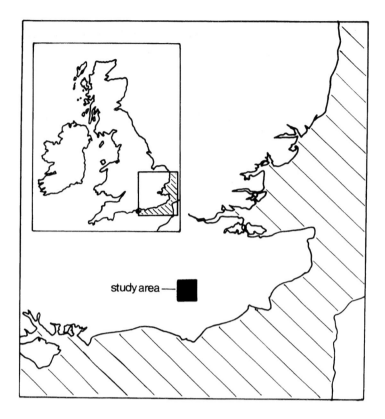

Fig. 1 WIRG study area: location plan

governing factor; the principal source of this ore in the study area is near
the base of the Wadhurst Clay formation, just above its junction with the
Ashdown Sand (Fig. 2). These strata are frequently exposed by relatively
insignificant streams which cut deep ravines, locally known as gills, through
these layers. Many examples were found of small quarries beside these streams
associated with accumulations of bloomery slag, often at different levels of the
same stream for the iron ore in the Wadhurst Clay, which are known to occur.
Iron ore also occurs, though sporadically, in the Tunbridge Wells Sands.

Other essential raw materials for the bloomery process would, at all the
sites, have been easily available. Experiments in furnace construction have
shown that silty clay from the upper layers of the Ashdown Sand is a suitable
material for this purpose and other lithologically similar layers from within
the series can be assumed to have been equally efficient. Raw material for
charcoal making would have been abundant in the wooded Wealden environment.

The probable accuracy of the field walking method was examined. It is
difficult to miss a bloomery site on a stream bank, as some slag inevitably
washes into the stream where it is easily seen. Away from a stream results
are less accurate. The county of Sussex, into which the study area falls,
has a higher percentage of woodland than any other English county, some 18%,
and in the Weald the percentage is probably higher. Much of the farm land
is permanent or ley pasture. On all these areas slag is difficult to locate.
The cultivated land is usually only available for field walking for a short
period after ploughing and as far as possible advantage was taken of this.

Thus it is considered that on the smaller streams where it is believed
most bloomeries are sited, few were missed. On the larger streams in the
main valleys where geological conditions make siting less likely, accumulation
of silt and damming for ponds would have covered all traces of any that were
there. Away from the streams the accuracy of the count is less certain.
Allowing for these factors, the results when plotted were nevertheless impressive. The map (Fig. 2) shows the position of all sites recorded in the study

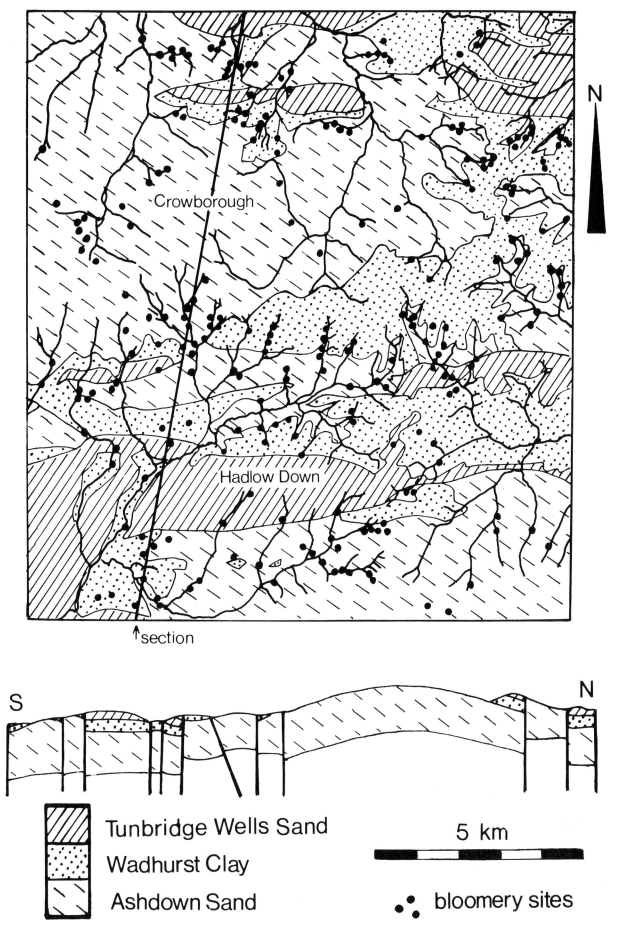

N

S   N

	Tunbridge Wells Sand	5 km
	Wadhurst Clay	
	Ashdown Sand	bloomery sites

Crowborough

Hadlow Down

↑section

Fig. 2 WIRG study area: bloomery sites in relation to geology

area including previous discoveries by Straker (1931) and others, a total of 246 giving an average density of 1.4 per km^2.

The next stage of the study was the difficult one of dating. The bloomery method of iron making in the Weald is known to have extended over a period of at least 1500 years, the slag produced being indistinguishable as to date. Straker (1931) and Money (1974) had recorded the occurrence of pottery among bloomery furnace debris and WIRG excavations had made similar discoveries (Tebbutt and Cleere 1973, Tebbutt 1979). It was therefore decided to conduct a number of simple excavations on slag heaps of sites in the study area where metre-wide trenches would be unlikely to affect the actual furnaces as slag heaps have usually been found sited a short distance away. Sites for this project were selected on grounds of favourable access, absence of tree roots and farm crops, and willingness of land owners. In almost every case this method proved successful and pottery was found among the slag, its presence reflecting the long hours spent away from home by the iron workers during smelting.

By this method of excavation thirty-three sites were dated. To these could be added a further seven in the study area dated by Straker (1931), Money (1971 and 1974) and Cattell (1970 and 1971), making a total of forty. Thus 16% of the recorded sites in the area were dated, a significantly large sample from which to draw conclusions as to the date of the remainder (Tebbutt 1981). Two of the sites could be attributed to the pre-Roman Iron Age and five were given a date within the medieval period. However, the large majority, thirty-three sites, were dated to the period of the Roman occupation of the Weald. This represents some 82% of the dated sites and, if this percentage is projected in respect of all the sites in the study area, the magnitude of the Wealden iron industry in that period must be regarded as very considerable.

Plate 1 Cow Park anvil site; pegs indicate position of wooden rods (Scale 1m)

The study of the pottery by Green (1981) is also illuminating. He recognised most of it to be native East Sussex Ware type, none of which need be
later than the second century AD, and where they were identifiable there was
a predominance of first century AD materials. None of the sherds suggested
a late Roman date.

Of the type of furnace used in the study area we have less knowledge,as
the superstructures have been largely destroyed. Two sites have been excavated
by WIRG, both on the former Ashdown Forest but now enclosed as private land.
The first known as Pippingford Furnace (Tebbutt and Cleere 1973) comprised a
single furnace of the type classified by Cleere (1972) as *domed type 1 ii*.
There was also a re-heating hearth and a nearby domestic hearth where pottery
of East Sussex Ware of first/second century AD date was found. The furnace
was built of clay at one end of a short trench and thus supported by the
trench sides. It was on a levelled platform in a steeply sloping valley above
a small stream. Immediately below at stream level a small opencast quarry
penetrated horizontally into the hillside.

The second excavated site known as Cow Park (Tebbutt 1979) lies some
750 m east of Pippingford Furnace. It is on a valley side approximately
500 m from the nearest stream but close to an active spring with no obvious
signs of mining nearby. It comprised a levelled working area of about six-
teen metres square on which were three furnaces apparently of *domed type 1 ii*
(Cleere 1972), each with a re-heating hearth. In association with these was
an anvil site which had consisted of two posts supporting a flat iron plate,
the whole revetted by a mound of clay reinforced by wooden rods (Plate 1).

Plate 2 Cow Park bloomery furnace (Scale 1m)

164

In addition there was a heap of roasted ore, domestic hearths, and a maze of post holes relating to ancillary buildings. As at the Pippingford site, the furnaces were each built at the end of a short trench supporting the furnace walls and two of them had large stone blocks forming the foundation of the side adjoining the open trench (Plate 2). It was apparent that while some slag had been tapped into the trench much still remained in the furnace after the last smelting.

A third bloomery site within the study area was excavated by Money (1971 and 1974).

In conclusion it is suggested that these results prove that a fieldwork study, supported by sample excavation, can produce worthwhile results provided the area is large enough to give significance to the samples taken. In the survey a large iron industry in the Roman period was revealed, probably officially organised, which seems to have come to an end after the second century AD. Earlier pre-Roman Iron Age techniques of furnace building seem to have persisted, at least on those sites fully excavated. By medieval times the industry appears to have reverted to one supplying small local needs.

Acknowledgements

The authors wish to acknowledge the contribution of D M Meades in helpful discussion and of M Tebbutt in preparing the illustrations.

References

Cattell, C S 1970. Preliminary research findings relating to the bloomery period of the iron industry in the upper basin of the eastern Rother (East Sussex). *Bulletin of the Historical Metallurgy Group*, **4i**, 18-20

Cattell, C S 1971. A note on the dating of bloomeries in the upper basin of the eastern Rother. *Bulletin of the Historical Metallurgy Group*, **5ii**, 76

Cleere, H F 1972. The classification of early iron-smelting furnaces. *Antiquaries Journal*, **52**, 8-23

Green, C M 1981. Pottery report. In Wealden bloomery iron smelting furnaces, C F Tebbutt. *Sussex Archaeological Collections*, **119**, 61-62

Money, J H 1971. Medieval iron workings in Minepit Wood, Rotherfield, Sussex. *Medieval Archaeology*, **15**, 86-111

Money, J H 1974. Iron Age and Romano-British iron working site in Minepit Wood, Rotherfield, Sussex. *Historical Metallurgy*, **8i**, 1-20

Straker, E 1931. *Wealden Iron*. London, Bell

Tebbutt, C F & Cleere, H F 1973. A Romano-British bloomery at Pippingford, Hartfield. *Sussex Archaeological Collections*, **111**, 27-40

Tebbutt, C F 1979. The excavation of three Roman bloomery furnaces at Hartfield, Sussex. *Sussex Archaeological Collections*, **117**, 47-56

Tebbutt, C F 1981. Wealden bloomery iron smelting furnaces. *Sussex Archaeological Collections*, **119**, 57-63

THE POLISH SMELTING EXPERIMENTS IN FURNACES WITH SLAG PITS

Elzbieta M Nosek

Archaeological Museum, Ul. Senacka 3, 31-002 Kraków,
Poland

Abstract

This paper presents the results of smelting
experiments which have been carried out on
reconstructed bloomery furnaces of the types
excavated in the Holy Cross mountain region of
Poland during the past twenty-five years. These
furnaces are typified by the presence of a sunken
slag pit. In addition a knife has been made from
one of the iron blooms and its metallographic
examination is reported.

Keywords: POLAND, IRON, BLOOM, SMELTING, FURNACE,
EXPERIMENTAL, SHAFT, BELLOWS

Introduction

In the northeastern part of the Holy Cross Mountains, which are southwest
of Warsaw, it is possible even today to find traces of an enormous smelting
region which dates back to the period of Roman influence. Since 1955 the
Museum of Archaeology in Cracow has been conducting a systematic research
programme on these remains in close collaboration with metallurgists and
technicians. Basically it consists of making detailed inventories of all
the traces of metallurgical activity, as well as excavating a selection of
sites.

Up to the present date over 3000 separate smelting sites have been
discovered by a combination of aerial photography and surveying on the
ground, and we have estimated that the total number of smelting places in
the area must be well over 4000 since only part of the region has so far
been covered by the inventory programme. Each of these sites contains an
average of about a hundred bloomery furnaces, and it has thus been estimated
that the Holy Cross mountain region must have had about 400,000 individual
bloomery furnaces. Up to the present time excavations have been carried
out at more than 120 of these sites.

The joint research programme has been conducted and supervised by
Professor Kazimir Bielenin, the Deputy Director of the Museum of Archaeology
in Cracow.

The ancient smelting region in the Holy Cross Mountains area has been
radiocarbon dated and the results backed up by ceramic discoveries. Both
these methods indicate dates during the first four centuries of our era.
The excavations have established that two kinds of smelting 'workshop' used
to operate in the Holy Cross Mountains area:

1. In the first place there are small, so-called random slag pits which
    are scattered among the contemporary habitation sites in the settle-
    ments of the time. These are the remains of small shaft furnaces
    with an internal diameter of about 20 cm.

2. The second kind of metallurgical site is represented by large smelting
    establishments. These were deliberately sited away from the living
    areas. The remains consist of slag pits arranged in parallel rows
    with a gap in the middle of each row (Fig. 1). The numbers of furnaces
    on each side of the gap are usually three, four or five and the largest
    site so far surveyed in the Holy Cross Mountains contained 123
    bloomery furnaces.

The bloomery furnace used in the area was of the immersed type, that
is to say its lower part was dug into the soil to a depth of 40-50 cm
(Fig. 2). This part formed a so-called slag pit which served as a recepta-
cle for the slag which formed during the smelting process. Above the slag
pit there was a shaft, probably about 1 m high, with blast holes in its
lower part. The furnace was charged through the opening at the top of the
shaft. The reduction zone was on a level with the blast holes and the
reduced nodules of iron collected here, forming iron sponge. In the
process the metal did not pass through a fluid state but formed a piece of
malleable iron by a solid-state reaction, while the gangue and some of the
unreduced ore formed a slag which dripped down through the charge into the
pit at the bottom of the furnace. This pit gradually filled with slag and
when its upper level reached the reduction zone, the smelting process was
over.

Afterwards the upper part of the shaft was dismantled so as to remove
the metallic sponge, and the lump of solidified slag in the pit was left
in situ. For the next smelting another furnace was built. As a result of
this technology in which the furnace site was only used once, the lumps of
slag remained to be found today, where they bear witness to the number of
smelting operations carried out in the past.

As the excavations raised a number of technological problems which
required further study, a series of experimental iron smeltings has been
carried out since 1960. At the very outset these were rather typical
laboratory experiments. At a later stage it was necessary to transfer this
research work to the region of the Holy Cross Mountains and in a place
called Nova Slupia, which was an ancient iron smelting site, the natural
conditions for our experiments could be provided.

The ore for iron smelting was the hematite ore from the nearby Rudki
mine. It should be mentioned here that the mine had been operating at the
same time as the iron smelting centre. There are remains of ancient mining
such as drifts and passages to be found in the modern mine. Wood samples
taken for carbon-14 analysis from the remains of the timber lining of the
passages put their age between the second and the fourth century of our era.
Gossan, that is to say the iron ore in the oxidised zone, was mined here in
antiquity down to a depth of twenty five metres. These deposits of hematite have the consistency of cream and are mixed with dolomite, siderite
and pyrite. For our experiments we have managed to obtain a certain
amount of hematite with the consistency of cream. The ore analysis is
given in the table.

Table: The chemical composition of the ore used for experimental smelting

ore	concentration %								
	Fe_{tot}	Fe_2O_3	SiO_2	CaO	MgO	MnO	P_2O_5	S	Al_2O_3
hematite raw	52.53	72.77	15.50	0.55	tr	0.85	0.08	1.06	7.77
hematite roasted								0.22	
hematite floated								0.05	

Sulphur content was high and amounted to 1.06%. Before smelting the ore was subjected to a roasting process just as it had been in ancient times. Next to the slag pits the archaeologists excavated traces of original ancient roasters which had been detected by the magnetic surveying method. The ore found in the roasters was maghemite. As regards the charcoal used for these smelting experiments, sampling of the hearths under the slag blocks has established that a mixed charcoal was used consisting of some charcoal obtained from hard woods like beech and oak, and some from coniferous trees like pine, fir and larch. Charcoal has also been identified from poplar and lime trees.

Experimental reductions showed that the optimum ratio of beech to pine was 1:2, and these proportions were maintained throughout the experiments so as not to introduce another variable factor into the smeltings. The charcoal for the experiments was obtained from our own kilns and the size of the pieces used was regulated by sieving to give lumps of about six cubic centimetres in volume.

The first experiments were carried out using an induced draught, without the aid of bellows, in shafts which were forty-five centimetres high. The charge solidified into a block, but did not produce any iron (Fig. 2).

In the next phase of the experiments the height of the shaft was increased to 100-110 cm and the result of this was that the smelting could be carried out with an induced natural blast from four holes in the side of the furnace (Fig. 3).

In the third phase of the experiments an artificial draught was used with a pair of bellows working continuously. This produced a sponge of iron and the slag ran down into the slag pit underneath the furnace.

The furnace for the experimental smeltings was made of clay, mixed with chaff and grass. The thickness of the wall was about ten centimetres. Before the experiments can start, the furnaces have to be air-dried for several days and then heated. For the first few hours the furnace is heated by burning wood which is then followed by charcoal. The duration of the heating had a direct impact on the whole course of our experiments. Our observations have led us to the conclusion that a twelve hour pre-heating results in proper functioning of the furnace. The heated furnace was then charged at the top with beech and pine charcoal in the ratio of 1:2 and with roasted and sifted iron ore. The ratio of the ore to the charcoal was 1:2. The weight of each charge of charcoal and ore was about 2 kg. During the first few hours the charge was fed into the furnace six-seven times per hour, then four times, depending on the rate of consumption of ore and charcoal in the furnace.

As a rule the smelting took twelve hours to complete. During the smelting the temperature inside the furnace was measured by means of Pt-PtRd thermocouples. The distribution of temperature for a two-bellows furnace are indicated in Fig. 4. It is evident that the zone of highest temperature is on the level of the blast hole, and it is there that the iron sponge is formed. The highest temperature recorded in the Holy Cross furnace did not exceed 1400°C. Simultaneously the concentration of oxides of carbon was established by means of an Orsat apparatus.

During the last two-three hours of the smelting no iron ore was charged but the furnace was fed with charcoal. Finally, the shaft was broken to pieces and the iron sponge and slag were left to cool. Unfortunately we have not yet been able to separate hot iron sponge from the slag, which must be separated by hammering when cold.

At present two variations in smelting technique are under investigation. First there is smelting in the tall furnace using an induced natural blast; and second there is smelting in a slightly shorter furnace 80-100 cm high using single bellows. The experiments have investigated the optimum angle for the blast hole and have shown that the smelting is improved if the angle of the blast holes is about 30° downwards with respect to the shaft and if a small hole with a diameter of about 2 cm is made in the opposite side of the furnace wall just above the level of the blast hole (Fig. 5). This allowed some gases to escape when the blast was applied and resulted in an increase in the size of the reduction zone. Figs. 6 and 7 illustrate the sequence of operations, described above, for the experimental smeltings.

No measurements of temperature and gas concentration have been made with the latest experiments, as we did not wish to disturb the progress of the reduction by the presence of thermocouples and sampling tubes. However, laboratory investigation of the iron sponge and slag has been carried out. Plate 1 shows the cross section of three iron sponges made during the experimental smeltings. The proportion of the cross section, which consists of metallic iron, amounts to an estimated 20%. The microstructure of the iron sponge is shown in Plate 2. The metallic iron nodules were surrounded by the oxides-slag mass and sometimes by charcoal. The carburization of the iron was very slight (about 0.15% of carbon). The microstructure of the iron was ferritic with a small amount of cementite III, and was independent of the type of bloomery furnace used. In our experimental smeltings we have never obtained highly carburized metallic iron, apart from the occasional small nodule of iron containing up to 0.8% carbon.

One sponge was then forged into a small bar (Fig. 8) from which a knife blade was made (Fig. 9). The blade of the knife was hardened by carburization and quenching. The following figures illustrate the microstructures of the bar. The carburization was higher because of the forging process and reached 0.4% carbon. In the microphotographs we can observe ferrite, pearlite and non-metallic inclusions. All the metallic inclusions were identified by means of microanalysis. We found many complex inclusions containing iron oxides, silicate and aluminium oxides. Plates 3 and 4 show the microstructures of the blade after the carburization and quenching process (martensite and austenite). A typical complex non-metallic inclusion is shown in Plate 5.

The results of the smelting experiments have led to the conclusion that the ancient iron smelting was carried out using a naturally induced draught without the aid of bellows. This is independently supported by the sites of the furnaces themselves, which are always on sloping or high ground, and also by the absence of clay tuyeres in the excavations, which would have been essential if bellows had been used.

Finally, I would like to add that for some years now the experimental smeltings have been included in an entertainment programme for tourists. Every year in September the 'show' is enacted on the slopes of the Holy Cross Mountains. The smelting is accompanied by folk art fairs and by folk music. The whole event lasts three days and as many as 100,000 people gather around to witness it.

References

Bielenin, K 1965. Badania doswiadczalne nad wytopem zelaza w Kotlince Swietokrzyskiej. *Wiadomosci Archaeologiczne*, **XXXI**, 417-421

Bielenin, K 1970. Komplexe technologischer und archäologischen Forschungen über die frügeschichtliche Eisenverhuttung im Gebiet von "Gory Swietokrzyskie". *Actes due VIIe Congres International des Sciences Prehistoriques et Protohistoriques*, 34-37. Prague

Bielenin, K 1973. Schmelzversuche in Halbeingetieften Rennofen in Polen. *Die Versuchsschmelzen und ihre Bedeutung für die Metallurgie des Eisens und dessen Geschichte*, 62-70. Schaffhausen-Prag

Bielenin, K 1977. Frühgeschichtliches Bergbau und Eisenhuttenwesen in Swietokrzyskie-Gebirge. *Eisenverhuttung vor 2000 Jahren Archäologische Forschungen in der VR Polen*, 11-26. Berlin, Dusseldorf

Bielenin, K 1977. Übersicht der Typen von altertumlichen Rennöfen auf dem Gebiet Polens. *Wissenschaftliche Arbetien aus dem Burgenland*, **50**, 127-146. Eisenstadt

Mazur, A & Nosek, E 1966. Od rudy do noza. *Materialy Archeologiczne*, **VII**, 19-50

Radwan, M 1961. Dalsze probne wytopy w piecykach dymarskich typu swietokrzyskiego. *Kwartalnik Historii Nauki i Techniki*, **IX**, 366-376

170

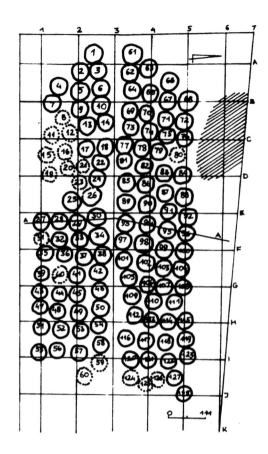

Fig. 1 Stara Slupia smelting site. The remains consist of slag pits
arranged in parallel rows with a gap in the middle of each row

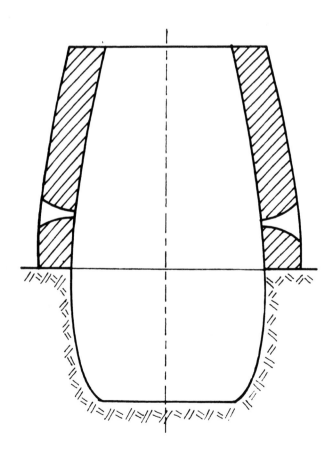

Fig. 2 Reconstruction of the Holy Cross Mountain type of bloomery furnace
with an induced draught (After K Bielenin)

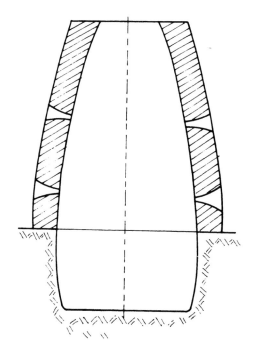

Fig. 3   Reconstruction of the taller
          bloomery furnace with an
          induced natural blast (After
          K Bielenin)

Fig. 4   The distribution of temperature
          for a two-bellows furnace

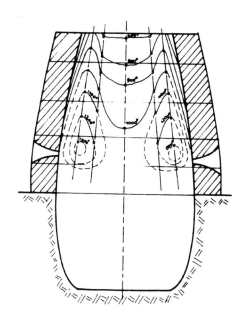

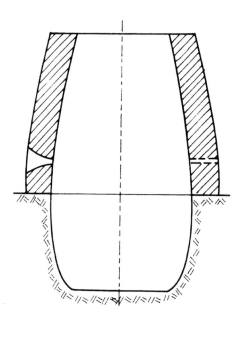

Fig. 5   The bloomery furnace with an
          induced draught (one bellow).
          Note the small hole opposite
          the blast hole

172

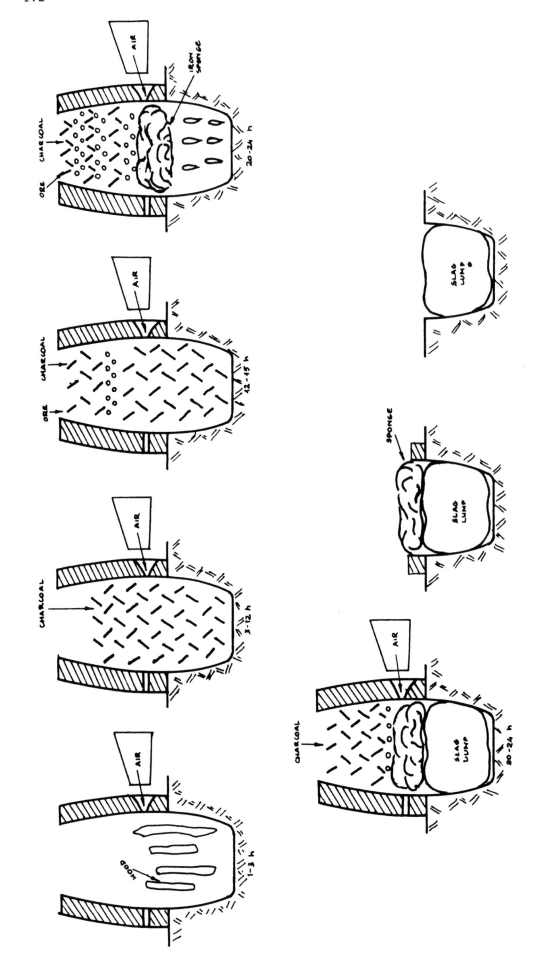

Fig. 6   The experimental smelting scheme for a furnace with an induced draught (one bellow) and a small hole opposite the blast hole

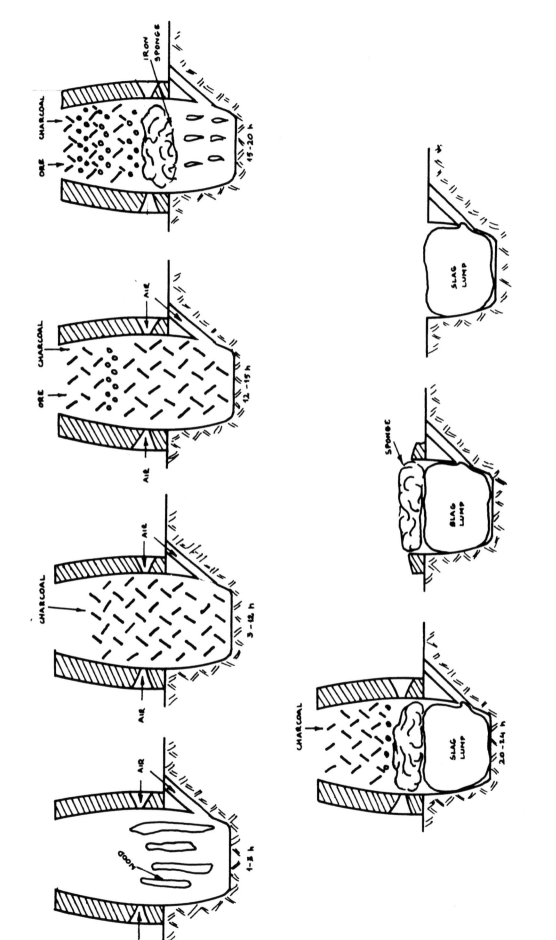

Fig. 7 The experimental smelting scheme for a furnace with an induced natural blast

Fig. 8 The bar forged from the iron sponge

Fig. 9 The knife blade forged from the bar

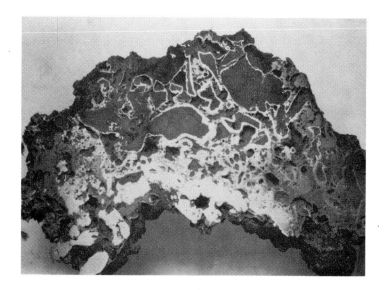

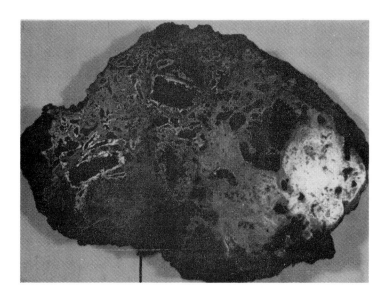

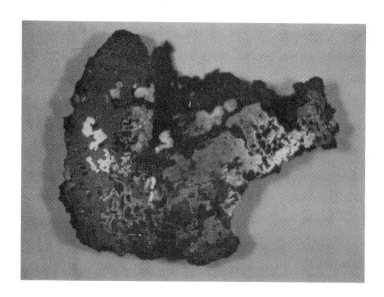

Plate 1 The cross section of three iron sponges from the experimental
         smeltings

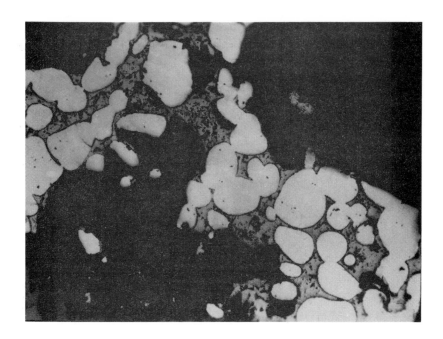

Plate 2   The microstructure of iron sponge.   Nodules of ferritic iron
            surrounded by oxide-slag

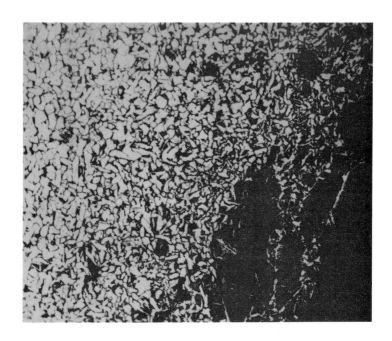

Plate 3   The microstructure of the bar.   Ferrite, perlite and non-metallic
            inclusions.   Magnifications: 250x (etched by nital)

Plate 4   The microstructure of the knife blade after the carburization and
           quenching process.   Martensite and austenite.   Magnification: 400x
           (etched in nital)

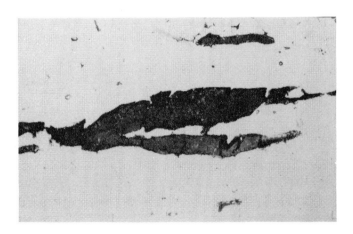

Plate 5   The microstructure of the knife blade.   A complex non-metallic
           inclusion

THE IRON INDUSTRY IN THE IRON AGE AND ROMANO-BRITISH PERIOD

R E Clough

Institute of Archaeology, University of London

Abstract

Current theories concerning the early iron
industry in Britain have their origins deeply
entrenched in nineteenth century ethnography.
The present model of 'bowl' furnace succeeded
by shaft furnace can be seen as far back as 1864
in Percy's volume *Iron and Steel*. From records
of early observations of the industry in India
he categorises furnaces into three types, ranging
from the primitive low hearth of the Agaria to
the more advanced shaft furnaces of Tendukera
whose equivalents can be seen in the European,
the Catalan furnace and the German Stucköfen
(Percy 1864, 255). Similar possibly derivative
models can be seen throughout subsequent archaeological literature: Gowland (1899), Coghlan
(1956) and Tylecote (1962). All accept the small,
non-tapping bowl furnace to be characteristic of
the Pre-Roman industry in Britain just as the
slag tapping shaft furnace is characteristic of
the Roman industry. In accepting this model a
growing body of archaeological, technological
and experimental literature supporting an
alternative interpretation was overlooked.

Keywords: IRON, SMELTING, FURNACE, BOWL FURNACE,
SHAFT FURNACE, STUCKÖFEN, ETHNOGRAPHIC
PARALLEL

Introduction

The nineteenth century saw a notable increase in the volume of literature on
'primitive' peoples and, of significance to this paper, observations of many
small scale iron industries were recorded in both the African and Asian con-
tinents (though it should be noted not always with great accuracy, as the
observers were unfamiliar with the process). Cline in the 1930s (Cline 1937)
collated the majority of studies on African metallurgy. What became obvious
from these works was the bewildering variety of furnace types and practices all
representing the same (bloomery) process. Tylecote attempted to extract a
hard core of information from this literature in his 1965 paper, but found it
difficult to generalise.

The processes, having been categorised into types based on European
standards of primitiveness or efficiency (i.e. size or simplicity), represent
the synchronic variation, that is, the variation of coexisting furnace types.
The archaeologist had inverted this to produce a diachronic array, or temporal
sequence, which was then used as a means of dating. For example, any primitive

structure such as a bowl furnace is interpreted as early in date which in Britain means Iron Age. The site of Gretton (Jackson 1979, 36) provides an excellent example of the process: furnaces found on the site were interpreted as shaft furnaces and therefore, without any dating evidence, were assumed to be Roman on typological grounds. West Brandon (Jobey 1962) on the other hand could be dated to the Iron Age and the furnace structure found there was accordingly interpreted as a bowl furnace.

One of the problems with furnaces is that they leave little in the way of intact structural remains or are found in industrial settlements with little or no dating evidence. As a consquence the type was used to date the furnace and, as mentioned above, a primitive structure was invariably interpreted as early. However, there is now sufficient evidence to refute many erroneous conclusions resulting from such an approach.

The Weald was one of the areas exploited by the Romans for iron, and although the sources (see p. 159) refer to an intensive native iron industry, there was little in the way of securely dated evidence to support the existence of such an industry. However, many of the sites with Roman material probably contain pre-Roman material which has been overlooked. Saxonbury, Footlands and Crowhurst Park (Money 1978, Tebbutt 1973) were until recently some of the few sites with pre-Roman industry. However, over the past decade sites such as Minepit Wood (Money 1974), Pippingford Park, Little Inwoods, Sandyden I (see WIRG 1972 no 3 for carbon-14 dates) and notably Broadfield (Gibson-Hill 1980) can be added to the record of pre-Roman activities.

We are now beginning to appreciate the range of these pre-Roman activities. Broadfield, for instance, has revealed over seventy furnaces of two basic types with a number of variations dated by carbon-14 from the second century BC to the third century AD. Both slag tapping and shaft furnaces here appear to be pre-Roman. Apart from the Weald, Wakerley in Northants (Jackson 1978) is another industrial settlement spanning the late Iron Age/ Roman transition with evidence for production on a moderate scale and slag tapping shaft furnaces.

Brooklands, Surrey, (Hanworth *et al.* 1977) provides some of the earliest evidence of iron production with the remnants of at least twenty-one furnaces excavated. Of these twelve had a base diameter of *c.* 30-35 cm, while another six were about 60 cm in diameter. Furnace F247 from this site can be dated on the basis of pottery to the fifth century BC. F247 has been interpreted as a shaft furnace, possibly with slag tapping facilities, as there was a 1.5 m long burnt trench in front of the furnace. A small amount of tapped slag was found on site along with plano-convex cakes and small pieces. In all only 44 kg of slag was recovered, but this is unlikely to be representative of the scale of production.

The pattern that is now emerging, therefore, is of a growing pre-Roman iron industry with variations in furnace structures and a degree of sophistication which the Romans would absorb and expand in their usual colonial manner. As a consequence of this emerging pattern we need to re-examine structures hitherto identified as small bowl furnaces such as Kestor (Penniman *et al.* 1958, fig. 2) and West Brandon (*c.* 30 cm in diameter), and also the numerous plano-convex cakes of slag (Pl. 1) which are found in many different contexts and attributed to bowl furnaces.

In order to investigate such structures experimental work was carried out by the author using a small cylindrical shaft furnace and a bowl furnace. In the earlier bowl furnace experiments of Wynne and Tylecote (1958) two charging techniques were employed: layered and catalan (Fig. 1). In the

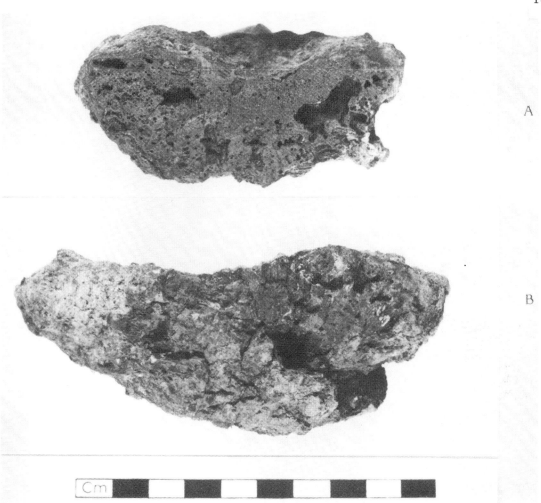

Plate 1 Furnace Bottoms (A) Cow Down (B) Towcester

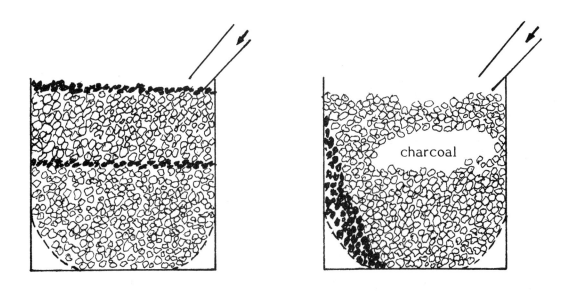

charcoal

Fig. 1 Charging Techniques (diagrammatic only, particle size not representative)

latter method the ore is pre-packed and the charcoal charged between it and the blast.

Wynne and Tylecote found that very little success could be achieved with the layered charge, but considerably more with the pre-packed catalan method, whch succeeded in producing small blooms and a characteristic slag structure (Fig. 2). Similar difficulties have been encountered in most attempts to produce iron in small bowl furnaces (Richardson 1934, O'Kelly 1957).

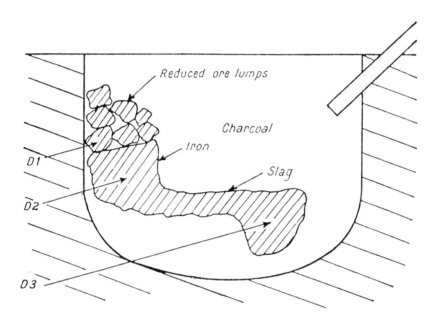

Fig. 2   Smelting iron in a bowl furnace. (D1) Reduced lumps of ore consisting of porous iron and slag. (D2) Agglomerated iron particles;
most of the slag has liquated from the iron which is now the pro-
spective bloom. (D3) Glassy black liquated slag; this forms the
'furnace bottom' (After Tylecote 1962, fig. 44)

One of the furnaces used by the author was a bowl furnace approximately 30 cm in diameter and height. In some experiments a ceramic cover was used to improve smelting conditions but only limited success was achieved. When the furnace remains were examined it became clear why such furnaces are not a practical idea for iron production. Some slag was formed, and in some experiments a small iron bloom, but a major part of the ore remained in a semi-reduced state, being black and magnetic but retaining the original morphology of the ore particles. When the thermodynamic requirements of the bloomery process are examined the efficiency of these small furnaces is easy to explain. Before a sufficiently reducing atmosphere is attained the blast must travel a certain distance through the charcoal. This is to some extent governed by the particle size of the fuel, and in such small furnaces it would result in only a small region with the necessary conditions for the production of iron (Fig. 3). A second point is that the amount of ore which can be pre-packed into these furnaces is small, being in the region of 5-10 kg, since a fuel to ore weight ratio of at least 1:1 is needed for reduction while charcoal occupies about ten times the volume of an equal weight of ore. This, in conjunction with the inherent inefficiency of such a furnace, results in only small quantities of iron being produced (a few hundred grams). This is far below that required to produce some of the early blooms which have been recovered, such as the 3 kg bloom from Wookey Hole (Tylecote 1962), which must originate from a larger furnace. Nor have any slag structures charac-teristic of a catalan charge been found on archaeological sites.

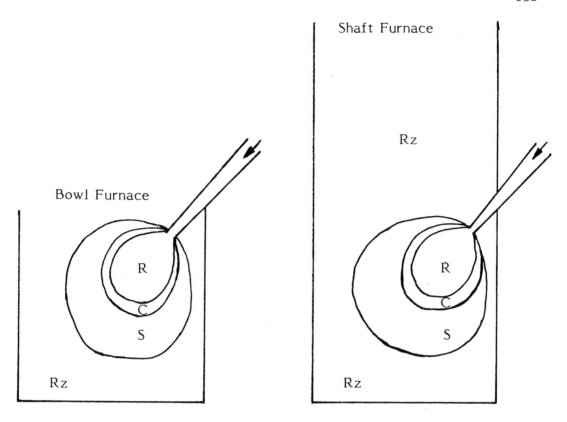

Fig. 3   Furnace Zones

R = Race

C = Combustion Zone $C + O_2 = CO_2$

S = Solution Zone $CO_2 + C = 2CO$

Rz = Reduction Zone (if temperature c. 800°C+)

A further doubt is cast on the use of small bowl furnaces for the production of iron when it is seen that the majority of the furnace bottoms thought to originate from these bowl furnaces (plano-convex) weigh in the vicinity of 0.5 kg. If these were from smelting they would represent at most the production of 200-300 grams of iron - less than an average currency bar!

Furthermore, archaeological evidence suggests that these plano-convex cakes of slag originate from smithing hearths. They are never found in association with furnace structures and come from Iron Age to medieval contexts: Cow Down, Odell, Gussage, Towcester and Wanborough (examined by the author), and Walton (J Haslam personal communication). Many of them have a glassy surface possibly resulting from the combination of fuel ash and slag in the oxidising tuyere zone of the forge. Sectioning of one specimen from the late Iron Age site of Bagendon, Gloucestershire, revealed a green corrosion product which on x-ray diffraction analysis proved to be a tin-bronze corrosion product. This would result from working both iron and bronze in the forge.

The Wiltshire site of Cow Down (Longbridge Deverill) has two such cakes with associated carbon-14 dates of sixth/fifth century BC. Kestor and West Brandon have often been cited as typical bowl furnaces of the Iron Age, but results from experimental work would suggest that both structures are likely to be the bases of shaft furnaces. A layered charge in a non-tapping furnace descends to give a characteristic structure: a furnace bottom often several kilograms in weight (the extreme represented by the slag pit furnaces which produce blocks of slag weighing up to 200 kg) and at times an accumulation of slag under the tuyere (or eating away of the furnace lining under the tuyere). Such an accumulation can be seen in the Kestor remains, while at West Brandon the remaining bowl had layers of charcoal, a bulk of

5 Cm

Plate 2   Experimental Furnace Bottom: 'Catalan' charge

slag and more charcoal covered with collapsed superstructure. The diameter
of this furnace (c. 30 cm) necessitates a shaft for successful operation.
(Note that the final diameter of the furnaces found at Gretton also necessitates a shaft superstructure). Furnace diameters of approximately 30 cm and
60 cm seen at the site of Brooklands are typical of many sites. From experimental work and thermodynamic considerations the 30 cm furnaces must have a
shaft superstructure (if used for smelting), while it is less certain what
form the superstructure of the larger furnaces (60 cm) would have required.

It is essential that the slag structures are closely examined as they
can provide additional information regarding the processes occurring on site.
Gussage All Saints, Dorset, produced the remains of a bronze-casting foundry
with thousands of mould and crucible fragments for the casting of horse har-
ness bits. The site report also notes a small bowl furnace for the production
of iron (Wainwright 1976, 1979 and 1973). Examination of the slag from the
site revealed some 700 kg of slag with pieces of varying size ranging up to
7 kg. These were certainly not the by-products of a small bowl furnace as
most of the pieces had a plate structure from being tapped out of the furnace.
The iron industry had been dismissed in a sentence in the shadow of the more
impressive bronze industry.

The conclusions put forward here are, in summary: that prior to the Roman
period there is little to suggest that small bowl furnaces were used for iron
smelting; that Britain had an expanding iron industry based on variety of
furnace types; and that both slag tapping and shaft furnaces were pre-Roman
innovations.

These conclusions should come as no surprise when the European background
is examined: the evidence from the continent, such as that from the Holy Cross

Mountains, Poland, (Bielenin 1973), Manching in Bavaria (Jacobi 1974), and Magdalensberg, Carinthia, (Alföldy 1974) must be considered. It is generally accepted that the wealth of the Hallstatt and La Tène world was based on the exploitation and trade of mineral resources, specifically salt, copper and iron, and their efficiency is certainly reflected in the iron industry. At Noricum in Carinthia there is evidence (as there is in the Holy Cross Mountain sites) for intensive exploitation of the rich iron resources throughout the La Tène and Roman periods with possible beginnings in Hallstatt times. Widespread trading of Noricum iron is well attested (*ibid.* p. 14, 28, and 44).

At Manching, Bavaria, a Celtic oppidum, there is evidence for extensive iron production with remains of slags, furnaces and an impressive array of iron artefacts (Jacobi 1974, pls. 1-81). Slag remains suggest that the furnaces were slag tapping shaft furnaces (*ibid.* pl. 101). Numerous cakes of smithing slag were also found (*ibid.* pls. 102-105), all indicating that a sophisticated iron industry existed at this oppidum for over 200 years of La Tène settlement before the time of Caesar.

The Polish sites such as Masowien and the Holy Cross Mountains have long been famous for their scale of operations: thousands of pit type furnaces located at hundreds of production sites provided iron for local requirements and export (see p. 165).

In brief, this was the pre-Roman continent in frequent contact with Britain whose peoples were therefore acquainted with a technology of far greater sophistication than that with which they are generally credited. Given this level of continental sophistication it is not surprising to find that the iron industry in Britain was also developed on a moderate scale.

This would also be in accordance with the historical observations of Caesar (*BG* 5.12), who found an industry on a limited scale (by his standards), and those of Strabo, writing a half-century later of an intensive iron industry which was exporting to the continent (Geography 4.5.2). The archaeological evidence also supports a developed local industry, as can be seen in the occurrence of large hoards of currency bars dating from the second century BC. Such hoards suggest production in excess of local requirements and trade.

Although it is beyond the scope of this paper to discuss the furnaces or sites in greater detail, it is likely that the furnace type adopted or used was influenced by the scale of the operation. Close examination of some of the ethnographic literature clearly indicates that furnace requirements for a single village producing on a seasonal basis were very different from those of an industrial site where iron was produced for a larger area and/or export, and thus we would expect to find a range of furnace types reflecting a range of requirements rather than a specific type of furnace being used by all iron producers at any given period.

Evidence from Britain should be regarded in this light because it is obvious that the type and size of settlement relates to the industrial remains from the site. This is not to say that settlement type can be rigidly correlated with furnace type, but that a small farmstead or village unit may only have a single idiosyncratic furnace, while an organised industrial site such as some of the Roman establishments on the Weald are much more likely to have a greater uniformity in furnace construction.

References

Alföldy, G 1974. *Noricum*. London, RKP

Bielenin, K 1973. Slag pit type furnace in ancient Europe (Polish). *Materialy Archaeologiczne*, **14**, 5-102

Cline, W 1937. *Mining and metallurgy in negro Africa*, General series in Anthropology. Menasha, Wisconsin

Coghlan, H H 1956. *Notes on prehistoric and early iron in the Old World*. Occasional Papers in Technology. Pitt Rivers Museum

Gibson-Hill 1980. Cylindrical shaft furnaces of the early Wealden iron industry. *Journal of the Metallurgical Society*, **14**(1), 21-27

Gowland, W 1899. The early metallurgy of copper, tin and iron in Europe. *Archaeologia*, **56**, 267-322

Hanworth, R & Tomalin, D J 1977. *Brooklands, Weybridge: the excavation of an Iron Age and medieval site*, Res. Vol. Surrey Archaeological Society No 4

Jackson, D A 1979. Roman ironworking at Bulwick and Gretton. *Northants Archaeology*, **14**, 31-37

Jackson, D A 1978. Excavations at Wakerley, Northamptonshire 1972-1975. *Britannia*, **9**, 115-242

Jacobi, G 1974. Werkzeug und Gerät aus dem Oppidum von Manching. In *Die Ausgrabung in Manching*, W Kramer, Band 5

Jobey, G 1962. An Iron Age homestead at West Brandon, Durham. *Archaeologia Aeliana*, **40**, 1-31

Money, J 1974. Iron Age and Romano-British iron-working in Minepit Wood, Rotherfield, Sussex. *Bulletin of the Historical Metallurgical Group*, **8**(1), 1-20

Money, J 1978. Aspects of the Iron Age in the Weald. In *Archaeology in Sussex to AD 1500*, ed. P L Drewett, Research Report 29, 38-40. Council for British Archaeology

O'Kelly, M J 1957. Review of Coghlan 1956. *Cork Historical and Archaeological Society*, 1957-8, 59

Penniman, T K *et al*. 1958. Ancient metallurgical furnaces in Great Britain to the end of the Roman occupation. *Sibrium*, 1958, 97-127

Percy, J 1864. *Metallurgy: iron and steel*. London, John Murray

Pleiner, R 1980. Early iron metallurgy in Europe. In *The coming of the age of iron*, eds. Wertime & Muhly

Richardson, H 1934. Iron, prehistoric and ancient. *American Journal of Archaeology*, **38**(4), 555-583

Tebbutt, C F 1973. Wealdon fortified camps and the iron industry. *Wealden Iron Research Group*, winter, 11-12

Tylecote, R F 1962. *Metallurgy in archaeology*. London, Edward Arnold

Tylecote, R F 1965. Iron smelting in pre-industrial communities. *Journal of the Iron and Steel Institute*, **197**, 340-345

Wainwright, G & Spratling, M 1973. The Iron Age settlement of Gussage All Saints. *Antiquity*, **48**, 109-130

Wainwright, G *et al.* 1976. Gussage All Saints - a chronology. *Antiquity*, 50, 32-39

Wainwright, G 1979. *Gussage All Saints: an Iron Age settlement in Dorset*, DoE, Arch. Report No 10. London, HMSO

Wynne, E J & Tylecote, R F 1958. An experimental investigation into primitive iron smelting techniques. *Journal of the Iron and Steel Institute*, 190, 339-348

PRELIMINARY INVESTIGATIONS OF SOME METALLURGICAL REMAINS AT KNOSSOS, HELLENISTIC TO THIRD CENTURY AD

E Photos[1], S J Filippakis[1] and C J Salter[2]

1 N R C "Demokritos", Aghia Paraskevi, Attiki, Greece
2 Metallurgy Department, Oxford University, Oxford

Abstract

The excavation of the post-Minoan levels above the Unexplored Mansion of Knossos, Crete, site of continuous settlement activity for a good part of fourteen centuries, brought to light among other finds a large variety of metal objects dating predominantly to the Hellenistic and Roman times. Among these objects were iron slag and furnace remains which have been analysed by a variety of methods. The degree of weathering in the slags was quite extensive while their high content in calcium led to the formation of calcium-rich crystalline and glassy phases. The slag microstructure was similar for most samples despite their external morphology, thus rendering their identification as smelting or smithing-slags difficult. . Analyses of various furnace wall fragments gave interesting insights into the construction of contemporary melting furnaces.

Keywords: KNOSSOS, HELLENISTIC, ROMAN, IRON SLAG, SMELTING, SMITHING, FURNACE REMAINS, METALLURGY

Introduction

Until recently the primary sources of information concerning the production and manufacture of iron in Greece have been the references to such operations by ancient authors as well as the representations on Attic vases of metal-smith's workshops. It is only a little over a decade since the first attempt was undertaken to compile all that was known on the subject of mining, smel-ting, and forging of iron (Pleiner 1969). In his concluding remarks Pleiner emphasized that ancient methods of production and manufacture of the raw metal would only be elucidated through the analytical and metallographic investigation of iron artefacts and slags. Following his suggestion, a number of studies have appeared relating to the nature and type of metallur-gical operations carried out from Mycenaean to Classical times in various parts of Greece (Conophagos and Papadimitriou 1981a, Rostocker and Gebhard 1981, Varoufakis 1982).

Through these and comparable studies in other regions, it became apparent

that if the development of metallurgical operations was to be reconstructed
for any particular site a more unified methodology would have to be undertaken. Apart from the furnace remains, the type of ores available, the
archaeology and morphology of the area as well as the metal artefacts would
all have to be considered appropriately.

With this approach in mind we turned our attention to the metallurgical
remains of the Unexplored Mansion (UM) at Knossos. The UM is the site of a
Minoan mansion which after the end of the Bronze Age was continuously occupied until the third century AD.

Knossos is supposed to have been a quite prosperous town during both
the Hellenistic and Roman times, as evidenced by the quantity of pottery and
other finds (Sackett 1973, Sackett and Jones 1979). Both the Hellenistic
and the early Roman occupation levels suffered severe damage from earthquakes
and man-induced causes; the levels dating to the second and third centuries
AD are the best preserved. The large number of the UM post-Minoan metal
artefacts, including metalsmith's tools, are currently being catalogued and
investigated (Branigan pers. comm.).

This study concerns the examination of some of the metallurgical remains
of the UM site at Knossos. Twenty-four samples of iron slag representing a
third of the total (c. 35 kg) of iron and bronze melting slags were analysed.
They date from the Hellenistic and Roman times and the investigated slags
were in the shape of furnace bottoms as well as small cakes and fragments,
weighing from a few grams to 2.5 kg. They varied from a few cm to 15-20 cm
in diameter and were of different degrees of porosity and were dark-brown-
to-black in colour, covered with a calcareous layer. In addition to the
iron slags, a number of furnace remains such as furnace walls and wall linings were analysed and will be discussed subsequently.

Results

Analyses of the slags were carried out by a number of methods. X-ray diffraction was applied to the identification of minerals and various crystalline phases within the slag while x-ray fluorescence was used to provide
elemental qualitative information. Atomic absorption spectrometry gave bulk
quantitative elemental concentrations for some of the samples and optical
emission spectroscopy was used for the chemical analysis of the non-metallic
furnace remains. Finally the scanning electron microprobe analyser (SEM-
microprobe) provided visual inspection and analyses of various phases within
the slag microstructure.

Of the twenty-four analysed samples of iron slag only three (small fragments) proved to have fayalite (see Plate 1). The phases encountered in their
slag microstructure of these include iron oxide globules (wüstite, FeO), the
elongated crystals of fayalite (Fe_2SiO_4) as well as a glassy phase (Bachmann
1982). To understand how the slag solidified in the phases that are evident
in each sample, one makes use of a ternary phase diagram. In the case of
these three slags the most appropriate phase diagram was expected to be the
$FeO-SiO_2$-anorthite diagram proposed by Morton and Wingrove (1969). These
slags had a large percentage of wüstite (between 20 and 40% by weight) and
were quite dense. Apart from the major elements (iron, silicon, aluminium,
calcium) minor elements were also present and distributed themselves between
the various phases. The anorthitic glass was rich in potassium, phosphorus
and sulphur while the fayalite contained mostly magnesium and manganese.

However, as already mentioned, this typical fayalitic slag microstructure
was only evident in a small number of the samples analysed. The majority dis-

Table 1   SEM-microprobe analyses of the kirschensteinite phase within some of the Knossos iron slags

	Na$_2$O	MgO	Al$_2$O$_3$	SiO$_2$	P$_2$O$_5$	SO$_3$	K$_2$O	CaO	MnO	FeO
24a	.44	.56	8.92	35.02	3.75	.19	1.72	21.83	–	23.97
34d	.28	.63	11.60	34.59	.41	.69	3.64	23.20	.40	24.57
44h	.23	.66	2.34	25.57	9.53	.81	.97	17.38	–	42.50
48b	.40	1.20	6.85	38.52	1.28	.40	3.29	23.74	.56	23.97
49g	.27	1.15	5.39	30.53	4.42	.45	1.01	30.83	–	25.95
55a	.37	2.59	6.92	25.04	4.50	.38	1.12	23.24	.39	35.42
109b	.46	2.25	4.62	33.52	.41	.34	.95	25.18	–	31.60

192

Plate 1 Fayalite grains with wüstite globules in an anorthitic glassy matrix

played three different types of microstructure as seen through the SEM-micro-probe: a) kirschensteinite, wüstite and a glassy phase; b) a calcium silicate glass with very little wüstite; and c) corroded iron oxides (mainly heamatite) and silica. Each one of the above types will be discussed separately. The appearance of the first two seems to be due to the high calcium content (up to 30% by weight). High calcium amounts have recently been reported to be present in slags from Isthmia, near Corinth (Rostocker & Gebhard 1981) as the result of ground water deposition. This could indeed have been the case with the Knossos material, since the area is rich in deposits of calcareous marls. Nevertheless the evidence from the SEM-microprobe proved otherwise: calcium was found to be present in a well crystallized phase of kirschenstei-nite, an olivine with the formula of $Fe.CaSiO_4$; the same phase was also detected with x-ray diffraction. Its composition analysed with the SEM-micro-probe is shown in Table 1 for a number of slags. The high calcium content required the use of another phase diagram, the $FeO-CaO-SiO_2$ (Levin *et al*. 1974). This diagram shows that this mineral has a relatively low melting point which is compatible with the range of temperatures existing in the various iron working processes of the period. The other mineral present was wüstite together with a glassy phase.

Further evidence that calcium was not deposited by ground waters comes from the appearance of a small number of samples of a second type with a glassy calcium silicate phase and very little wüstite.

Together with the above two types of microstructure, a third type with corroded iron oxides plus silica was often identified with the SEM-microprobe. This mixture was thought to have originated from the corrosion of wüstite crystals or metallic iron with further deposition of silicates by ground waters. However, the appearance of up to 30% silica in some samples rendered this assumption rather unlikely. It was also unlikely that this phase was the result of weathering of fayalite into iron oxides and silica as similar microstructures were evident within corroded iron nails of the same period which could have not contained fayalite.

As indicated previously, the twenty-four samples analysed consisted of furnace bottoms of varying sizes as well as small fragments. Samples of both types showed mainly microstructures of kirschensteinite and wüstite as well as corroded iron oxides and silica. Thus, slags with differing external morphology (furnace bottoms and small fragments) show evidence of similar microstructure. On the basis of this observation and at this preliminary stage of investigation it is rather difficult to identify any of the slags as the products of different metallurgical operations, namely smelting or smithing.

It is quite possible that both the slag furnace bottoms and small fragments may have originated from primarily smithing operations, but before any conclusions are reached it is essential to investiage firstly the origin of the high calcium content and its role in the formation of slag, and secondly the nature and mechanism of the weathering process. When these questions have been answered it may then also be possible to establish whether essentially the same type of metallurgical operations pertaining to the manufacture of iron were taking place during both Hellenistic and Roman times.

The metallurgical remains at Knossos included six furnace remains, the analyses of which are shown in Table 2. Three of these had a characteristic layered structure consisting of a beige calcareous layer (Pl. 2, section 1), a green malachite layer, another beige layer of similar composition to the first, and a grey layer. The two beige layers are of highly refractory clays while the grey is more calcareous (Table 2). The neighbouring grey and beige must have been mixed while both were still dry and thus fused well during firing. The three fragments (A3, A4, A6) were too thick to have belonged to crucibles so it is assumed that they may have been part of a furnace wall. This furnace was probably used for the melting/alloying of copper and was similar to those presented on Attic vases such as the foundry cup (Conophagos & Papdimitriou 1981b). It may have been designed as a cupola type furnace.

Plate 2   Layered structure of furnace wall (sample A3):

     (1) Beige calcareous layer; relining

     (2) Green malachite-rich-slagged lining

     (3) Beige layer similar in composition to (1); initial lining

     (4) Grey; main furnace wall

Table 2 Chemical analyses by Optical Emission Spectroscopy of furnace walls and linings

		%Al$_2$O$_3$	%CaO	%MgO	%Fe$_2$O$_3$	%TiO$_2$	%Na$_2$O	%MnO$_2$	%Cr$_2$O$_3$	%NiO
A1	wall frag.	14.3	3.5	.7	7.7	.44	.66	.04	.04	.01
A3a	wall lining beige	14.0	>30*	2.0	4.7	.60	.04	.07	.04	.01
A3b	wall grey	9.8	>30	1.5	3.5	.45	.04	.04	.03	.01
A4a	wall lining beige	10.1	25.0	3.6	2.9	.57	.02	.05	.02	.01
A4b	wall grey	13.6	>30	2.0	5.1	.61	.04	.05	.04	.02
A6a	wall lining beige	12.8	29.0	7.4	5.0	.87	.04	.07	.05	.02
A6b	wall grey	11.7	>30	2.1	3.8	.56	.55	.05	.03	.01
A7	wall frag.	10.5	2.0	.8	7.1	.68	1.55	.04	.01	-
A9	wall frag.	15.5	1.5	.7	7.3	.82	.25	.22	.02	.04

*>: greater than

without crucibles for the melting of large quantities of bronze (Tylecote 1976). Such a furnace would have been heated using a pure charcoal charge and when the working temperature was achieved bronze and charcoal would be added. Slag would form at the sides of the furnace as the fuel ash reacted with the furnace lining; hence it was necessary to reline the furnace wall using clay of the same composition as the initial lining.

Another piece of furnace remains (sample A9) proved to be equally interesting, showing evidence of mending of the furnace wall while the furnace was still in operation. Apparently a leak must have developed through which the bronze must have run out (Plate 3). Having noticed the hole and the possible loss of metal one can picture the bronzesmith rushing to patch the furnace with fresh clay. It would be unlikely that a smith would have bothered to patch a hole in a melting furnace that made use of crucibles, as such a leak would indicate that the crucible itself had failed. Analysis showed 2% tin within the copper grains but the corrosion layer contained a higher percentage in the form of tin chloride.

Plate 3   Section of a furnace wall (A9). Bronze leaked out at the point
          above the furnace mending. Black holes indicate locations from
          which drillings for analyses were taken

The interpretation of the furnace representations on Attic vases has been the subject of many studies (See Oddy & Swaddling p. 43). The examination and analysis of the furnace wall fragments from the UM dating to the Hellenistic and Roman times may be a step forward to the better understanding of the subject not only through the interpretation of representations on vases but through the material itself.

Conclusions

These are the preliminary results of the examination of metallic and non-metallic furnace remains from the Unexplored Mansion of Knossos dating from the Hellenistic period to the third century AD. The relatively small number of iron slags analysed at both the bulk and microstructure level brought to light a number of questions. Calcium and silicon are present in high percentages within the various phases in the majority of slags. Although silica, together with corroded iron oxides, may be the product of weathering through extended burial, the presence of high amounts of calcium cannot be explained in the same way. Calcium appears in a glassy (calcium silicate) phase as well as in a crystalline (kirschensteinite) phase, a fact which suggests that calcium was present when the slag was formed. The understanding of the role of weathering together with the mechanism of formation of the above phases will possibly lead to the identification of the metallurgical processes that created these slags, i.e. smelting or smithing.

The study of the other type of metallurgical material, namely furnace wall fragments, has provided for the first time direct evidence for the construction of furnaces used in the melting and alloying of copper. Examination points to the use of a small furnace, resembling the cupola type, which would be relined from time to time as soon as the initial lining was slagged away. The furnace wall remains date to Hellenistic times and onwards, i.e. later than the appropriate representations on the well known Attic vases. The finds suggest that similar types of furnaces may also have been in operation at Knossos.

Acknowledgements

The authors wish to acknowledge the kind assistance of Dr R Jones of the British School of Athens for the chemical analysis of the non-metallic furnace remains. Thanks are also due to the excavator Mr L H Sackett and Prof K Branigan for the helpful discussions on the UM stratigraphy and metallurigcal operations as well as to Dr K Apostolakis and Mr J Elpiziotis, N R C Demokritos, for their valuable technical assistance.

References

Bachmann, H G 1982. *The Identification of slags from archaeological sites*, Occasional Publication No. 6. London, Institute of Archaeology

Conophagos C & Papadimitriou G 1981a. La technique de production de fer et de l'acier par les Grecs anciens en Attique pendant la periode classique. *Praktika tis Akadimeias Athenon*, **56**, 148-172

Conophagos C & Papadimitriou G 1981b. Interpretation du pot place par les grecs anciens sur le gueulard des fours pendant la periode classique, *Praktika tis Akadimeias Athenon*, **56**, 191-211

Levin, E M Robins, C R & McMurdie, H F 1974. *Phase diagrams for ceramicists*, ed. M K Reser, 3rd ed. Columbus (Ohio), The American Ceramic Society

Morton, G R & Wingrove, J 1969. Constitution of bloomery slags, Part I: Roman. *Journal of the Iron and Steel Institute*, **207**, 155´-1564

Pleiner, R 1969. *Iron working in ancient Greece*. Prague, National Technical Museum

Rostocker, W & Gebhard, E R 1981. Iron smelting at Isthmia. *Journal of the Historical Metallurgy Society*, 15(1), 41-43

Sackett, L H 1973. Post-Minoan occupation about the unexplored mansion. *Annual of the British School of Athens* 1972-1973, 50-71

Sackett, L H & Jones, J E 1979. Knossos: A Roman house revisited. *Archaeology,* 32(2), 18-27

Tylecote, R F 1976. *A History of metallurgy.* London, The Metals Society

Varoufakis, G. 1982. 'The Origin of Mycenaean iron'. In *Early metallurgy in Cyprus 4000-500 BC*, eds. J D Muhly, R Maddin & V Karageorghis. Nicosia

THE INVESTIGATION OF A SMALL HEAP OF SILVER SMELTING DEBRIS FROM RIO TINTO, HUELVA, SPAIN

P T Craddock[1], I C Freestone[1], N H Gale[2], N D Meeks[1], B Rothenberg[3] and M S Tite[1]

1 British Museum Research Laboratory, London
2 Department of Geology and Mineralogy, Parks Road, Oxford
3 Institute for Archaeo-Metallurgical Studies, Institute of Archaeology, 31-34 Gordon Square, London

Abstract

The remains of ancient metallurgy are prolific: enormous slag heaps cover the ancient smelting sites. Only rarely are the remains still *in situ*, more usually the furnace fragments, other refractories and even spillages of the metals are buried in slag heaps, an apparently unpromising source of information. In fact their burnt and vitrified state is an accurate record of the actual process within the furnace. This paper describes the scientific investigation of the remains from one small but typical heap at Rio Tinto.

Keywords: SILVER, IBERIAN, RIO TINTO, SPAIN, SMELTING, ROMAN, FURNACE, REFRACTORY, CUPELLATION, SLAG, TEMPERATURE

Introduction

The gigantic heaps of the debris of ancient metal production at Rio Tinto are only matched in scale by the modern open cast mining. In a very few years this will bodily remove a mountain, the old village of Rio Tinto and almost all of the ancient remains. During the last eight years the IAMS, greatly supported by the present Rio Tinto Company, has been carrying out a programme of survey and excavation above and below ground of the ancient remains prior to their removal. The team has already found extensive evidence of metal production, mainly for silver from the Late Bronze Age, spreading out from the Corta Lago area (Fig. 1). The main silver ore was jarosite which consists of mixed hydrated sulphates of various metals (Williams 1950); this silver ore was most probably one of those mentioned by Pliny (Gale *et al.* 1980). The technology seems to have changed little through the centuries from the Late Bronze Age until the appearance of the Romans.

The Romans seem to have been much more concerned with the day to day running of the enterprise in that they developed processes and dramatically increased output, as documented by much more extensive slag heaps remaining both from silver and copper production. The task of the IAMS, led by Professor B Rothenberg, has been to chart the spread of metal working and the changes in technology at Rio Tinto over the centuries. The first volume of the survey dealing with the whole of the province of Huelva has recently been published (Rothenberg & Blanco-Freijeiro 1981). The purpose of this paper is to illustrate the range of information stored within the debris itself and how this may be revealed by scientific investigation. The material from just one small heap of second-first centuries BC date is used to exemplify the exciting potential of such apparently unrewarding debris.

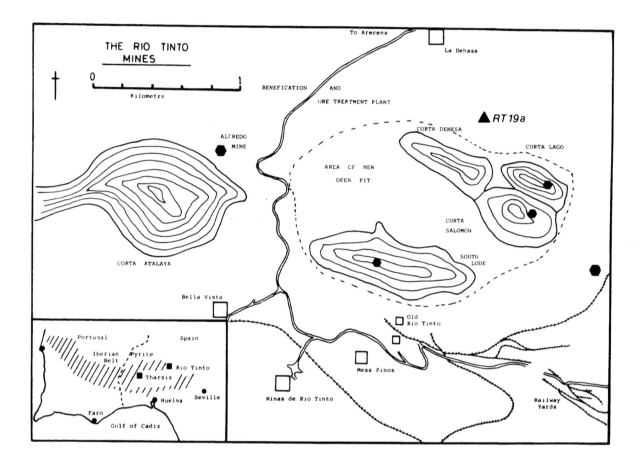

Fig.1   Location of RT 19A. Plan reproduced by kind permission of Dr Lyn Willies, Peak District Mining Museum

The site

RT 19A lies near the centre of ancient operations (Fig. 1). At this point the continuous slag cover is about 15 metres thick but it has recently been partially cleared prior to mining operations and a section has been cut through the slag. At RT 19A the base of the slag cover consists of a small heap of tap slags and fragments of refractories. The slags are very loosely packed and there is no soil infilling suggesting that the heap formed as a result of dumping over a very short period, possibly hours, probably days, but certainly not more than a few weeks. Thus the material in the heap may be considered as forming part of one related operation and as the product of a limited number of furnaces. The Iberian pottery in the heap indicates a date in the second-first centuries BC. The machine-cut section was cleaned down by hand, photographed, drawn and then excavated and sampled in the manner developed for all such sample excavations at Rio Tinto (Plate 1).

Physical description of material from the heap

The bulk of the heap is formed of loosely-filled tap slags. Most of them are in the form of thin plates, approximately 15-40 cm diameter and 1-8 cm thick, and would seem to represent the frequent tapping of a mobile slag from a small furnace. There are also smaller quantities of ropey slag cakes formed of runners from continuous tapping. The chemical compositions and significance of the two are discussed below (see pp. 205-6).

There were numerous curved furnace fragments. These were up to 20 cm in length and between 2-4 cm thick; they appear to come from small hemispherical furnaces approximately 60 cm in diameter. Some fragments had regular concave edges, approximately 20 cm diameter, suggesting that they came from the rim of the opening at the top of the furnace through which the charge was added and the fume escaped (Plate 2). With such a concentration of well-preserved fragments it was hoped to find joins, but this did not prove possible. This failure may not have been entirely due to erosion of the edges. During recent smelting experiments by John Merkel very similar cracks were seen to develop in the clay walls during the firing. It is very probable that this is the cause of at least some of the major breaks in the fragments from RT 19A, and further heat warping and distortion of the walls would make a join unrecognizable. This heat damage further emphasises the extremely ephemeral nature of most ancient furnaces.

The other refractories recovered from the heap in quantity were the distinctive clay wedges approximately 8-10 cm square and tapering from about 5 cm thick (Plate 3). One face is concave and usually glazed with a high surface concentration of lead containing silver. The opposite face is heavily slagged and vitrified. Although heavily burnt none of the wedges was fused to anything else, or even to each other.

Only one small fragment of tuyere was recovered. This was sufficient to show that the original internal diameter was about 3 cm and the tuyere wall about 1.5 cm thick. The city was similar to that of the wedges (see next section). A few small fragments of ceramic were found of identical composition to the furnace walls but much thinner (0.4-0.8 cm) and were probably from crucibles. Several pieces of metal were recovered including three spills of lead (89.4 gm), a quarter section of a small button of raw silver (32.5 gm), and a fragment of impure litharge weighing 200 gm.

Scientific investigation

The following section shows the scope of our investigations so far. They are necessarily not complete, but already give some idea of the varied information to be obtained from the debris.

(a)   Refractory ceramics

The furnace wall fragments are of clay formed from the local heavily weathered shales. Shale fragments are very abundant in all sizes from under 20μm up to several cm. The majority are rather weathered, lozenge-shaped fragments only a few mm long. The larger pieces are more angular, suggesting some crushing, but there is no evidence that this represents a deliberate separate addition of unweathered shale, beyond that which was present within the clay bed. The wedges are of a different, finer clay containing fragments of tuff, porphyry and occasionally shale; the tuyere fragment was also of this clay. The two clays have fairly similar refractory properties. The massive amounts of shale in the furnace wall clay render it more friable and therefore unsuitable for the more precise forms required for the wedges or tuyeres.

The examination of ceramics by scanning electron microscopy (SEM) is now a well established technique (Tite & Maniatis 1975). The method can also be applied to refractories to determine the duration and temperature of the process carried out within the furnace (Tite *et al.* 1982). Expressed very simply, the higher the temperature, the greater will be the degree of vitrification into the clay wall. The parameters can be quantified by the controlled refiring of unvitrified portions of the same refractory taken from areas not exposed to the maximum temperature. The fragments of furnace wall are highly vitrified on their inner (concave) surfaces, on which discontinuous lead-rich, glassy areas and fayalite particles are present. The outer (convex) surface is still extensively vitrified on one fragment (68) but is only slightly vitrified on the second (95). Refiring experiments indicate that the clay is relatively refractory and suggest maximum temperatures of around 1200°C at the inner surface, dropping to between 1100° and 900°C at the outer walls of the furnace. The relatively high temperature of the outer face and deep penetration of vitrification into the clay for fragment 68 would suggest a firing time of about ten hours, but a firing time of about three hours for fragment 95. This difference is possibly due to these fragments coming from different parts of the furnace.

The refractory wedges are much more complex and it must be admitted more puzzling. The concave surfaces were exposed to an oxidising atmosphere and are covered with a lead-rich glaze containing some silver (Table 2, column 6). The clay beneath is not vitrified, suggesting temperatures below 900°C. From the phase diagram for the binary system $PbO-SiO_2$ (Levin *et al.* 1956), it is clear that the complex glass composition found here would melt well below 800°C. On the opposite face the situation is totally different. There the clay surface is penetrated by sinuous fingers of slag to depths of up to 1 cm. Analysis of the slag using the defocused microprobe beam showed that it closely resembled the plate slags in composition (Table 2). The vitrification at the clay surface suggests that these temperatures were held for many hours. Clearly therefore this was the side exposed to the heat. The similarity of the temperature and time suggest that the wedges and curved furnace fragments belong to the same structure, and the similarity between the compositions of the slag on the wedges and the plate slags suggests that the latter were generated within these structures. The furnace fragments are not heavily slagged and this might suggest that they formed the dome of the furnace above the wedges which formed a hearth. Lead isotope analysis suggests ore roasting may have been taking place on the relatively cool concave face (see p. 209).

(b)   Slags

Only recently has the full potential of metallurgical slags as a source of process information begun to be realised (Bachmann 1980 and 1982; Morton & Wingrove 1969 a and b. 1972). Two plate slags (180, 181) and one ropey slag (182) were examined in detail. All contained fayalite, but fayalite was not invariably dominant. Instead the rare mineral andremeyerite, $BaFe_2Si_2O_7$ (Sahama *et al.* 1973) predominated in slag 180. Other phases present included barium-potassium feldspars in the series celsian ($BaAl_2Si_2O_8$, Cn) - sanidine ($KAlSi_3O_8$, Sa), iron oxides (magnetite or wüstite) and iron sulphide, pyrrhotite (FeS). Microprobe analyses of some of these phases are given in Table 1. The mineralogy of the slags depends on their chemical composition. Slag 180, with 11.1% BaO, contains andremeyerite as a major crystalline phase, needles of which are intergrown with fayalite (Plate 4). In addition this slag contains celsian-rich feldspar ($Cn_{55}Sa_{15}$). Slag 181 (BaO=6-9%) contains hyalophane feldspar ($Cn_{55}Sa_{45}$) and minor sanidine (Cn_3Sa_{97}) but only minor, interstitial andremeyerite; skeletal crystals of fayalite are predominant. The ropey slag, 182, is significantly different with only 1.4% BaO, no andremeyerite, and no feldspars. Fayalite is the only crystalline silicate present.

Table 1

Microprobe analyses of some minerals from the Rio Tinto slags

	1	2	3	4	5	6
SiO_2	37.44	30.25	44.10	53.17	30.41	30.20
Al_2O_3	24.68	1.96	23.23	23.03	b.d.	b.d.
FeO	2.79	31.81	1.53	1.23	63.83	66.21
MgO	b.d.	0.57	b.d.	b.d.	4.44	0.96
CaO	b.d.	0.92	b.d.	b.d.	1.33	3.84
BaO	32.37	33.22	23.27	2.40	b.d.	b.d.
Na_2O	b.d.	0.67	0.37	b.d.	b.d.	b.d.
K_2O	2.56	1.41	6.35	19.82	b.d.	b.d.
	99.84	100.81	99.85	99.65	100.01	101.21

1. Barium-rich feldspar (celsian) from slag no. 180

2. Andremeyerite from slag no. 180

3. Intermediate barium-potassium feldspar (hyalophane) from slag no. 181

4. Potassium feldspar from slag no. 181

5 & 6. Fayalite from slag no. 181

b.d. = below detection limit

Iron oxides, wüstite or magnetite, occur in all the slags either in dendritic form or as irregular blebs embedded in glass interstitial to the silicate phases. Pyrrhotite is confined to interstitial areas, and is generally associated with iron oxides (Plate 5). Minute blebs of lead and lead sulphide, a few microns in diameter, were detected with the SEM.

All the slags are rich in iron (Table 1); this is expressed as FeO, as indicated by the high fayalite content, but some ferric iron is present as magnetite, and probably in the interstitial glasses and the feldspars (Table 1). The BaO and K_2O in the plate slags are probably derived from the jarosite ore. The K-Ba feldspar component is essentially replacing anorthite ($CaAl_2Si_2O_8$) which is more typical of slags. Thus, based on the three samples examined so far, there would appear to be a significant difference in chemistry as well as morphology between the plate slags and ropey slags. The plate slags have much higher barium, calcium and magnesium content. This would seem to indicate that at some stage in the process a slag low in alkaline earth metals is run from the furnace to form the ropey slags. Analysis of slag adhering to the wedges showed it resembled the plate slags most closely, the relatively high K_2O and SiO_2 coming from the adjoining clay (Table 2).

Assuming equivalence of $BaAl_2Si_2O_8$ and $CaAl_2Si_2O_8$, then the slags lie close to the low temperature regions of the appropriate phase diagrams. Given the low magnesium contents of the fayalites and the multicomponent nature of the slags, the temperatures of c. 1200°C for the smelting process determined by the ceramic examination would seem to be confirmed by the slags.

Viscosity

The viscosities at 1200°C for selected slags were calculated using the method of Bottinga and Weill (1972) and are shown in Table 2. According to Urbain et al. (1982) this method yields values for viscosity which are typically accurate to within a factor of 2; a further approximation in the present instance was the assumption that $BaAl_2O_4$ and $CaAl_2O_4$ are equivalent but even so it is clear that the viscosities of the slags are low, of the order of 10 poise or less. For density (Table 2) the method of Bottinga and Weill (1970) as revised by Bottinga et al. (1982) was used, data for BaO are included in the method and accuracy within 5% relative is expected. As part of the silver collecting process lead would have been periodically sprinkled into the furnace. The density of molten lead at 1200°C was extrapolated from data in Hofmann (1970) to be 9.68 g cm^{-3}. Then from Stoke's law, it was calculated that a 1 mm diameter droplet of lead would settle at a rate of 20 cm min^{-1} and a 0.1 mm droplet at a rate of 0.2 cm min^{-1}. The implication is that even very fine droplets of metal would have settled quickly through the slags.

It will be observed from Table 2 that there are no significant differences between the viscosities of the plate and ropey slags. Furthermore, as they are of approximately the same bulk, cooling rates for a single tap would have been similar. This suggests that the morphological differences represent differences in technology rather than in physical properties (contra Koucky & Steinberg 1982). This was confirmed by Merkel's experiments which indicated the ropey slags were formed by slow continuous tapping (Merkel 1982) and by thin section photomicrographs (Plate 6) of slag 182 which clearly showed internal chilled boundaries where one 'rope' of slag had time to cool before the next covered it.

Table 2

Analysis of slags from Rio Tinto

	1	2	3	4	5	6
SiO_2	23.20	30.66	33.31	28.42	36.29	19.24
Al_2O_3	2.66	4.46	4.19	5.91	4.94	5.83
FeO	42.0	36.57	34.97	50.54	38.89	1.66
MgO	0.32	0.70	0.83	0.20	0.50	0.34
CaO	1.95	3.75	3.82	0.15	3.09	0.62
BaO***	11.12	8.56	5.92	1.36	9.70	b.d.
Na_2O	0.07	0.20	0.20	0.13	0.70	b.d.
K_2O	0.73	1.75	n.a.	0.71	3.27	1.37
PbO	0.55	1.12	1.07	0.66	1.02	67.57
CuO	0.13	0.09	0.03	0.05	n.a.	n.a.
TiO_2	0.19	0.36	0.38	0.32	n.a.	b.d.
TOTAL***	82.97	88.30	84.79	88.49	100.04*	99.67**
Ag	70 ppm	23 ppm	14 ppm	46 ppm		
Phases	Fay, Cn, And, Py ? Wu, Pb Gal	Fay, Hy Or, Gal ? Mag Py, gl		Fay, Py, Fe-ox, gl		
ρ_{1200}		3.82		3.57		
η_{1200}	4.72	9.3		4.96		

* includes 1.67% S; ** includes 2.00% As; *** BaO is a minimum in 1-4

1-4 by AAS, 5 and 6 by Microprobe.

Phases: Fay = fayalite, Cn = celsian, Hy = hyalophane, Or = orthoclase,
          Py = pyrrhotite, Pb = metallic lead, Gal = galena, Wu = wüstite,
          Mag = magnetite, Fe-ox = unspecified iron oxide, gl = glass,
          ? = signifies that only major line observed by XRD.

ρ_{1200} = density at 1200°C (g cm^{-3})   1. Plate slag 180
η_{1200} = viscosity at 1200°C (poise)   2. Plate slag 181
  n.a. = not analysed   3. Repeat of 2
  b.d. = below detection limits   4. Ropey slag 182
                                   5. Slag inclusion in wedge-shaped
                                      ceramic 154 (Average of 4 200 μm
                                      defocussed microprobe spots)
                                   6. High-PbO glass on low temperature
                                      side of 154

(c)   Reducing conditions within the furnace

Some rough estimates can be made of the typical oxygen partial pressures
(pO_2) in the slag during the smelting process.   Fig. 2 shows the pO_2
(atm)/T°C relationships for a number of metal and mineral reactions
involving oxygen.   Firstly, it is clear that as lead was present as metal,
the pO_2 was below curve (1), corresponding to the reaction $2Pb+O_2=2PbO$.
Fayalite (Fe_2SiO_4) is always present, with about 0.1 mole fraction Mg_2SiO_4
plus Ca_2SiO_4, which necessitates only a minor correction to curve (2) for
the breakdown of fayalite.   Thus pO_2 was below curve (2).   Both magnetite
and wüstite have been identified in the slags, suggesting pO_2 around curve
(3).   The absence of metallic iron indicates pO_2 above curve (4).   Finally,
the shift in curve (1) for typically 0.5 mole % PbO in the slag, i.e.
$2PbO$ (slag)=$2Pb$(metal) + O_2(gas), is estimated to lie along curve (5),
assuming ideal mixing of oxide components in the slag (i.e. activity of
PbO=mole fraction of PbO).   This estimate of the reducing conditions is
considered to be broadly in agreement with the mineralogical indicators,
given the approximations made.   The shaded area in Fig. 2 therefore includes
the probable operating conditions for a typical smelting operation within
the RT 19A furnaces, given the earlier estimates of temperature.

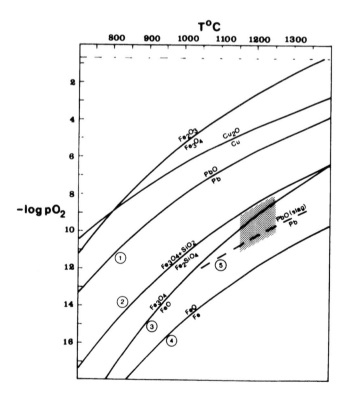

Fig. 2   Plot of partial oxygen pressure against temperature.   Shaded area
represents most likely conditions within the furnaces represented
by RT 19A

Estimate of ore grade

Analysis of the slags may give an indication of the lowest grade of ore
that it would have been feasible to smelt after beneficiation. The
maximum silver content of the slag is 70 ppm and thus the ore must have
contained at least 70 ppm of silver assuming that nothing else contributed
to the slag, and no silver was actually produced. In practice some gossan
would almost inevitably have been added as a source of iron to flux the
smelt. The gossan itself contains some silver, but only small amounts compared to the jarosite. If a 1:1 mixture of gossan and jarosite was used
the ore would need to contain at least 140 ppm of silver just to account
for the silver in the slag. This suggests that a figure between 100-200
ppm silver in the ore would represent the lowest level that was worth processing. Striking confirmation of the validity of these figures is provided by a heap of jarosite found abandoned in a Roman Gallery (RT 67).
This assayed at 120 ppm silver and the circumstances of its discovery
suggest it was abandoned as not worth smelting. (We are grateful to
Dr Lyn Willies for permission to use this information prior to his own
publication). Analyses of jarositic ores from Rio Tinto record silver
concentrations ranging from 160 ppm to 3110 ppm, so that both rather poor
and very rich silver ores were certainly available there (Williams 1950).

(d)   Metal and mineral samples

In antiquity lead played a vital role in the smelting of silver (Gale &
Stos-Gale 1982). Even the richest ore contains only a minute quantity of
silver and this would be dissipated throughout the furnace. Lead readily
takes up silver and in the furnace acted to concentrate the silver into
itself. The molten argentiferous lead was then run from the furnace and
cupelled. In this process a stream of air was played over the molten metal
on a refractory 'saucer', i.e. the cupel. The lead oxidised away to
litharge leaving a button of silver behind.

At Rio Tinto the mixed jarosite ores contain varying amounts of iron,
lead, copper, arsenic, antimony, bismuth, gold and silver.

The iron went chiefly into the slag or combined with the arsenic to
form speiss; some arsenic would also have been lost in the furnace fumes.
The analyses of the argentiferous lead, cupellation litharge, recovered
lead, raw and refined silver in Table 3 show clearly the destination of
the remaining elements in the ore. Copper, bismuth, gold, silver, antimony and some arsenic were collected by the lead. On cupellation, copper,
antimony and part of the bismuth remained in the litharge, but most
bismuth stayed in the silver together with the gold and some copper.
Bismuth is well known to be a difficult metal to remove from silver, and
Table 3 shows that even the 'refined' metal contained 0.42%, which is
much higher than usually found in ancient silver. Otherwise the Rio Tinto
silver seems typical of that found in other parts of the ancient world
(Hughes & Hall 1979).

The contrast shown in Table 3 between the high silver content of the
raw argentiferous lead and the low content of the presumed refined lead
suggests that the latter may be the result of the resmelting of litharge
from the cupellation process.

The practise of reducing cupellation litharge to lead is in direct
contrast to Laurion in the Bronze Age where this was not done at all (Stos-
Gale & Gale 1982); unpublished data on lead from Archaic and Classical

Table 3

Sample	Pb	Ag	Au	As	Bi	Sb	Sn	Cu	Zn	Cd	Fe	Ni	Co	Mn
(Palmer 1927) Argentiferous Lead	86.93	combined analysis (0.233)			2.81	8.79	0.35	0.8			0.17			
Litharge RT 19A 63*+	90					5.0		1.0			present			
Litharge (Palmer 1927)*	68.05	combined analysis (0.02)		0.89		1.22		0.45			6.99			
RT 19A 85 Raw silver**	0.55	91.0	1.2	0.03	4.6	0.04	0.1	1.3			0.07	0.02	0.001	
(Palmer 1927) Refined Lead	0.14	97.0	0.1		0.42			2.25			0.09			
(Palmer 1927) Refined Lead	99.92	0.007			0.01			0.01			0.00			
RT 19A 84 Refined Lead**	96	0.03			0.04	0.07		0.1		0.005	0.015		0.003	
RT 19A 87 Refined Lead**	100	0.025			0.01	0.01	0.2	0.03			0.005		0.001	

+ Semi Quantitative. Sample observed to be very inhomogeneous.

* Results expressed as appropriate oxides rather than metal.

** Quantitive analysis by Atomic Absorption details of method given in Hughes et al.1976. Precision ± 1% for major elements, ± 20% for trace elements, all elements could be detected down to 0.005% in the sample.

strata at Thorikos show that neither was the practice adopted in the Laurion at times contemporary with site RT 19A in Rio Tinto. Undoubtedly this reflects the contrast between the scarcity of lead at Rio Tinto compared with its great abundance in the Laurion. Litharge found with lead slags and furnace remains at Margenthol near Mount Nideggen in North Eifel, Germany, dating from the second century AD have been interpreted as remains of silver cupellation (Bachmann 1977). That litharge contained about 5% copper and only 0.15% antimony in contrast to the 1% copper and 5% antimony found in the RT 19 sample.

Our analyses permit us to suggest a scheme, outlined in Fig. 3, for the silver recovery processes in use at Rio Tinto in the second-first centuries BC. The scheme accords well with that suggested by the experimental work of Pernicka and Bachmann (1982), McKerrell and Stevenson (1972), and Tylecote & Merkel (see pp. 3-20, esp. Table 1).

Lead isotope analyses

In general Rio Tinto is rather poor in lead ores, though some galena was available from the altered porphyry wall rocks along the surface of the North, South and San Dionisio Lodes; the surfaces of these rocks are scored by ancient tool marks (Allan 1970). From an early period it was, however, probably necessary to import lead to supplement the local supply.

Isotopic analyses of several samples of metallic lead excavated at Rio Tinto when compared with analysis of the ore show (Table 4) that the lead from the Late Bronze Age site RT 26 is local, but that by the fourth-third centuries BC at RT 19A the lead has a non-local component. This appears also to be true, as would be expected, of the litharge, the raw silver and the plate slag. However the isotopic composition of the lead contained in the enigmatic clay wedges is close to that of the one jarosite ore sample so far analysed. Could this be a hint that the wedges are associated with a preliminary roasting of the ores prior to smelting?

The evidence at RT 19A for the importation of lead recalls the story recounted by Timaeus of the Phoenician sea traders discovering so much silver in Spain that they were obliged to replace their lead anchors with those of silver. Allan (1970) has already suggested that this story could symbolise a highly profitable trade in lead and silver carried on by the Phoenicians. These lead isotope analyses provide further evidence for such a trade. By Roman times at least some of the lead was coming from within Spain, as two lead pigs stamped NOVA CARTAGO (modern Cartagena) were found in the heaps at Rio Tinto (Palmer 1927) and are now preserved in the Huelva Museum.

One important consequence of the extensive use of imported lead at Rio Tinto from an early date is to jeopardise the use of lead isotope analyses to recognise silver from Rio Tinto. This is particularly unfortunate since Rio Tinto was one of the major sources of silver in the ancient world, especially in the late Republican and early Imperial period. On the other hand the limited evidence so far established suggests that it may be possible to trace Rio Tinto silver in the Bronze Age.

Conclusions

Examination of the furnace refractories, slag fragments and metal has revealed a great deal of information on the process and allowed at least a partial reconstruction of the operation.

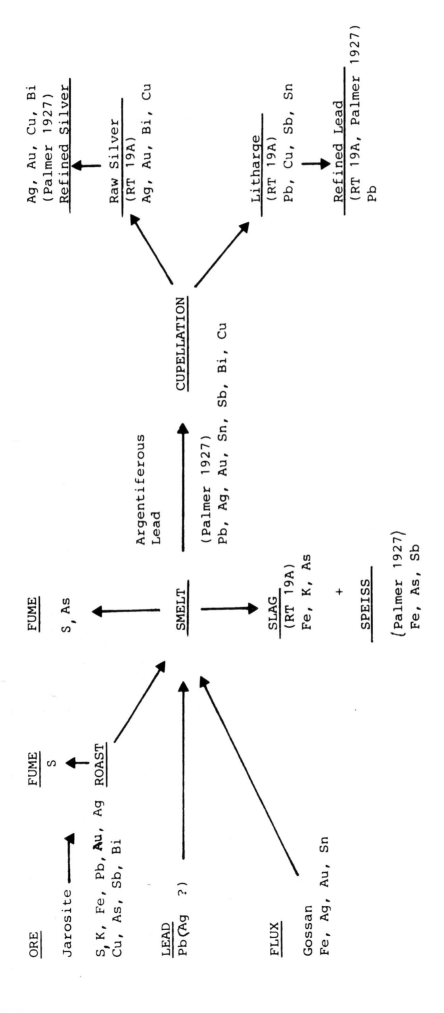

Fig. 3 Flow diagram depicting the course followed by the trace elements during the smelting of jarosite silver ores

Table 4

SAMPLE	DESCRIPTION	208 206 Pb/ Pb	207 206 Pb/ Pb	206 204 Pb/ Pb
Jarosite Ore	Corto Lago Rio Tinto	2.09571	0.85303	18.317
RT 26A 83	Lead from late Bronze Age Deposit	2.09694	0.86062	18.73
RT 19A 86	Lead	2.09253	0.84503	18.59
RT 19A 87	Lead	2.09112	0.83946	18.779
RT 19A 63	Litharge	2.09040	0.84425	18.599
RT 19A 85	Raw Silver	2.08729	0.84507	18.516
RT 19A	Plate Slag	2.08564	0.83839	18.730
RT 19A	Concave Surface of Wedge	2.09610	0.84842	18.522

Crushed jarosite ore, to which iron-rich gossan was added where necessary to act as a flux, was smelted in small hemispherical furnaces approximately 60 cm in diameter. The furnace walls were made of a very shaly refractory clay and were approximately 4 to 8 cm thick. The heavily slagged clay wedges may have been incorporated into the lower part of the furnace and have been associated with roasting of the ore prior to smelting, although their arrangement and function is still far from clear. The smelting process operated at about 1200°C for a period of the order of ten hours. Lead brought in from outside Rio Tinto was added to collect the silver, and the resulting argentiferous lead run out and was subsequently cupelled. This separated the silver from the lead but left some metals in the silver, notably bismuth.

The remains of early metallurgy are prolific but are usually just heaps of apparently formless debris no longer *in situ*. At first sight an ancient slag heap is a rather unpromising not to say daunting prospect. This report has been prepared primarily to demonstrate the range of information contained within the material and to show how systematic examination by a combination of techniques can reveal the ancient processes. Of course laboratory investigation is only one aspect of the work and must be considered together with the archaeological discoveries both above and below ground, the geological surveys and experimental reconstructions of the processes in the laboratory. Scientific examination has provided much

212

new information but certainly not all the answers. The examination of the
wedges for example produced valuable data, but their function is still
uncertain; new methods of analysis and investigation will doubtless one
day provide more information on them. The main duty of those concerned
with ancient metallurgy now is to ensure that stratified material is
excavated from the many sites likely to be destroyed by modern mining and
preserved for the future.

Acknowledgements

This work would have been impossible without the continued support of Rio
Tinto Minera, Spain and Rio Tinto Zinc, England. The advice, enthusiasm
and friendship of a great many individual members of the two companies
have greatly aided our exploration and interpretation of one of the great
mines of the world. We thank Dr A C Bishop, Keeper, Department of
Mineralogy, British Museum (Natural History) for access to the microprobe.
We are grateful to Dr M J Hughes and Ms M Fabrizi for the atomic absorption
analyses of the slags.

References

Allan, J C 1970. *Considerations on the antiquity of mining in the Iberian
Peninsula*. London, Royal Anthropological Society

Bachmann, H-G 1977. Bleiglätte-Fund aus der Nordeifel. *Bonner Jahrbücher*,
617-622

Bachmann, H-G 1980. Early copper smelting techniques in Sinai and in the
Negev and deduced slag investigations. In *Scientific studies in early
mining and extractive metallurgy*, ed. P T Craddock, 103-134. London

Bachmann, H-G 1982. *The Identification of slags from archaeological sites*.
London, Institute of Archaeology

Bottinga, Y & Weill, D 1970. Densities of liquid silicate systems calculated
from partial molar volumes of oxide components. *American Journal of
Science*, **269**, 169-182

Bottinga, Y & Weill, D 1972. The viscosity of magnetic silicate liquids: a
model for calculation. *American Journal of Science*, **272**, 438-475

Bottinga, Y, Weill, D & Richet, P 1982. Density calculations for silicate
liquids I: Revised methods for aluminosilicate compositions. *Geochemica
et Cosmochimica Acta*, **46**, 909-919

Gale, N H, Gentner, W & Wagner, G A 1980. Mineralogical and geographical
silver sources of Archaic Greek coinage. *Metallurgy in Numismatics* 1,
3-49. London, Royal Numismatic Society

Gale, N H & Stos-Gale, Z A 1982. Cycladic lead and silver metallurgy. *Annual
of the British School of Archaeology at Athens*, **76**, 169-224

Hofmann, W 1970. *Lead and lead alloys*. Berlin, Springer Verlag

Hughes, M J, Cowell, M R & Craddock, P T 1976. Atomic absorption techniques
in archaeology. *Archaeometry*, **18**, 19-36

Hughes, M J & Hall, J A 1979. X-Ray flourescence analysis of late Roman and Sassanian silver plate. *Journal of Archaeological Science*, 6, 321-344

Koucky, F & Steinberg, A 1982. Ancient mining and mineral dressing on Cyprus. In *Early pyrotechnology*, ed. T A & S F Wertime. Washington, Smithsonian

Levin, E M, McMurdie, H E & Hall, E P 1956. *Phase diagrams for ceramists.* Columbus(Ohio), American Ceramic Society

McKerrell, H & Stevenson, R B H 1972. Anglo-Saxon and oriental coinage. In *Methods of chemical and metallugrical investigation of ancient coinage*, ed. E T Hall & D M Metcalf, 95-210. London, Royal Numismatic Society

Merkel, J F 1982. 'Reconstruction of Bronze Age copper smelting experiments based on archaeological evidence from Timna, Irsrael'. Unpublished thesis, London University

Morton G R & Wingrove, J 1969a. Slag cinder and bear. *Bulletin of the Historical Metallurgy Society,* 3, 55-61

Morton, G R & Wingrove, J 1969b. Constitution of bloomery slags Part I: Roman. *Journal of the Iron and Steel Institution*, 207, 1556-1564

Morton, G R & Wingrove, J 1972. Constitution of bloomery slags Part II: Medieval. *Journal of the Iron and Steel Institution*, 210, 478

Palmer, R E 1927. Notes on some mine equipments and systems. *Journal of the Institute of Mining and Metallurgy*, 36, 299-336

Pernicka, E & Bachmann, H-G 1982. 'The Partition of copper, antimony, tin and bismuth during the cupellation process'. Synopsis of the 22nd Symposium on Archaeometry, Bradford

Rothenberg, B & Blanco-Freijeiro, A 1981. *Studies in ancient mining and metallurgy in south-west Spain.* London, Institute for Archaeometallurgical Studies

Sahama, Tb. G, Siiovla, J & Rehtijarvi, P 1973. Andremeyerite, a new barium iron silicate from Nyiragongo, Zaire. *Bulletin of the Geological Society of Finland*, 45, 1-8

Stos-Gale, Z A & Gale, N H 1982. The sources of Mycenaean silver and lead. *Journal of Field Archaeology*, 9, 467-485

Tite, M S & Maniatis, Y 1975. Examination of ancient pottery using the scanning electron microscope. *Nature*, 257, 122-3

Tite, M S, Maniatis, Y, Meeks, N D, Bimson, M, Hughes, M J & Leppard, S C 1982. Technological studies of ancient ceramics from the Near East, Aegean and South East Europe. In *Early pyrotechnology*, ed., T A & S F Wertime. Washington, Smithsonian

Urbain, G, Bottinga, Y & Richet, P 1982. Viscosity of liquid silica, silicates and alumino-silicates. *Geochimica et Cosmochimica Acta* 46, 1061-1072

214

Williams, D 1950. Gossanised breccia ores, jarosites and jaspers at Rio
     Tinto, Spain. *Transactions of the Institute of Mining and Metallurgy,*
     LIX, 509-520

Plate 1   RT 19A during cleaning and sampling

Plate 2   Furnace fragments. The curve on the fragment on the right probably
represents the original rim

216

Plate 3   Enigmatic clay wedge

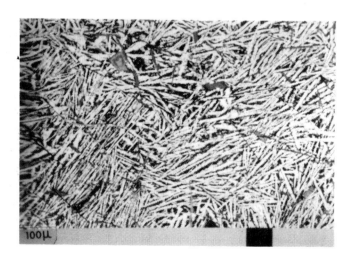

Plate 4   SEM photomicrograph of slag 180 showing abundant needles of
          andremeyerite

Plate 5   Detail of Plate 4 showing andremeyerite (light grey), magnetite and
          pyrrhotite (mid-grey), a large grain of celsian (centre) and
          fayalite (dark). A small droplet of lead (white) is seen centre-
          left

Plate 6   Section through ropev slag 182, showing internal chilled boundary;
          i.e. the individual 'ropes' of slag had time to cool before being
          covered by the next. Field of view is 3.6 mm

THE ARCHAEOLOGICAL EVIDENCE FOR GOLD SMELTING AT KRAKU'LU YORDAN, YUGOSLAVIA, IN THE LATE ROMAN PERIOD

Michael R Werner

Department of Classics, State University of New York
at Albany, Albany, New York 12222

Abstract

The metal resources of the upper Pek river in
Serbia worked in antiquity consisted of gold,
silver, copper and iron. Roman intervention in
the area most likely was primarily concerned with
gold extraction. Political conditions in the late
empire dictated fortified processing centres for
gold such as the industrial complex at Kraku'lu
Yordan. In the fourth century AD there is evidence
that in addition to iron smelting the process of
cementation for gold refining was practiced there;
numerous cylindrical ceramic vessels interpreted
as crucibles were recovered on the site. The condition of the crucibles and their find contexts
indicate the locations of probable gold refining
activities. The whole metallurgical complex was
destroyed suddenly by fire at the end of the fourth
century AD.

Keywords: GOLD, SMELTING, CEMENTATION, CRUCIBLES,
LATE ROMAN, SERBIA, YUGOSLAVIA, MOESIA,
PEK RIVER, METALLURGY, IRON, SLAG

Introduction

The metallurgical complex at Kraku'lu Yordan (the modern Vlak name for the
site) is located in northeastern Serbia along the upper reaches of the Pek
river, the ancient Pincus (Fig. 1). The region was once part of the late
Roman province of Moesia Prima and formed one of the principal mining
districts there, the *metalla Aeliana Pincensia* which we know from numismatic evidence (Dŭsanić 1977, 76). Intensive excavations on the site
were conducted by a joint Yugoslav-American team in the summers of 1976 and
1977 (for preliminary report, including site plan and illustrations, see
Bartel, Kondić & Werner 1979).

The upper valleys of the Pek abounded in metal resources which were
exploited in very ancient times, as the excavations of the Eneolithic
mining site at Rudna Glava have demonstrated (Jovanović 1982). The principal metals mined were gold, silver, copper and iron (Dŭsanić 1977, 76).
For the Roman period, however, historical and archaeological evidence indicates that Roman attention was first drawn to the upper valleys of the
river to wash placer gold from the river beds and extract it from the
quartz veins in the Homolje mountains which form the western limit of the
valley systems. Modern verification of gold sources in the region was made

220

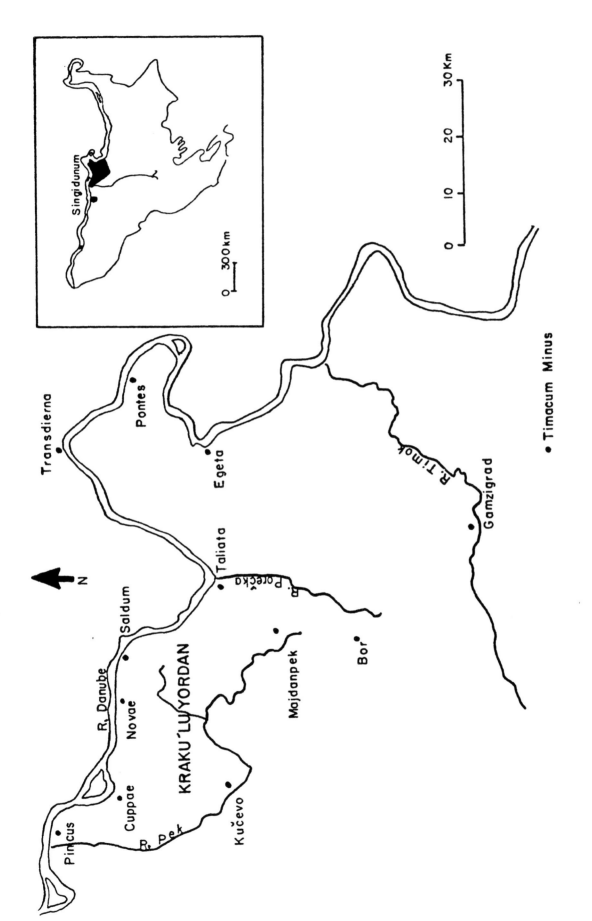

Fig. 1 Map of Northeast Moesia and the Kraku'lu Yordan Region; inset shows the Danube and Central Balkans

in the early part of this century. In 1908 Maclaren confirmed the continued existence of placer gold in the upper Pek and some of its tributaries (1908, 156-160). From his travels in the region in the late 1920s Davies noted both remains of placer-mining and reef-working in these valleys with associated Roman materials (1935, 217-218).

The earliest Roman metallurgical and habitation sites date from the reign of the emperor Hadrian or possibly his predecessor Trajan. Hadrian's family name, of course, was attached to the official title of the mining district in the form *Aeliana* (Dušanić 1977, 57). The largest concentration of Roman mining and processing remains have been reported west of Kucevo at Majdan Kucajna; the major settlements, whose growth can only be attributed to the mining industry, occupied reasonably level and accessible areas in the Pek valleys at Voluja and near modern Kučevo (Riznić 1888, 32-35; Garasanin 1951, 142-143). On the basis of the scanty evidence available, large-scale exploitation in the region probably ceased during the political upheavals and Gothic invasions around the middle of the third century AD; the latest coins from the two major hoards recovered in the region date to the 230s and 240s AD (Mócsy 1974, 205-206; Mirnik 1981, 65, 74). The apparently substantial archaeological remains of the imperial mining centre at Kučajna were obliterated by nineteenth and early twentieth century mining operations, while the habitation centres on the valley floors have long since disappeared beneath modern cultivation and agricultural settlements (Simić 1951, 311-314, 316-327).

The metallurgical complex at Kraku´lu Yordan belongs to a later phase of mining activity in the area, the fourth century AD, with a terminal point probably right at the end of that century. A sudden and intense conflagration destroyed the site, causing tools and other utilitarian objects to be abandoned in the ruins. The latest coin from a hoard of poorly preserved bronze coins found buried beneath the north circuit wall dates to the reign of Theodosius I (Kondić 1982, 107).

The excavated portions of the site occupy the top and south slope of a low hill situated near the centre of its valley and cover a surface area of approximatley 608 m^2. The average depth of fill in the excavated area was 1.00 m. Before the construction of the Belgrade-Bor railway line in 1947, the hill was flanked by the Brodica stream on the north and the Pek on the south. Significant to the design and hilltop location of the complex is the close proximity of the site to the Danubian frontier of the empire, a border which was subjected to increasing barbarian attack and invasion in the late fourth century AD. To the north of the Kraku´lu Yordan region, this frontier was protected by a dense line of fortifications because the Danube tributaries offered relatively easy access to the mining regions for invaders moving south (Kondić & Zotović 1971; Soproni 1968, squares VIII-X/g-h). The complex itself was fortified with a wall circuit, and the point of easiest access, the west end, was further protected by the addition of a square tower.

Architecture in the complex was primarily utilitarian and consisted of an irregular series of interior spaces defined by half-timbered walls built upon mortared stone foundations. The irregular spatial locations of concentrations of fallen roof tile, even in fragmentary form, indicate that many of the interior spaces lacked roof covering and permit the conclusion that several of the enclosures could have been used for smelting activities, where open-air ventilation would be the norm. The destruction debris filling the enclosures consisted primarily of a thin band of charcoal over the working floors, followed by a deep deposit or fall of burnt daub from the superstructures of the walls. Much of the daub had disintegrated, but large fragments, presumably fired by the heat of the final conflagration, were not infrequent occurrences. Although it was originally supposed that daub fragments might represent the remains of furnace walls, it is now apparent that the majority of the fragments, which lack the curved profiles that might be associated with either the rounded domes or cylindrical walls of furnaces, originate from the upper zones of the walls. Further confirmation of this interpretation is offered by the well-preserved flat impressions of some type of wooden shuttering or formwork on many of the larger daub fragments (Bartel, Kondić & Werner 1979, figs. 19, 20). Microscopic examination of daub samples has also shown that the material had not been exposed to high temperatures of the type to be encountered in the smelting of metals (personal communication, P T Craddock, 26 March 1982).

Table: Kraku'lu Yordan 1976-77 material inventory chart

MATERIAL	NUMBER	PERCENTAGE
Ceramic*	10,449	80.88
Animal Bone	1,739	13.45
Metal	439	3.39
Glass	263	2.03
Stone**	26	0.20
Bone Tool	2	0.01
TOTAL	12,918	

*Excludes 37 sherds classified as
Early Bronze Age.

**Excludes 2 stone tools classified as
Early Bronze Age.

The industrial character of the site is also affirmed by the artifact assemblage (see Table). With a high recovery rate due to screening of all excavated earth and debris, the artifacts recovered from excavation were counted on a piece by piece basis and grouped into the major categories shown in the Table. Since many of the bone statistics are represented by very small fragments and others are clearly the result of rodent intrusions, that category should be reduced from its dominant position. Among the metal artifacts, excluding the tools (e.g. spades, pick heads, a saw serrated on both edges), the most numerous objects fall into different classes of hardware, from nails to doorlocks, types of artifacts that one would expect to find where major components of the architecture are executed in wood. In the largest category, ceramics, many whole vessels were recovered, another indication of the sudden abandonment of the site. The dominant type was a range of containers of various sizes. Notably absent from the assemblage were any type of eating vessels, such as plates, cups and bowls. Two large pithoi and fragments of others were recovered from the complex.

By far the most numerous and, at first, the most puzzling kind of
ceramic artifact to come to light was the group of cylindrical jars, many
of which were equipped with tops (Pls 1, 2). The jars varied in height
from 57 cm to 45 cm with rim diameters of 22.5 cm and 21 cm respectively
(one exceptional example stood 54 cm high with a rim diameter of 12 cm).
The walls of the vessels were not exceptionally thick for their size, ranging between 1.0 cm and 1.5 cm thick. The cylinder jars were apparently
designed to be used as covered containers to judge from the number of tops
that were recovered with them. The tops came in two varieties, one with
a rim that would overlap the jar mouth and the other with a vertical flange
that would penetrate into the jar mouth (Bartel, Kondić & Werner 1979, figs.
21, 26). Unless some type of clay sealer was applied right on the spot,
there were no provision for actually fastening the tops to the vessels, and
the jars were most likely used in a vertically upright position. The find
contexts were what were ascribed generally to be furnace or smelting areas.
Some of the vessels were in mint condition, while others were badly distorted from heat and in many cases had slag adhering to them. Microscopic
examination of the heat-damaged jars indicated that the distortion was not
caused by temperatures as intense as those appropriate to metals with a
high melting point, such as copper or iron (personal communication,
P T Craddock 26 March 1982).

Another suggestion is that the pots were actually part of the furnace,
forming the base to act as insulators. This requires careful consideration.
A simple clay furnace set into the ground is likely to become damp very
quickly. When fired the steam generated would rapidly cause the floor
and lower walls to disintegrate. Thus furnaces set in damp ground from
Bronze Age China (Anon 1980) onwards have a substantial cavity beneath for
protection against excessive moisture. The use of clay pots set in walls
as structural elements is known from the classical world (the church of
St Vitale in Ravenna, consecrated in 457 AD, for example) although the
practice did not become common until the early nineteenth century (Hamilton
1959). However, none of the pots at Kraku´lu Yordan were found set in a
floor or wall, and pots have never been found set in an ancient furnace
elsewhere. It is also a little difficult to explain why a furnace built
on a rocky outcrop such as Kraku´lu Yordan should need special protection
against damp. Finds of similar cylinder jars in supposed metallurgical
contexts have been noted at Gamzigrad and other late Roman sites in Moesia
(Werner forthcoming 1984; Srejović et al. 1983, 100-1, 102, fig. 71; Janković
1981, 154-6).

On the basis of the find contexts and associated materials, the function of the cylinder jars would seem to be connected to the smelting
process. (Here the author must gratefully acknowledge the kind suggestions
made during the Symposium by Drs Bachmann, Craddock and Tylecote regarding
the functional interpretation of the cylinder jars; analysis of samples by
emission spectrography from the jar walls for traces of precious metals
has failed to show any trace of silver or gold, but there are areas of zinc
oxide 'glazing' on the outside of the one complete jar examined).

To the best of the author's knowledge there is no published evidence
for contemporary and analogous examples of these jars from other metallurgical sites outside the Moesian mining districts. However, from what is
known of ancient gold refining (Healy 1978, 153-155; Davies 1935, 56) the
most likely supposition is that these ceramic containers were used as crucibles in the cementation process of separating gold from other metals.
This process involved long heating of the containers and their contents at
relatively low temperatures, which would account for the lack of evidence

Plate 1   View of ceramic crucible group as excavated in south furnace room

Plate 2   Ceramic crucible with partial heat damage

225

for the exposure of the crucibles to extremely high temperatures. An
interesting sidelight is the fact that the crucibles were recovered in both
used and unused condition; this could indicate that the work of smelting
might actually have been in progress when the site was destroyed. Hanfmann
and Waldbaum (1970, 311-313) posit the existence of similar refining processes and artifacts at early sixth century BC Sardis in Asia Minor where
the remains of probable ceramic crucibles and heating furnaces were observed.

One of the probable furnace areas at Kraku´lu Yordan is located on the
southern slope near the crest of the hill (Bartel, Kondić & Werner 1979,
figs 4, 19, 20: for reasons beyond the control of the excavators, this
area was not excavated to bedrock which lies approximately one metre below
the final level of excavation). The rectangular enclosure encompasses an
area of 23.25 m^2 and is bounded by clay- and mortar-packed stone wall foundations, varying in thickness from 0.65 m to 1.10 m (the latter is the
south wall, a major retaining wall in the complex). The single entrance
to the area, a doorway 1.25 m wide, is located at the west end of the north
wall. The proposed identification of this area as a furnace room rests on
the large number of used and unused ceramic crucibles found there (at least
33 in all) and the locations and heavy concentrations of slag in the fill.
Most of the room was filled with destruction debris, primarily stone and
daub wall fall, but in the lower levels of the fill there were increasing
amounts of slag, some vitrified, and groups and single occurrences of the
cylindrical crucibles (Pl.1). Noteworthy were three large masses of slag
(maximum dimensions of 1.50 x 1.23 m, 0.80 x 0.60 m, and 0.50 x 0.40 m
with irregular thicknesses from 0.20 to 0.30 m) situated in an approximate
semicircle in the middle of the enclosure. As mentioned above, the burnt
daub fragments in the fill should be associated with the superstructures
of the walls, and it now seems reasonable to conclude that the actual furnace remains reside in the as yet unexcavated portion of the fill. Roof
tiles in whole (imbrices only) and fragmentary condition were recovered
from the room, but their location on the periphery of the area points up
the probability that they had fallen from the adjacent areas. Examination
of the slag in the British Museum Research Laboratory has shown that it is
a fayalite tap slag, produced under intensely reducing conditions and is
wholly typical of Roman bloomery iron production.

Other archaeological evidence from Kraku´lu Yordan, and our knowledge
of the historical context for this region in the late fourth century can
perhaps allow more positive conclusions, at least with respect to gold
processing.

The late fourth and early fifth centuries in Moesia witnessed
successive periods of unrest, caused by intrusions of Goths and Huns
(Mócsy 1974, 339-352). By the mid-fifth century, the region had been
overrun and occupied for a time by the Huns. If we view our basic datum
of a fortified metal-processing site against this background, the types of
metals potentially worked there can be limited. The site occupies a relatively small area and, from the amounts of slag observed, it does not
appear that huge quantities of ore were processed there. Certainly in
comparison with the Hadrianic workings which Davies (1935, 217-222) observed in the region, or with the immense amount of ancient slag around the
Roman metallurgical centre at Stojnik in the Mount Kosmaj region in northwestern Serbia (1,049,653 tons estimated in 1875; Simić 1951, 193), the
amount of smelting debris at Kraku´lu Yordan is minimal. Small amounts of
raw material, processed in a fortified location, would point to one of the
precious metals, and gold, some of it possibly panned in the Pek and its

neighbouring tributaries, is the most likely candidate for this region, being processed along with small amounts of iron presumably for the immediate needs of the fort itself.

Supporting this conclusion is the isolated location of the complex itself. The usual pattern of processing iron and copper ores on or near the mining sites themselves obviated the need for time-consuming and labour-intensive transport of the ores (Davies 1935, 209-222). However, the value of the final product might well have made feasible the transport of ore of a precious metal like gold to a central and defended processing site. Kraku′lu Yordan itself is certainly not a mining site, but rather a fortified processing centre with an ample supply of water available from the Pek or the Brodica for ore washing and other functions.

The fiery destruction of the complex, which produced the large concentrations of burnt daub in the debris layers, marked the end of activity which had operated without much direct Roman presence. Today Kraku′lu Yordan is the only excavated site of its type in the region, but unpublished survey data from the Museum of Mining and Metallurgy in Bor indicate that this site is most probably typical for metallurgical processing in its period and not a unique or isolated example of technological development for the late empire.

Acknowledgements

The 1976-77 excavations at Kraku′lu Yordan were funded with a grant from the National Science Foundation (BNS 76-10174). Work on the site was directed by Dr Vladimir Kondić, then Director of the National Museum, Belgrade, Professor Brad Bartel, Department of Anthropology, the San Diego State University, and the author. The project was designed to investigate the effects of the Roman imperial system on the indigenous peoples of the region. The context of a metallurgical site was considered particulalry appropriate because of the assumed interest that the central Roman government would have had in the mineral resources of the region. Excavation was limited to two seasons of work. The author would also like to acknowledge the participation and generous assistance of Ilija Janković, Director, Museum of Mining and Metallurgy, Bor (where the artifacts from the excavations are stored), and Zorka Stanojevic, Curator at the same institution. Karen Collins Werner was photographer for the excavations.

References

Anon 1980. *Tonglushan (Mount Verdigris Daye). A Pearl among ancient mines.* Beijng, Cultural Relics Publishing House

Bartel, B, Kondić V & Werner, M R 1979. Excavations at Kraku'lu Yordan, Northeast Serbia: Preliminary Report 1973-1976. *Journal of Field Archaeology*, **6**, 127-149

Davies, O 1935. *Roman mining in Europe.* Oxford, O.U.P.

Dušanić, S 1977. Aspects of Roman mining in Noricum, Pannonia, Dalmatia and Moesia. *Aufsteig and Niedergang der römischen Welt*, 2, 6, 53-94 Berlin

Garasanin, M & D 1951. *Arheološka Nalazišta u Srbiji.* Belgrade

Hamilton, S B 1959. The History of hollow bricks. *Transactions of the British Ceramic Society*, **58**, 41-62

Hanfmann, G M A & Waldbaum, J C 1970. New excavations at Sardis and some problems of western Anatolian archaeology. In *Near Eastern archaeology in the twentieth century: Essays in honor of Nelson Glueck*, ed. J A Sanders, 307-326. New York

Healy, J F 1978. *Mining and metallurgy in the Greek and Roman world*. London, Thames and Hudson

Janković, Dj 1981. *Podunavski deo oblasti Akvisa u VI i početkom VII veka*. Belgrade

Jovanović, B 1982. *Rudna Glava: Najstarije Rudarstvo Bakra na Centralnom Balkanu*. Belgrade-Bor

Kondić, V 1982. Poznorimska galerija u Rudnoj Glavi. In *Rudna Glava: Najstarije Rudarstvo Bakra na Centralnom Balkanu*, ed. B Jovanovic, 106-109. Belgrade-Bor

Kondić, V & Zotović, Lj 1971. Rimske i ranovizantijske tvrdjave u Djerdapu. *Materijali VI* (VIII Kongres arheologa Jugoslavije, Bor 1969), 37-54 Belgrade

Maclaren, M 1908. *Gold: its geological occurrence and geographical distribution*. London

Mirnik, I A 1981. *Coin Hoards in Yugoslavia*. BAR International Series 95. Oxford

Mócsy, A 1974. *Pannonia and Upper Moesia*. London, R.K.P.

Riznić, M 1888. Starinski ostaci u srezu Zviškom (Okp. Pozarevački). *Starinar*, 5, 31-39, 54-62

Simić, V 1951. *Istoriski Razvoj Našeg Rudarstva*. Belgrade

Soproni, S (ed.) 1968. *Tabula Imperii Romani*. L 34: Aquincum, Sarmizegetusa, Sirmium. Amsterdam

Srejović, D et al. 1983. *Gamzigrad: Kasnoantički Carski Dvorac*. Belgrade

Tylecote, R F 1962. *Metallurgy in archaeology*. London, Arnold

Werner, M R (forthcoming). The Moesian Limes and the Imperial Mining Districts. *Akten des 13. internationalen Limeskongresses, Aalen 1983. Forschungen und Berichters sur Vor- und Fruhgeschichte in Baden-Württemberg*. Stuttgart

ZINC PRODUCTION AT ZAWAR, RAJASTHAN

I C Freestone[1], P T Craddock[1], K T M Hegde[2], M J Hughes[1]
and H V Paliwal[3]

1 British Museum Research Laboratory, London WC1
2 M S University of Baroda, Baroda 390002, India
3 Hindustan Zinc Ltd, 6 New Fatehpura, Udaipur 3130001, India

Abstract

A field survey of the mines and remains at Zawar and the
preliminary scientific examination of a retort have enabled
a tentative reconstruction of the zinc smelting process to
be made.

Keywords: ZINC, INDIA, MINING, SMELTING, DISTILLATION,
MINERALOGY, ANALYSIS

Introduction

Impressive evidence of the production of metallic zinc in antiquity is to
be seen at Zawar, in the Aravalli Hills in Rajasthan, North-West India
(Fig. 1, Plate 1). Carsus (1960) estimated that there are 130,000-170,000
tons of zinc extraction debris at Zawar but a recent survey by the authors
suggests that there are in the region of 800,000 tons of debris in the
heaps which surround the site. The most complete report on this material
to date is that of Straczekk and Srikantan (1967).

The British Museum Research Laboratory, in conjunction with the
Department of Archaeology of Baroda University and with the generous cooperation and assistance of Hindustan Zinc Ltd, who are currently exploiting
the Zawar lead-zinc deposit, is carrying out an investigation of the zinc
production process (Craddock et al. 1983). The present report concerns
essentially the detailed investigation of a single retort, and should be
seen in its context as a preliminary study to a full investigation to be
carried out both in the laboratory and at Zawar itself (Craddock et al. 1985).

Background

The extraction of zinc presents its own special difficulties because the
boiling point of the metal at one atmosphere is lower than the minimum
temperature at which zinc oxide may be reduced by carbon. Thus, before the
advent of modern high pressure technology, it was necessary to collect a
zinc *vapour*, rather than separate a metallic liquid from a slag as in more
familiar smelting processes. This vapour readily oxidizes to clouds of
zinc oxide in air, so its collection requires a distillation system composed of a retort and an external condenser. On account of these problems
brass was produced by cementation from the time of its discovery in
Anatolia in the second century BC (Craddock et al. 1980) until the late

230

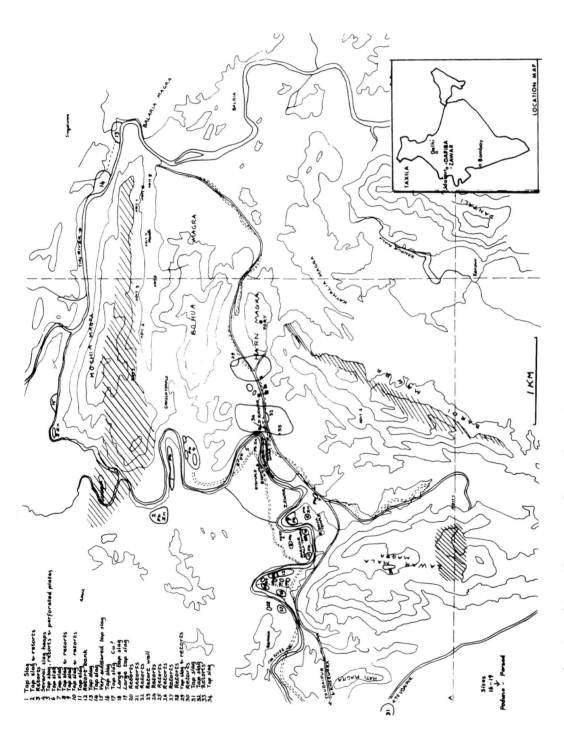

Fig. 1 Locality map showing distribution of metal production debris. (We are grateful to B Craddock for producing this map)

eighteenth century in the West. In the cementation process finely divided copper metal, zinc oxide and charcoal were sealed together in a crucible and heated to about 1000°C to produce brass.

Dating

There are analytical and textual grounds, discussed in detail by Craddock (1981), to suggest that metallic zinc was extracted considerably earlier in India than in the West, and that brass was produced by the direct alloying of zinc metal with copper by the sixteenth century. The remains at Zawar include a large number of retorts and make it a likely candidate as a major production centre in this early period. Preliminary thermolumine- scence tests on Zawar ceramics are consistent with an age of several cen- turies. However, attempts to obtain a C^{14} date on carbon extracted from the filler material from two of the zinc retorts yielded anomalous (post- Bomb, i.e. 1951) dates in both cases, suggesting contamination of some sort. Further work is needed to resolve this problem. In contrast radiocarbon dates obtained on timbers from an adit and a scaffold in the Zawar Mala Magra mines give dates of about 2,000 years bp (Craddock et al. 1983). It appears that zinc extraction at Zawar had ceased by the nineteenth century for James Tod, writing in *Annals and Antiquities of Rajputana* (1829) recorded that 'the miners are now dead and the mines filled with water'.

Materials

Retorts, condensers and furnaces

At least two groups of retorts may be distinguished at Zawar on the basis of size. The large retorts are 30-35 cm long and 10-15 cm diameter (Plate 2) and the small ones about 20 cm long and 10 cm in diameter. The collapsed and distorted states of many of the retorts, due to the high temperatures to which they have been subjected, do not allow greater pre- cision. Both large and small retorts are found within and around Old Zawar itself, and along the Tiri river but near the ancient mines in the Zawar Mala Magra hills there is a small heap of zinc smelting debris containing only the small retorts (Fig. 1). Within Old Zawar the retorts are commonly built into walls (e.g. Craddock et al. 1983).

A very few undistorted retorts were found on the 1982 survey and this showed the original shape of the larger types to be cylindrical, ending in a cone (Plate 2). The retort walls are about 1 cm thick and of clay, containing large fragments of quartzite and phyllite, both local rocks (Mookherjee 1964). They were prepared in two parts: a condenser was luted onto the open main body of the retort after it had been filled with the charge. Of the condensers, only the heads survive, usually embedded in the retorts (Plate 2). These heads appear to be of at least two types: a relatively large, thin-walled tulip-shaped variety (Plate 3, left) and a thicker, more robust cone which was formed in a polygonal mould. Droplets of zinc-rich material are found just inside the broken, tapered ends of the heads. They appear to have tapered into tubes (Plate 3), but the length of these is a matter for conjecture at present as none has been found complete. The tubes were probably broken up to extract the zinc which collected within them. They are likely to have passed into a collecting vessel in which the zinc condensed. In the fourteenth century Indian alchemists describe the process of *tiryakpatanam* in connection with zinc distillation:

> Place the chemicals in a vessel provided with a long tube, inserted in
> an inclined position, which enters the interior of another vessel
> arranged as receiver. The mouths of the vessels and the joints should
> be luted with clay. Now urge a strong fire at the bottom of the
> vessel containing the chemicals, whilst in the other vessel place cold
> water. This (process) is known as *tiryakpatanam*. (Ray 1956:190)

Before the 1983 excavations the extraction process was uncertain. It
had been suggested that the retorts were fired together as they stand in
the walls at Old Zawar. However, this was considered unlikely by us for a
number of reasons. Firstly, the more complete walls form quite recogniz-
able houses. Furthermore, in the double thickness of the walls occasional
retorts point into the centre of the wall rather than outwards. Many of
the retorts in the walls have fragments of other retorts fused to them,
the bulk of which is missing, suggesting that the necessary strong heating
took place elsewhere. Finally, the mortar which now binds the wall shows
no sign of strong heating. Examination by optical microscopy and X-ray
diffraction revealed no evidence of reaction between the calcite and quartz
components to produce high temperature phases, which would certainly have
happened at the temperatures and times implied for the heating of the
retorts (see below).

During the 1983 excavations two groups of furnaces were uncovered. A
single bank of seven furnaces upon Zawar Mala (site 30) contained small
retorts (Plate 1), whilst down in Old Zawar itself there was a more extensive arrangement of furnaces using the larger retorts. In this latter group
a row of lined and paved enclosures was excavated, each of which contained
a bank of three furnaces. In both groups thirty-six retorts in a six by
six arrangement were contained within the truncated pyramid of each furnace.
The retorts were supported vertically on perforated bricks, through which
the condenser tubes passed into the cooler zinc collectors beneath (Plates
4, 5) (Craddock *et al.* 1985).

A single retort, one of the larger type which was broken on arrival in
the laboratory, was selected for detailed examination. The clay is extensively vitrified and bloated through the thickness of the walls. There
appears to be less bloating at the sides and the ends of the retort than at
the top and bottom towards the centre. Spent charge is fused to the
interior walls towards the centre of the retort but not at the rear, nor at
the front towards the cone. A glassy layer had developed on the exterior
of the body in some areas (Plate 6). The clay matrix was analysed with an
electron microprobe (EPMA; Freestone 1982). It is not notably refractory
in composition but, on the other hand, neither does it have a high concentration of fluxes, 5% Na_2O + K_2O being typical of many potting clays used
in antiquity (Table 1). The glass on the external surface was found to
consist essentially of four components: K_2O, FeO, Al_2O_3 and SiO_2 (Table 1).
The K_2O content of 9% in this surface glass suggests it is the result of a
degree of partial melting of the ceramic (which contains 3% K_2O overall)
of 30-40%. In order to obtain some idea of the bulk composition of the
retort, a thin slice through the body was crushed and analysed by atomic
absorption spectrometry (AAS; Hughes *et al.* 1976). The higher SiO_2 content
relative to the microprobe analysis of the clay matrix (Table 1) reflects
the inclusion of the large quartzite grains in the AAS analysis. An interesting feature of the body is that it has absorbed 2% zinc; apparently the
formation of zinc spinels in the clay bodies of zinc retorts was recognised
early in the present century (Smith 1918), although in the present case at
least some of the zinc is dissolved in the glass phase (Table 1).

Table 1

Zawar zinc retort: analysis of ceramic materials

	(1)	(2)	(3)	(4)
SiO_2	62.49	53.82	64.85	57.96
TiO_2	0.71	0.27	0.44	0.59
Al_2O_3	13.90	17.49	13.75	13.97
FeO	2.48	4.16	7.49	15.39
MnO	0.04	b.d.	b.d.	b.d.
MgO	1.44	1.29	0.93	1.35
CaO	0.64	0.34	0.39	0.70
Na_2O	0.94	1.81	0.67	0.55
K_2O	3.08	3.11	9.90	7.54
P_2O_5	n.a.	0.50	0.28	b.d.
Cl	n.a.	0.16	b.d.	b.d.
S	n.a.	b.d.	b.d.	b.d.
ZnO	2.18	3.22	0.61	0.61
TOTAL	87.90	86.17	99.11	98.66

(1)   Bulk analysis of retort body
         (crushed slice) AAS

(2)   Clay analysis, EPMA

(3)   Partial melt (glass) from
         outer surface of retort, EPMA

(4)   As (3)

n.a. = not analysed

b.d. = below detection limits

234

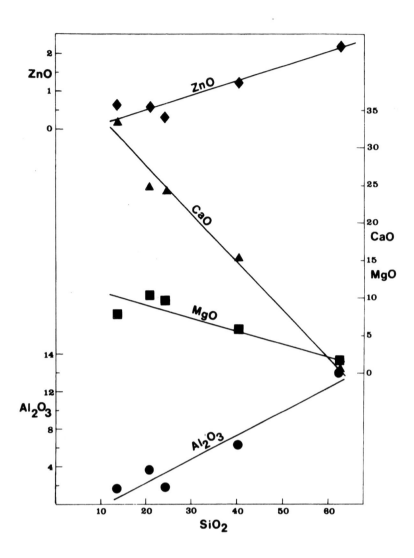

Fig. 2 Selected oxides plotted against SiO_2 for retort wall (high SiO_2),
fine fraction of distillation residue inside retort (intermediate
SiO_2) and three spent charge pellets (low SiO_2)

Residue

The retort was filled with somewhat less than 1 kg of spent charge, most
of which could be tipped out but some of which was fused to the walls.
This material was retrieved typically in the form of cindery pellets 1 cm³
along with a fine dust fraciton. This residue was sieved and divided into
two fractions, greater than and less than 2 mm. A sample of the fine fraction and three of the pellets were analysed by atomic absorption spectro-
metry (Tables 2, 3). Fig. 2 shows concentrations of selected oxides
displayed against SiO_2 for the pellets (low SiO_2), the fine dust (intermediate SiO_2), and the retort body (high SiO_2). The linear relationships
shown indicate that the fine fraction is essentially a mixture of the
pellets and material that has spalled off the retort walls. Thus the
pellets may be considered most representative of the charge. A significant
departure from the linearity of Fig. 2 is shown by FeO (Tables 1, 2);
petrographical examination reveals linings of goethite in vesicles and pores
in the pellets indicating that iron oxides were mobilised during weathering after the retorts had been discarded.

Table 2

Analysis of silicates from Zawar zinc retort

	(1)	(2)	(3)	(4)
SiO_2	54.36	50.50	20.82	40.48
TiO_2	b.d.	0.28	0.15	0.27
Al_2O_3	0.45	8.97	3.61	6.42
FeO	4.42	5.72	8.30	8.97
MnO	1.93	3.11	1.60	0.96
MgO	14.10	0.28	10.16	5.94
CaO	21.85	6.43	24.54	15.25
Na_2O	0.34	7.13	0.34	0.80
K_2O	b.d.	5.07	0.51	1.06
P_2O_5	b.d.	0.27	n.a.	n.a.
Cl	b.d.	0.70	n.a.	n.a.
S	b.d.	0.43	n.a.	n.a.
ZnO	3.44	12.45	0.61	1.22
	———	———	———	———
TOTAL	100.89	101.34	70.65*	81.37*

(1)   Diopside, from carrier material, EPMA

(2)   Glass, from carrier material, EPMA

(3)   Example of carrier fragment, AAS

(4)   Fine fraction from within retort, AAS

* Most of CaO and MgO present as carbonates,
  accounting for low totals.

Table 3

Silver, lead and zinc contents of Zawar materials

		%Ag	%ZnO	%PbO
Coarse fraction of carrier	(a)	0.023	0.61	0.36
	(b)	0.029	0.65	0.03
	(c)	0.012	0.30	0.04
Fine fraction of carrier		0.010	1.22	0.26
Retort Body		-	2.19	0.03

X-ray diffraction and polarised light microscopy of polished thin-sections show the pellets to be composed primarily of carbonates (calcite), but their state of aggregation and rigidity is imparted by a skeleton of silicate glass, in which are embedded numerous crystals of diopside (Plate 7). In addition fine grains of metallic iron are common (Plate 8). Micro-probe analyses of glass and diopside are presented in Table 2. The glass is rich in zinc, containing up to 15 wt % ZnO. However, the total concen-tration of ZnO in the pellets as determined by atomic absorption spectro-metry is only of the order of 0.5 wt % (Table 2). Other notable features are the high MnO/FeO ratios and the high Na_2O and particularly chlorine contents of the glass. Although metallic iron has been precipitated from the glass, the FeO content of the glass (excluding metallic iron particles) is quite low at around 5%.

Discussion

The charge

The zinc ore at Zawar is the sulphide, sphalerite, occuring with galena (PbS) in an impure dolomite host (Mookherjee 1964). Prior to distillation it would have been necessary to roast the sulphide to convert it to the oxide, a process most effective when temperatures of the order of 900-950°C are attained (Smith 1918). At these temperatures any dolomite present, $(CaMg[CO_3]_2)$ will have decomposed to calcium and magnesium oxides. The high MgO and CaO contents of the residue in the retort (Table 2) are a clear indication that a high proportion of dolomite was included. During the distillation process some of this material reacted with silica to form diopside and glass, but much of it appears to have remained as the free oxides, which recarbonated during cooling or after the retort had been discarded.

Most, if not all, of the components now present in the residue are likely to have been derived from the ore and the associated gangue, the

mineralogies of which are documented by Mookherjee (1964). The high manganese content derives from mangano-calcite and the relatively high silver
content reflects the native silver and argentite in the ore. K_2O, Al_2O_3
and SiO_2 reflect impurities in the dolomite such as biotite, orthoclase
and quartz. Sodium may also be derived from the gangue (as albite,
$NaAlSi_3O_8$) but the high chlorine content of the glass (Table 2) is less
easy to explain. The solubility of chlorine in a glass containing 15.8%
Na_2O at 1400°C was determined as 1.42% by Bateson and Turner (1939). Thus
the 0.7% chlorine in the residue glass, with 7% Na_2O, is probably close
to saturation. While a source for this high chlorine content in a gangue
mineral with an unusual composition (e.g. biotite) cannot be ruled out, it
is noted that the writings of medieval Indian iatrochemists specify salt
as one of the ingredients in the distillation of zinc.

For the production of zinc the fourteenth century *Rasaratnasamuccaya*
states (Ray 1956): '...... Rub calamine with turmeric, the chebulic
myrobalans, resins, the salts, soot, borax, and one fourth its weight of
semicarpus anacardium, and the acid juices ......'. Or 'Calamine is to be
powdered with lac, treacle, white mustard, the myrobalans, natron and borax
and the mixture boiled with milk and clarified butter and made into balls'.
When simplified into their basic ingredients, these recipes can be seen to
consist essentially of calamine (zinc ore), organic reducing agents, and
compounds of sodium (the salts, natron, and borax). Thus it may be that
the high chlorine and sodium in the Zawar residues reflects the addition of
a small amount of salt to the charge. Alternatively, ammonium chloride,
which is still used locally as a flux, called 'Nausadar' (L Gurjar *pers.
comm.*) may have been added. Furthermore, the procedure of making the
charge into balls is referred to, and it is difficult to account for the
regular size of the fragments from the retort unless this was inherited
from the charge, possibly as prepared pellets or balls about 1 cm diameter.

The open structure of the charge, formed by the ore pellets, would
have facilitated the extraction process by enlarging the surface of reaction between the zinc oxide and the reducing carbon monoxide gas, as well
as allowing the escape of spent gases and zinc vapour from the reaction
chamber. The minor glass phase formed a skeletal adhesive which stabi-
lized the pellets formed by the gangue minerals. Sodium is a potent flux
and its presence promoted the formation of the melt. Given the high ZnO
content of the glass (Table 2) it is clear that too much melting would
have limited the yield of zinc, thus a high proportion of refractory CaO
and MgO relative to the alkali fluxes was clearly desirable. If salt was
added to promote glass formation it was in very low concentrations, probably less than 1% of the charge. As well as the inorganic constituents,
it is emphasised that a considerable quantity of carbonaceous material
(? charcoal) would have been mixed with the charge to effect the reduction.

One of the surprising aspects of the analytical data is the relatively
low lead content of the charge (Table 3). Zawar is a lead-zinc deposit
with minimum lead/zinc ratios of at least 0.1 in the main ore body
(Mookherjee 1964). If this ratio had been obtained in the charge, then
the low lead concentrations measured in the residue would imply an initial
zinc content of only 3% or so, and very low yields of only a few tens of
grams of zinc per retort.

Even given that a certain amount of lead would have been lost from
the retort during the process, such low yields are improbable and the
implication would appear to be that the ore was carefully selected to be
essentially free of galena (PbS). This would have been desirable, for
the presence of lead inhibits the decomposition of sphalerite during

roasting as a lead silicate glass forms, preventing reaction with air and removal of SO_2. For this reason, the processing of lead-zinc ores was avoided in the West until the 1890s (Smith 1918). Lead was smelted from galena only a short distance away from Old Zawar, as evidenced by heaps of slag (Fig.1), which have yet to be investigated in detail.

Given that the ore was carefully selected to be free of galena, or perhaps even hand-picked to separate sphalerite and galena, then it might be expected that the gangue minerals such as dolomite would also have been removed. However, it has been noted that the presence of these components in the charge was necessary to provide the open carrier framework in the retort. The dolomite was deliberately retained - or perhaps even mixed with the ore - to produce a suitable charge.

Conditions of distillation

The walls of the retort are highly vitrified with very coarse bloating pores throughout, and distortion of the retort has occurred giving a 'sagged' appearance. This suggests that temperatures of the order of 1000°C or more are likely to have been attained. Indeed, the liquidus temperatures of the glasses on the exterior of the body, which lie in the system K_2O-FeO-Al_2O_3-SiO_2 (see above), are likely to have been considerably higher, suggesting temperatures of the order of 1100°C (see Freestone and Powell 1983, for sources of phase equilibrium data on this system). Such temperatures are desirable for zinc distillation for, according to Smith (1918), temperatures over 1125°C were required to achieve 'reasonable' rates of reaction in the nineteenth and early twentieth century processes. Temperature /pO_2 relations for a number of reactions of archaeological interest are shown in Fig. 3, based on data from a variety of sources (Kubaschewski and Evans 1958; Eugster and Wones 1962).
It is observed that within the range of temperatures attainable by the ancient technologist (up to 1300°C), the production of metallic zinc requires extremely reducing conditions below the pO_2 required to reduce wüstite (FeO) to metallic iron. These were achieved by isolating the reaction inside the retort from the air blast necessary to raise the temperature of the furnace sufficiently to obtain the required yield of zinc. Thus the presence of metallic iron in the spent charge is to be expected of the process. Indeed, taking mole fractions of 0.05 FeO and 0.10 ZnO in the glass in the charge (as analysed), assuming that the metallic zinc and iron phases were pure and making some gross thermodynamic simplifications such as ideal mixing of oxide components in silicate liquids, then the FeO-Fe and ZnO-Zn reactions were displaced to the dashed curves in Fig.3 during the distillation process. As can be seen, both the FeO and the ZnO contents of the glass are consistent with the operation of the process 1-2 log units of pO_2 below the Zn-ZnO reaction curve, within the temperature range of interest. The probable range of conditions within which the reaction in the retort occurred are shaded (Fig. 3). If the activities of FeO and ZnO in the glass were known accurately, together with the activities of iron and zinc in the metallic phases, then the conditions of the reaction would be defined precisely by the intersection of the dashed curves. However, the approximations made here are so great that no significance is attached to this point.

Scale of production

The concentrations of zinc in the various fractions of the retort have been determined (Tables 1-3). From the weights of these fractions it is estimated that 50g of zinc remains in the retort. According to Smith (1918)

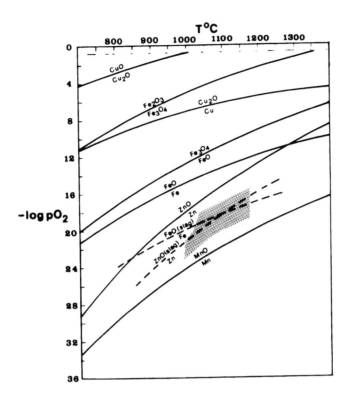

Fig. 3 Temperature/oxygen partial pressure relationships for selected
reactions for interest (see text). The shaded area represents the
range of suggested conditions within the retorts during firing

10-15% of the zinc was lost during the process in the nineteenth century.
Assuming that at Zawar 20% zinc was lost and that all the material lost
remains in the retort, then 200g of zinc would have been produced. From
another perspective let us suppose that zinc oxide made up 50% of the
original charge (excluding carbon). Then, as the spent charge weighs
about 1 kg, about 750g zinc would have been produced. Using these
speculative figures as limiting values, then the amount of zinc extracted
per retort is likely to have been of the order of hundreds of grams,
perhaps 0.5 kg. If, of the estimated 800,000 tons of debris at Zawar,
600,000 tons are made up of spent retorts, and assuming each retort weighs
3 kg and produced 0.5 kg zinc, then total production at Zawar is estimated
at 100,000 tons, over a very long time-span. The potential errors
associated with this figure are very great, but it gives some idea of the
order of magnitude of the production.

Conclusions

The conclusions to be drawn from a limited study such as this are inevitably speculative, but they are useful in that they indicate those areas
which must be covered in further work. To summarize:

(1)   Sphalerite with impure dolomite gangue was selected or processed to
       ensure that it was relatively free of galena.

(2) The ore is likely to have been roasted at 900-950°C to convert the starting materials to oxides.

(3) A small quantity of salts was added and the ore may have been shaped into pellets about 1 cm^3.

(4) The prepared ore plus carbon (? charcoal) was loaded into the retort and a cone-condenser unit luted on with clay.

(5) The vertically mounted retort was heated externally to temperatures of 1000-1150°C. A small amount of partial melting of the charge occurred, forming a skeletal adhesive framework which prevented collapse of the charge, maintaining an open structure. This enlarged the surface of reaction and allowed spent gases and zinc vapour to escape. pO_2 in the retort was several log units below that defined by the Zn-ZnO reaction curve.

(6) Hundreds of grams of zinc are likely to have been produced per retort.

(7) Prior to 1820, Zawar produced of the order of 100,000 tons of zinc by the distillation process over an unspecified period.

Acknowledgements

We thank Hindustan Zinc Ltd for support and encouragement at Zawar and Mr Lalit Gurjar, Senior Geologist, for advice and discussion. The British Academy and the Historical Metallurgy Society generously provided financial support for the visit to Zawar. Mr Keith Buck gave invaluable help in setting up the project and Mr S W K Morgan kindly donated the retorts. We thank Dr A C Bishop, Keeper of the Department of Mineralogy, British Museum (Natural History), who allowed us to use the electron microprobe in his department.

References

Bateson, H M & Turner, W E S 1939. A note on the solubility of sodium chloride in a soda-lime-silica glass. *Journal of the Society of Glass Technology*, **23**, 265-267

Carsus, H D 1960. Historical background. In *Zinc*, ed. C H Mathewson, 1-8. American Chemical Society Monograph

Craddock, P T 1981. The copper alloys of Tibet and their background. In *Aspects of Tibetan Metallurgy*, ed. W A Oddy & W Zwalf, Occasional Paper No. 15, 1-31. London, British Museum

Craddock, P T, Burnett, A M & Preston, K 1980. Hellenistic copper-base coinage and the origins of brass. In *Scientific Studies in Numismatics*, ed. W A Oddy, Occasional Paper No. 18, 53-64. London, British Museum

Craddock, P T, Hegde, K T M & Gurjar, L 1983. Zinc production in medieval India. *World Archaeology*, **18**, 2

Craddock, P T, Freestone, I C, Gurjar, L K, Hegde, K T M & Sonawane, V H 1985. Early zinc production in India. *The Mining Magazine*, (Jan), 45-82

Eugster, H & Wones, D R 1962. Stability relations of the ferruginous biotite, annite. *Journal of Petrology*, 3, 82-125

Freestone, I C 1982. Applications and potential of electron probe microanalysis in technological and provenance investigations of ancient ceramics. *Archaeometry*, 24, 99-116

Freestone, I C & Powell, R 1983. The low temperature field of liquid immiscibility in the system $K_2O-FeO-Al_2O_3-SiO_2$. *Contributions to Mineralogy and Petrology*, 82, 291-299

Hughes, M J, Cowell, M R & Craddock, P T 1976. Atomic absorption techniques in archaeology. *Archaeometry*, 18, 19-38

Kubaschewski, O & Evans, E 1958. *Metallurgical thermochemistry*. Oxford, Pergamon

Mookherjee, A 1964. The geology of the Zawar lead-zinc mine, Rajasthan, India. *Economic Geology*, 39, 656-677

Ray, A P C 1956. *History of chemistry in ancient and medieval India*. Calcutta, Indian Chemical Society

Smith, E A 1918. *The zinc industry*. London, Longmans, Green

Straczekk, J A & Srikantan, B 1967. The geology of Zawar zinc-lead area, Rajasthan, India. *Memoirs of the Geological Survey of India*

Tod, J 1829. *Annals and Antiquities of Rajputana*. Esp. Vol. 1, p. 399. London, Smith and Elder

Plate 1 Bank of furnaces on Zawar Mala (site 30).

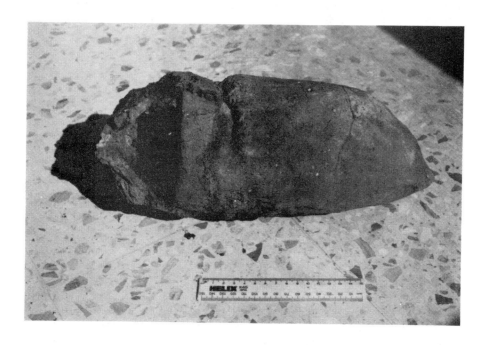

Plate 2 One of the larger type of retorts. The condenser end is partially
broken away, showing the cone-shaped head in section.

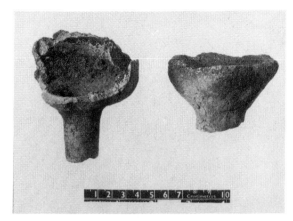

Plate 3   The two principal types of condenser head.

Plate 4   Chamber beneath the furnace where the zinc was collected, exposed
by removal of the perforated plates.

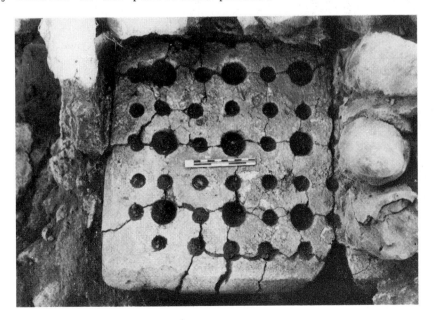

Plate 5   One complete perforated plate *in situ* in furnace I on Zawar Mala
(site 30).

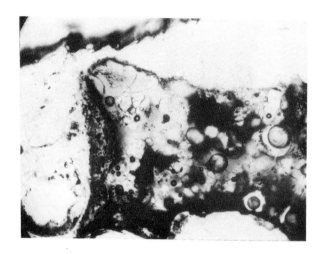

Plate 6   Thin-section photomicrograph showing high degree of melting (glass) at outer surface of retort. Field of view is 1.4 mm.

Plate 7   Thin-section photomicrograph of spent charge pellet, showing numerous crystals of diopside embedded in glass. Field of view is 0.7 mm.

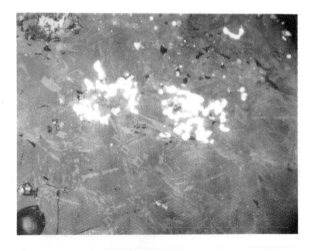

Plate 8   Reflected light photomicrograph of spent charge pellet, showing grains of metallic iron (white) in silicate (glass plus diopside) matrix. Field of view is 0.44 mm.